KEY CONCEPTS IN FEMINIST
THEORY AND RESEARCH

D1615660

KEY CONCEPTS IN FEMINIST THEORY AND RESEARCH

CHRISTINA HUGHES

SAGE Publications
London • Thousand Oaks • New Delhi

First published 2002

 SAGE Publications Ltd
6 Bonhill Street
London EC2A 4PU

SAGE Publications Inc.
2455 Teller Road
Thousand Oaks, California 91320

SAGE Publications India Pvt. Ltd
32, M-Block Market
Greater Kailash – I
New Delhi 110 048

British Library Cataloguing in Publication data
A catalogue record for this book is available from the British
Library

ISBN 0 7619 6987 X
      0 7619 6988 8 (pbk)

Library of Congress control number

Typeset by Mayhew Typesetting, Rhayader, Powys
Printed and bound in Great Britain by The Cromwell Press,
Trowbridge, Wiltshire

For Malcolm

Contents

Acknowledgements

I have been so fortunate in the contributions and help I have received in writing this book. First, I must acknowledge the support I have received from the University of Warwick, and from my colleagues in the Department of Continuing Education, for a period of study leave. This certainly eased the task of researching and writing at length.

I am also very appreciative of those colleagues who willingly gave up their precious time to read and comment on earlier drafts of the material and whose responses have also been so generous in spirit. So thank you Linda Perriton, Arwen Raddon, Elaine Millard, Jane Martin, Morwenna Griffiths and Lynn Clouder. Just at the moment of a crisis of confidence your thoughts were very helpful and welcome indeed.

I also have to thank Mal Leicester who, a few years ago now, pointed me in the direction of Wittgenstein and Cathie Edwards who so kindly lent me her Wittgenstein resources. Thank you both.

Karen Phillips at Sage has been delightful to work with. Not only has she facilitated the production process but she has engaged with the ideas in the text in such a developmental way. Loraine Blaxter has continued to be the person who has listened to me and challenged me throughout the writing of this book and I count myself fortunate to have such a colleague.

And of course, last but not least, Malcolm Tight has not only continued to walk the dog and cook the meals during what has been for me a lengthy and intensive period of academic writing but I know I have also benefited from his clarity of thought and intellectual rigour.

List of Figures and Tables

Figures

Tables

List of Case Studies

Introduction
Not Talking about the Same Thing:
Introducing Conceptual Literacy

> In none of the sciences, and not even the perspectives within them . . .
> were people talking about the same thing.
>
> (Adam, 1990: 5)

F or those who are new to social theory and research the multitude of
meanings that are given to the same term gives rise to a certain
amount of concern. Students feel muddled and confused as they search
for the correct meaning of a particular term or try to sort out the variety
of meanings from a wide range of literatures. Recourse to a dictionary is
one response. Recourse to a tutor is of course another. Giving up and
learning to live with confusion is perhaps a third. Giving up altogether is
a fourth option! The search for a fixed, unified and indeed accessible
meaning becomes something like the search for the 'philosopher's stone'
that in myth promised to turn base metal into gold.

It is, of course, not only those who are new to an area or students
more generally who have concerns about multiple and changing
meanings. This is an issue that has been noted by researchers for a
considerable time. In researching the literature on all the key terms used
in this text – time, choice, experience, difference, care, equality, theory
and research – there was an abundance of commentary on the
variability of their meanings. Thus, the complete quote from Adam is:

> In none of the sciences, and not even the perspectives within them . . .
> were people talking about the same thing when they made use of the idea
> of time. They seemed to be talking about phenomena, things, processes,
> qualities, or a dimension, a category, and a concept, using the word
> unproblematically as if it had only one meaning. (Adam, 1990: 5–6)

Similarly, Anderson (1998) comments that conceptualizations of choice
are vague and ill-defined and thus methodologically fraught with

problems. Scott (1992) refers to the use of the term experience as ubiquitous and Barrett (1987) makes a similar comment about the use of the term difference. Thomas (1993) reflects on how conceptualizations of care tend to be presented as generic rather than taking into account that the meanings of care are domain specific. Evans (1995) suggests that there are two major conceptualizations of equality but these are not the same as those noted by Brine (1999). Poovey (1988: 51) comments, 'There are as many deconstructions as there are feminisms.' Butler and Scott (1992: xiii) note that '"Theory" is a highly contested term within feminist discourse.' They ask whether theory is singular or multiple. Or is theory defined in opposition to something that might be described as atheoretical, pre-theoretical or post-theoretical? Or is theory distinct from politics? In response to the question 'What is research?' my colleagues Loraine Blaxter and Malcolm Tight and I (Blaxter et al., 2001) identify 20 'views' of research. We also suggest that 'even a brief review of writings on research will uncover a lengthy and potentially baffling list of types of research' (ibid.: 5) and we offer four different representations of the research process.

One response to this diversity has been to try to work towards a unified schema of conceptualization. This is because if we are not 'talking about the same thing' (Adam, 1990) how can we be sure that our research is comparable or that our results are valid? Thus, Burgess (1984) explored the varied conceptualizations of terms such as 'race' and ethnicity, age, gender, health and illness, education, social class and occupation, leisure, politics and voluntary associations with a clear recognition of their ambivalent and transient meanings. The contributors to Burgess' text may have been initially concerned that researchers used the same meanings for the same terms. In this their aim was to improve the validity of comparative research. Nonetheless, in line with much thinking in the postmodern, they also recognized the impossibility of this. Thus:

> If the contemporary diversity of sociology and social research makes the emergence of a unified conceptual scheme unlikely, it is nevertheless essential to be aware of how one's work relates to that of others. Researchers need to consider how the concepts and indicators that they use relate to those used in local and national studies both now and in the past, in an attempt to find some common ground and with a view to enabling comparisons to be made. (Burgess, 1984: 261)

More recently postmodern and poststructural theorizing has brought to prominence the significance of language in understanding the changing nature of meaning. Thus Scheurich (1997) comments on how post-modern theorization has illustrated how the relationship between language and meaning shifts in small and large ways, between people, across time and according to varied situations. What is shaping the difference between the approaches evidenced by Burgess and Scheurich is whether or not meanings can be fixed and whether a consensus could be achieved on the conceptualization of key research terms.

This text enters the terrain of conceptual meaning with some sympathy for Burgess' position. In this I would reiterate that researchers need to consider how the concepts they use relate to other conceptualizations. Indeed, I would go further than this and argue that researchers need to be conceptually literate. Conceptual literacy is no more, and no less, than an act of sensitization to the political implications of contestation over the diversity of conceptual meanings. In this it draws attention to the multiplicity of meanings that are invoked by the use of key terms; to the dualistic framing of language; to the art of deconstruction; and to the salience of focusing on language in use. However, more broadly, conceptual literacy is concerned to develop an understanding of the effect of epistemic games that surround conceptual contestation in producing warrantable knowledge that justifies the directions through which a field of enquiry and its associated political concerns may proceed.

My point of divergence with Burgess is his starting point that there might be some common ground in the operationalization and conceptualization of key terms. As a sensitizing act the exploration of conceptual literacy in this text does not aim for closure on conceptual usage in the sense of offering a 'last word', a complete review or a definitive operationalization of any term or any theorization of language and its meaning. Indeed, my purpose is quite the reverse. Rather, I imagine that you will enter into the analysis at many points in terms of your own experience, knowledge, politics and purposes. At most, I hope that some of what I have to say will provide food for further thought as part of an open-ended and ongoing exploration for understanding conceptual usage in your own work and intellectual development.

I make these points because if my own experience is relevant, the existence of divergent and plural meanings not only has implications for the development of a field of knowledge but also for our learning careers. For all its postmodern provenance, plurality stands in contradiction to a more modernist desire for fixity and boundedness, for neatness and framing. It contradicts, in fact, a desire for absolute knowing that is a mark of scientific enquiry. Thus, when, for example, I come across a new term or theory my response is very similar to those of my students. I want to know what it 'really' means *as if this were possible*. My desire for the boundedness of knowing also leads to a sense of muddle and confusion when that feeling of safe boundaries, clear frameworks or absolute meanings is absent. And, this sense of muddle quickly moves into a sense of self-blame. Somehow it is my fault there is this confusion and this is probably due to some personal failing in my education, my IQ, the fact that I haven't read enough, and so forth. In terms of my learning career, therefore, I experience confusion and failure. I want to give up. I am inclined to close down rather than open up to this veritable array of diversity of meaning.

Relatedly, my concern that the text is perceived to open up, rather than close down, understanding is not simply due to a commitment to these elements of postmodern discourse. Rather, it is because I am acutely aware of what I have not said, what I have edited out and, of course, what I do not know. In this I am drawn to Crick (1976: 11) who, in the introduction to the publication of his doctoral thesis, comments on how his work was to a large extent 'the result of a situation brought about by the naiveté thesis'. Naiveté is a relative term that is usually used with pejorative overtones. As such, one's naiveté can only be understood by looking back from some point of greater and more respectable wisdom. The ignominious nature of naiveté means that we have a tendency to refuse it a place in our learning careers. Rather, we focus on the progressive myths of learning that are concerned with the acquisition of expertise as the only credible prize. Such myths focus us on the end points of education – the book, the thesis, the dissertation, the exams passed – as ends in themselves and ultimately as acts of closure. A phrase that was popular in Britain a couple of years ago rather sums this up. 'Been there. Done that.' In this progressive myths disallow the importance of foolishness, naiveté and not knowing as moments of continual beginnings that absolutely require openness and openings.

It is, therefore, for these reasons that I offer the term conceptual literacy as an act of sensitization that opens us to the variety of ways that we can understand the evidence of multiple meanings. Fuzzy, blurred and multiple meanings are not signs of the personal failure of the naïve. Their recognition is a prelude to unveiling the broader political significance of conceptual contestation. As such, this text explores the contested and varied meanings of equality, difference, choice, care, time and experience within their usage in feminist theory and research. To this end I now offer an overview of my pedagogic approach to the construction of this text and, of course, a brief commentary on what is to come.

Pedagogic Concerns

As the brief review of the contents of this text will indicate, an analysis of key concepts draws on a range of theoretical and methodological terms. I am conscious that for many students even the word 'theory' is off-putting and acts as a point of closure. Many students comment that they do not understand theory, they are not 'theoretical' people or they are more concerned with practice. My response is usually to say that theory simply means explanation and how are we to explain our social worlds or what we find in our research if we do not have some kind of theory? However, I am also conscious that any form of writing is a pedagogic act. By this I mean that it is an opportunity for teaching and learning. For this reason I need to say a few words about how I have responded to my pedagogic concerns.

Whenever I hear a student say that they are not interested in theory, I understand this as reflecting on the mental barriers that are set up by the expectation that theory is a difficult subject. I agree that it can be. However, I would also suggest that finding many and varied ways into a topic can greatly facilitate understanding. Texts such as Brooks (1997), Beasley (1999) and Freedman (2001) that outline key theoretical positions are an excellent way of developing knowledge about the social theory that underpins feminism. Yet they are only one genre through which knowledge can be enhanced. In turning to this text I appreciate that readers may focus their attention on single chapters because of their particular relevance or importance. However, I would suggest that you may find it valuable to consult those chapters that are not necessarily of immediate or primary concern. This text offers an alternative approach to understanding some of feminism's more formal theoretical concerns because particular theoretical perspectives give rise to alternative conceptual meanings and implications for how to proceed. These theoretical perspectives form cross-cutting ties within the text. Therefore within the discussion of each of the concepts you will find commentary on, for example, liberal, cultural, materialist, postmodern, poststructural and postcolonial feminism.

In addition, and somehow, theory is often viewed as detached from empirical research. One either 'does' theory or one 'does' research. Moreover, there is another form of detachment that operates across this binary. This is that theory is abstract and empirical research is concrete. Because of my concerns about these kinds of false separation, you will find interleaved within the discussion of the varied conceptualizations of equality, difference, choice, care, time and experience a number of illustrative case studies. These are drawn from contemporary research in the fields of education, employment and family and have been selected to concretize the more abstract nature of the discussion. As I am primarily concerned to illustrate how concepts are applied in different forms of research I mainly focus on the methodological approaches and theoretical frameworks of these case studies. This allows us to understand the 'results' of research with the necessary contextualization of how these results were obtained and theoretically framed.

Finally, as a text focused on developing a form of literacy, I have included suggested further readings. This text provides an introduction and an overview of the central issues of meaning, as I see it, in the varied definitions of feminism's key concepts. The further reading has been selected to provide examples of work that can build on the material that has been presented here.

Conceptual Concerns

Any text is built on some kind of theoretical or conceptual framework that may or may not be made explicit. This places the knowledge presented in a broader epistemological and ontological field. This further allows us to judge its claims and justifications. Chapter 1 therefore outlines the field of language theorizing that has informed my own development of conceptual literacy. A key point to note here is that this review is necessarily selective because it is based on what has been personally relevant in terms of my own learning journey. In developing your own conceptual literacy other theorizations may well be equally if not more relevant. As part of opening up rather than closing down, therefore, this chapter provides a useful starting point to which further theoretical frameworks might be added.

Chapter 1 includes a number of issues related to the analysis and theorization of multiple meaning. I begin by discussing Derridean notions of différance and analyses of meaning that focus on language dualism. I next turn to Wittgenstein's analysis of language with particular attention to his conceptualization of language games. This is to illustrate the place of context as giving meaning to specific discourses within language. Finally, I explore the politics of conceptual contestation. Here I illustrate the conditions for contestation in terms of Connolly's (1993) analysis of cluster concepts. In addition, I discuss how contestation may masquerade as a simple issue of accurate description that requires the correct indicators. However, as Tanesini (1994) comments, such descriptors also invoke particular judgements about what is warrantable knowledge that have a justificatory role in terms of how a field of study should proceed. In these ways a particular field changes direction or extends its purview both in respect of its empirical and political concerns.

One of the consequences of the changes that arise from debates about what counts as adequate ways to proceed is that there is a tendency that *post-hoc* analyses and thus the veracity of earlier work are primarily read within the terms of these later debates. My concern that any development of conceptual literacy takes account of situating meaning within historical and cultural contexts is therefore taken up in Chapter 2 by illustrating how eighteenth- and nineteenth-century feminist theorizing of *equality* drew on Enlightenment ideas of liberalist rights. In Chapter 2 I explore two basic conceptualizations of equality. These are equality as sameness and equality as difference. In respect of equality as sameness I explore the problems of measurement that are central to such conceptualizations and the policy and legislative outcomes of rights-based equality arguments. In respect of equality as difference I focus on the centrality of motherhood to such conceptualizations and illustrate the varied meanings of this in terms of the eighteenth-century writings of Wollstonecraft and more contemporary Italian feminists' conceptualizations. Because it is becoming a neglected area, my final concern in Chapter 2 is to discuss material inequalities. Here I specifically focus on Fraser's (1995) theoretical conceptualization through her analysis of the politics of recognition and the politics of redistribution that are part of post-socialist political life.

As will be evident from Chapter 2, it is impossible to talk of equality without invoking issues of *difference*. In Chapter 3 I explore a variety of conceptualizations of difference. These include difference as sameness, identity differences, sexual difference, poststructural and postcolonial analyses of difference. Difference has, of course, been of enormous importance to feminism with the consequence that there is a plethora of writings that could be drawn upon to illustrate its meanings. The question for any academic or student, then, is 'How does one organize and manage this wealth of material?' I begin Chapter 3 by comparing two conceptual schema of difference (Barrett, 1987, and Evans, 1995). One of my purposes here is to illustrate how feminists approach a field as rich and diverse as difference in terms of the imposition of alternative organizing frameworks. For example, Barrett separates experiential, sexual and positional difference and draws up her framework of three key differences accordingly. Evans draws on particular schools of

thought such as cultural, liberal and postmodern feminism as underpinning her three key differences. I continue the discussion in Chapter 3
by exploring the key differences through a concern with conceptualizations of group difference, deconstructive approaches and postcolonial
theorizing of multi-axial locationality.

Chapter 4 explores the concept of *choice* within a broader framework
of agency and structure. This enables me to situate conceptualizations of
choice within debates about these two concepts. I offer two conceptualizations of choice. The first is that of rational choice. Here I
illustrate how rational choice most closely fits with common-sense,
everyday conceptualizations and is also central to economic theory. By
way of critique I explore feminist economists' analyses of rational
choice theory in terms of its predominant assumption of agentic,
rational personhood. I then outline poststructural conceptualizations of
the choosing subject. These focus on the processes of subjectification
through keeping in simultaneous play issues of mastery and submission.
Whilst poststructural theorizing is critical of humanist conceptions of
personhood, the primary aim is to go beyond the agency-structure 'ping-
pong' (Jones, 1997) that has been a central feature of much theorization
in the social sciences.

Thomas (1993) suggests that *care* is primarily an empirical rather
than a theoretical category. Her point is important because it highlights
how terms are conceptualized through the theoretical frameworks
within which they are placed. For example, within sociological frameworks of care giving and care receiving, care has mainly been imbued
with negative meanings. Within some philosophical and psychological
writings, and particularly those of care ethicists, care takes on more
positive evaluations. Care is also interesting because in some domains
the empirical facets of care giving and receiving are renamed. In
employment contexts, for example, caring is redefined as service or
support (Tronto, 1993). However, one idea recurs. That is that care is
primarily women's responsibility. In Chapter 5 I explore these meanings
of care through an analysis of its economic character in both family and
employment domains and its ethical implications for a deconstruction of
rights-based discourses. A conceptualization of care as economic has
enabled feminists to rename care as work whether this is unpaid work
or paid work. A conceptualization of care as an ethic has facilitated a
critique of individualist rights and associated policies that continue to
neglect a further central feature of care. This is that we all need care and
we are all equally capable of care giving (Sevenhuijsen, 1998).

Time is feminism's latent concept. It is for this reason that Adam
(1989) was able to write an article illustrating why feminist social

theory needs time. Time is so imbued in our everyday language that we most often fail to notice its expansiveness. When we do we tend to focus on clock-time as the all-encompassing only time. In Chapter 6 I explore three aspects to conceptualizations of time. The first is the linear time of the clock. This is the most predominant conceptualization of time in social theory and can be found in a body of research that ranges from historical analyses to adult development theories to work–family balance policies. Feminist research has primarily referred to linear, clock time as male time and has contrasted this with female time. Female time arises from women's relationship to the reproduction of family and organizational life. It is relational and repetitive as tasks, such as feeding, cleaning or counselling, regularly interrupt the linearity of the clock. I next turn to analyses of time that are concerned with the development of the self and I outline here conceptualizations of time that view the past, the present and the future as simultaneous. For example, I discuss issues of authenticity and the role of time in creating a sense of the continuous self. Finally, I turn to issues of time–space relationships. Here I particularly focus on Grosz's (1995) analysis of the body and Kristeva's (1986) conceptualization of feminist politics that both incorporate issues of time, space and identity.

Arising from feminist consciousness-raising and summarized within the phrase 'The personal is the political' *experience* is central to feminist politics. Experience also forms the cornerstone of empirical research as the very stuff of narrative and interview. In Chapter 7 I discuss the development of standpoint theory from its original conceptualization in the late 1970s to the present. Standpoint theory originally posited that the experiences of those who were positioned outside the dominant order gave rise to a more adequate, even superior, view of dominant social relations. Identity politics and postmodern theorizing subsequently raised significant questions about whose experience was being used as the normative standard and whether experience could have such a fixed, ontological status. By focusing on debates that surround standpoint theory this allows me to illustrate the theoretical roots of standpoint theory in materialist feminism and the impact of subsequent debate in developing alternative conceptualizations, and politics, which surround experience. Given the centrality of experience to feminist epistemology I also discuss feminist debates on objectivity and the role of the personal in feminist theory and research.

Chapter 8 forms the concluding chapter to the text. I have one primary purpose here. This is to offer ways in which conceptual literacy can be further developed. As will be clear, my primary purpose in writing this text is to offer an approach that will enable students to go beyond simply learning to live with the multiple conceptualizations of key terms. It is to suggest that such multiplicity offers an opportunity for the development of conceptual literacy through which awareness and sensitivity are developed to the political implications of the diversity of conceptual meanings. Thus I am concerned to indicate that one of the dangers of viewing contests over meaning and the politics of language games is that it can suggest an anything goes, relativist and even cynical approach to debate. Conceptual literacy is a recognition that debate and contestation impact on the development of a field of study, on the production of different forms of knowledge and on changing the language of theory and research. Each of these, in turn, impacts on what is viewed as the necessary politics of that field. Thus the consequences of debate are real in very material and tangible ways.

And so all that remains for me to now say is that I hope some of the material in this text is useful to you. I know that I learnt a lot in researching it!

Christina Hughes
University of Warwick
October 2001

Concepts: Meanings, Games and Contests

I am suggesting neither that there are differences of opinion about concepts which possess an uncontestable core, nor that concepts are linked to incommensurable theories. Rather I see concepts and categories as shaped by political goals and intentions. Contests over the meaning of concepts, it follows, are contests over desired political outcomes.

(Bacchi, 1996: 1)

'I did not have sexual relations with that woman.' When I first heard this statement from President Clinton in respect of his relationship with Monica Lewinsky my first response was to judge it in terms of its truth or non-truth. While, of course, there are many kinds of sexual activity surely, I thought, he either had or had not. Yet the Clinton case is a classic example of what would be defined as conceptual contestation. By this I mean two things. First, that in the everyday the meanings of particular terms are varied. Second, that in certain circumstances different protagonists will forcefully and protectively deploy their specific definitions in a contest over meaning. Thus Clinton drew on what I personally would understand as an extremely narrow, even technical, definition of sex. Others deployed a wider meaning that might accord with more everyday meanings. The truth did not lie in the physical act that was or was not undertaken. The truth lay in which definition was going to take precedence.

For those of us who might have some vicarious enjoyment from the contest over meaning in the Clinton case, the turn to the drier academic field of texts and theory has perhaps rather less of a hold on our attention. Yet such texts are full of issues of conceptual contestation that are enacted in much the same way as the Clinton case. Here the contests over meaning are central to the development of a particular field of theorization and, in consequence, to the political implications of that field. Moi (1999) offers a useful example in this respect when she discusses the sex/gender distinction that provides the basic framework for much feminist theory in the English-speaking world. In contrast to the Clinton case where discussion of the term sex was related to the physicality of sex acts, within feminism the term sex is primarily used to make distinctions about what is meant when we use the term 'woman'. Thus sex is the term that is used when referring to woman as a biologically sexed body and gender is the term that denotes the socially produced meanings of woman.

What is useful about Moi's analysis is that she illustrates two important features of conceptual contestation. The first point is that we need to take account of the historical and cultural situatedness of meaning. As Moi notes, prior to 1960, feminists used the term sex to include the social and cultural meanings now associated with gender. In the 1960s English-speaking feminists introduced the sex/gender distinction as a strong defence against the biologically deterministic meanings that were predominant in understandings of the term woman in masculine theorizing. In addition, there is no sex/gender distinction in French (*sexe*) and Norwegian (*kjønn*). The second point to note is that dominant meanings are always open to challenge. As in the case of the original call for a distinction between sex and gender, more recent poststructural theorization has challenged the meanings of sex as being confined to a reference to a biologically sexed body. Moi (1999: 4) notes that the purpose of this challenge is to shift our understandings of the sexed body as an essence and to refocus the meanings of sex as incorporating concrete, historical and social phenomena. In this way poststructuralist theorizing seeks to avoid the biologically deterministic meanings of the term sex and to develop an account of sex and the body as historically located.

In the Clinton case the debate ensued over the meanings of sex but there never appeared to be any doubt about what constituted woman. Monica Lewinsky's sexed body was sufficient evidence. Indeed, in the everyday we rarely spend time analysing and discussing the meanings of the most common terms in our language. However, the feminist debates that Moi sets out in terms of the sex/gender distinction were concerned with the meanings that constitute woman. Indeed, it is the theme of 'What is "woman"?' that provides the illustrative framework for this chapter as I draw on the varied debates and issues that have been of concern in answering this question. This serves as the context for my primary purpose, which is to set out the theorizations of language, meaning and acts of conceptualization that have appeared to me to be most relevant to the development of my own imminent understandings of the conceptual literacy that I outlined in the Introduction. I therefore draw on the theme of 'What is "woman"?' for exemplification.

I begin with poststructuralist understandings of language and meaning. These draw on Derridean notions of the deferral of meaning through différance. There are several points that I have found important here. The first is the recognition that is given to the role of language in shaping our understandings of reality. The second is the attention that has been given to the instability of meaning. This has given a focus, for example, to the lack of guarantee over the transference of meaning. A third point is the attention that is given to the power relations of language.

In the section that follows I explore issues of power and language through Plumwood's (1993) deconstruction of dualism. Plumwood's work is exceptionally useful in highlighting the embedded nature of power relations within language. This is because she illustrates how we need to look beyond the coupling or pairing of terms in language. For example, language operates in terms of binaried pairs through which each term in the binary draws its meaning. However, Plumwood's analysis illustrates something of a rhizomatic quality as she also explores how meaning draws from networks and webs of connection that extend beyond the binaried pair.

The third section of this chapter is illustrative of how my own conceptual literacy draws from what I now understand to be Wittgenstein's philosophy of language. There is considerable debate in the literature on Wittgenstein in terms of whether he is a deconstructionist or a pragmatist (see, for example, Nagl and Mouffe, 2001). For example, Moi (1999) suggests that the central point where Wittgenstein and Derrida part company is on the Derridean idea that meaning is *always* deferred. Such debate is, of course, evidence of the multiple ways in which we might read a particular author. My own concerns with Wittgenstein are rather more mundane. My beginnings here arose from a concern to recognize the contextual dependency of meaning and to find an analytic framework that offered a useful explanation. Meaning may be multiple, varied and diverse. It may carry on beyond our intentions and it may be taken up in a host of ways. However, meaning is not idiosyncratic in the sense that any meaning goes at any time. If it were, it would be virtually impossible for us to communicate. These issues are not denied in poststructuralist theorizing. Meaning is derived from the discourse within which it takes place (Weedon, 1997). Yet my (mis)reading of work in this field has left me with a strong impression that within standard accounts of poststructuralism the contextualization of meaning is usually in the background of a more fully foregrounded concern to emphasize the transience of meaning. In my brief acquaintance with Wittgenstein I do not believe that his analysis encourages such backgrounding. Rather, for Wittgenstein, context is key.

In the fourth section of this chapter I explore the political terrain of contestation of meaning. Here I set out Connolly's (1993) analysis of essentially contested concepts and his associated term of cluster concepts. It seems to me that Connolly's analysis bears a strong resemblance to Wittgenstein's and Plumwood's rhizomatic approaches with their attention to networks and diverse forms of meaning that branch out in all directions. I also draw on Tanesini's (1994) analysis of the politics of meaning where she highlights that we need to understand contestation over meaning as claims about how a word ought to be used rather than as attempts to describe how a word is used.

The Non-Fixity of Meaning

> The plurality of language and the impossibility of fixing meaning once and for all are basic principles of poststructuralism.
>
> (Weedon, 1997: 82)

As a 'post'-theorization, poststructuralism follows on from the work of structuralist theories of language. This is an important point because it draws attention to what is both common and distinctive to structuralism and poststructuralism. In particular, it is de Saussure's structuralist linguistics that is viewed as being a significant forerunner to poststructuralist approaches. Beasley (1999: 90) notes that for de Saussure 'meaning is formulated within language and is not somehow to be found outside the ways in which discourse operates'. Language is, therefore, not simply an expression of a preconceived meaning but instead language creates meaning. This point is not at issue for poststructuralist theorists. Poststructuralism places considerable emphasis on the role of language in shaping how we know.

In addition, de Saussure argued that language has an underlying structure. This underlying structure is comprised of oppositions through which meaning derives. I indicated in the Introduction that the meanings of naiveté are drawn from what we would also understand as not being naïve. In this case naiveté's meanings arise through ideas of wisdom and experience. In this way we can conceive of meaning as derived from a 'web of other concepts from which it is differentiated' (ibid.). Again, poststructuralism gives considerable attention to the structuring of meaning through oppositional and dualistic relations.

There are two points of divergence, however, between de Saussure's structural linguistics and poststructuralist accounts of meaning. One of these is that whereas de Saussure stressed the fixity of a central underlying structure to language, poststructuralism stresses quite the opposite. That is that meaning is fragmented and shifting. Indeed, as Weedon (1997) notes, the impossibility of fixing meaning is central to poststructuralist theorizing. Alvesson and Skoldberg comment that a major implication of moving away from a belief in a central structure of language is that language becomes an open play of never-ending meaning within time relations. Thus, poststructuralism: 'breaks with the conception of a dominating centre which would govern the structure, and with the conception that the synchronic, timeless, would be more important than the diachronic, narrative, that which goes on in time' (2000: 148).

Finlayson (1999) illustrates how the approach to meaning as multiple and temporal draws on the notion of hierarchical binary oppositions. The most classic example of this is that of the binary male–female. It is this relational nature of meaning that is seen to give rise to its instability. This is important because it draws attention to how meanings are derived. In the male–female binary, to be a woman requires us to have a corresponding concept of man. Without this relation the terms alone would have no reference point from which to derive their meaning. Nonetheless, it is the relation between these binaries that gives rise to the instability of meaning production and reproduction. In particular 'the first term in a binary opposition can never be completely stable or secure, since it is dependent on that which is excluded' (Finlayson, 1999: 64). As understandings of male change, so do those of female and vice versa.

Although meanings cannot be fixed, we live our lives as though they are. The appearance of fixity is maintained through 'the suppression of its opposite' (ibid.: 63). In everyday discourse the fact that what it means to be masculine relies on what it means to be feminine is hidden from view. We are not conscious, for example, that every time we use the word 'woman', we are using the reference point of man to derive our meanings. As Davies (1997a: 9) notes, 'This construction operates in a variety of intersecting ways, most of which are neither conscious nor intended. They are more like an effect of what we might call "speaking-as-usual".'

The notion of an array of deferred meanings is often summarized in terms of Derrida's conceptualization of différance. Différance is derived from the French verb 'différer', which means to defer or to put off. Johnson (2000) notes that while the closest English translation is that of 'deferment', this loses the complexity of associations that arise in the French. These are particularly those of temporality, movement and process that institute difference 'while at the same time holding it in reserve, deferring its presentation or operation' (ibid.: 41). Thus:

> Each linguistic signifier comes laced with deferrals to, and difference from, an absent 'other' – the negated binary – that is also in play. Différance – Derrida's term for these deferrals and différance – is not a name for a *thing*, but rather 'the movement according to which language, or any code, any system of referral in general, is constituted "historically" as a weave of differences'. Thus, the terms 'movement', 'is constituted' and 'historically' need to be understood as 'beyond the metaphysical language in which they are retained' (1968, p. 65). (Battersby, 1998: 91–100)

Weedon (1997) comments that the issue of différance does not imply that meaning disappears completely. Différance does focus our attention on the temporal implications of meaning and how meaning is open to challenge. However 'the degree to which meanings are vulnerable at a particular moment will depend on the discursive power relations within which they are located' (Weedon, 1997: 82). Thus, a second point of divergence between de Saussure's linguistics and poststructuralism is the attention that is given to the relations of power within language. One way of illustrating this is through the attention that has been given to the analysis of dualism and the processes of deconstruction.

Dualism

> A dualism is more than a relation of dichotomy, difference, or non-identity, and more than a simple hierarchical relationship. In dualistic construction, as in hierarchy, the qualities (actual or supposed), the culture, the values and the areas of life associated with the dualised other are systematically and pervasively constructed and depicted as inferior. Hierarchies, however, can be seen as open to change, as contingent and shifting. But once the process of domination forms culture and constructs identity, the inferiorised group (unless it can marshall cultural resources for resistance) must internalise this inferiorisation in its identity and collude in this low valuation, honouring the values of the centre, which form the dominant social values . . . A dualism is an intense, established and developed cultural expression of such a hierarchical

relationship, constructing central cultural concepts and identities so as to make equality and mutuality literally unthinkable.

(Plumwood, 1993: 47)

Plumwood illustrates an important feature of the organization of language and its relations to power. This is that of the embedded nature of hierarchization that goes beyond a simple binary. The key elements of dualistic structuring in Western thought include culture/nature, reason/nature, male/female, mind/body, reason/emotion, reason/matter, public/private, subject/object and self/other (ibid.: 43). These, however, are not discrete pairs that bear no relation to other concepts in language. Rather, dualisms should be seen as a network of strongly linked and continuous webs of meanings. For example, 'the concepts of humanity, rationality and masculinity form strongly linked and contiguous parts of this web, a set of closely related concepts which provide for each other models of appropriate relations to their respective dualised contrasts of nature, the physical or material, and the feminine' (ibid.: 46). In this respect, as Hekman (1999: 85) notes, rationality, humanity and masculinity form 'the ideal type that forms the central core of modern social and political theory'.

Plumwood sets out five features that she argues are characteristic of dualism. These are:

- Backgrounding (denial) Plumwood comments that the relations of domination give rise to certain conflicts as those who dominate seek to deny their dependency and reliance on those they dominate. Denial of this dependency takes many forms. These include making the depended upon inessential and denying the importance of the other's contribution. The view of those who dominate is set up as universal 'and it is part of the mechanism of backgrounding that it never occurs to him that there might be other perspectives from which *he* is background' (1993: 48).
- Radical exclusion (hyperseparation) Plumwood argues that radical exclusion is a key indicator of dualism. Radical exclusion or hyperseparation arises because those who are superior need to ensure that their distinctiveness is perceived to be more than mere difference. For example, there may be a single characteristic that is possessed by one group but not the other. This 'is important in eliminating identification and sympathy between members of the dominating class and the dominated, and in eliminating possible confusion between powerful and powerless. It also helps to establish

separate "natures" which explain and justify widely differing privileges and fates' (ibid.: 49).

- Incorporation (relational definition) Incorporation or relational definition occur where masculine qualities, for example, are taken as primary. While the meanings of femininity and masculinity rely on each other, this is not a relationship of equals. Rather, 'the underside of a dualistically conceived pair is defined in relation to the upperside as a lack, a negativity' (ibid.: 52).
- Instrumentalism (objectification) Instrumentalism or objectification is the process whereby those on the lower or inferior side of the duality have to put their interests aside in favour of the dominant and indeed are seen as 'his instruments, a means to his ends. They are made part of a network of purposes which are defined in terms of or harnessed to the master's purposes and needs. The lower side is also objectified, without ends of its own which demand consideration on their own account. Its ends are defined in terms of the master's ends' (ibid.: 53).
- Homogenization or stereotyping Homogenization or stereotyping are ways through which hierarchies are maintained because they disregard any differences amongst the inferiorized class. Such a view would suggest, for example, that all women are the same.

Plumwood's approach to this analysis of dualism would be described as deconstructive. Deconstruction has been a significant tool in the politics of feminism that has facilitated an understanding of how truths are produced (Spivak, 2001). In this, deconstruction is not simply concerned with overturning binaried thinking but in illustrating how terms draw on their meaning from their dualistic positioning.

Deconstruction

Building on the notion of différance, deconstruction sees social life as a series of texts that can be read in a variety of ways. Because of this multiplicity of readings there is, therefore, a range of meanings that can be invoked. Moreover, through each reading we are producing another text to the extent that we can view the social world as the emanations of a whole array of intertextual weavings. While there is this variety, as we have seen, texts contain hierarchical concepts organized as binaries. Deconstruction does not seek to overturn the binary through a reversal of dominance. This would simply maintain hierarchization. Deconstruction is concerned to illustrate how language is used to frame meaning. Politically its purpose is to lead to 'an appreciation of hierarchy as illusion sustained by power. It may be a necessary illusion, at our stage in history. We do not know. But there is no rational warrant for assuming that other imaginary structures would not be possible' (Boyne, 1990: 124).

To achieve this deconstruction involves three phases (Grosz, 1990a). The first two of these are the reversal and displacement of the hierarchy. In terms of reversal we might, for example, seek to reclaim the terms Queer or Black for more positive interpretations of their meaning. However, it is insufficient simply to try to reverse the hierarchical status of any binary. At best, this simply keeps hierarchical organization in place. At worst, such attempts will be ignored because the dominant meanings of a hierarchical pairing are so strongly in place. This is why it is necessary to displace common hierarchized meanings. This is achieved by displacing the 'negative term, moving it from its oppositional role into the very heart of the dominant term' (ibid.: 97). The purpose of this is to make clear how the subordinated term is subordinated. This requires a third phase. This is the creation of a new term. Grosz notes that Derrida called the new term a 'hinge' word. She offers the following examples:

> such as 'trace' (simultaneously present and absent), 'supplement' (simultaneously plenitude and excess); 'différance' (sameness and difference); 'pharmakon' (simultaneously poison and cure); 'hymen' (simultaneously virgin and bride, rupture and totality), etc . . . These 'hinge words' (in Irigaray, the two lips, fluidity, maternal desire, a genealogy of women, in Kristeva, semanalysis, the semiotic, polyphony, etc.) function as undecidable, vacillating between two oppositional terms, occupying the ground of their 'excluded middle'. If strategically harnessed, these terms rupture the systems from which they 'originate' and in which they function. (ibid.)

Grosz comments that this is both an impossible and necessary project. It is impossible because we have to use the terms of any dominant discourse to challenge that discourse. It is necessary because such a process illustrates how so much of what is said is bound up with what cannot be, and is not, said.

In this respect, Plumwood's analysis illustrates the systematization of power relations that operate through networks of conceptual dualisms. She refers to the five features she has identified as a family and thereby indicates that they each have complex kinships with each other. Finlayson (1999) denotes the attention given to issues of power relations within poststructuralist analyses of language in terms of the turn to discourse. Accordingly, Finlayson defines discourse as referring both 'to the way language systematically organizes concepts, knowledge and experience and to the way in which it excludes alternative forms of organization. Thus, the boundaries between language, social action, knowledge and power are blurred' (ibid.: 62). Foucault (1972: 25) also illustrates how the meanings of discourse rely on what is left in the background. He comments that

> all manifest discourse is secretly based on an 'already-said'; and . . . this 'already-said' is not merely a phrase that has already been spoken, or a text that has already been written, but a 'never-said', an incorporeal discourse, a voice as silent as a breath, a writing that is merely the hollow of its own mark.

Gee (1996) comments on how dominant discourses are intimately related to the distribution of social power and hierarchical structure in society. Thus, control over certain discourses can lead to the acquisition of social goods such as money, power and status in a society.

The significance of this focus on discourse is that it directs our attention to the constellations of language. Language is not free-standing and nor are dualistic frameworks but part of what Wittgenstein defined as language games.

Language Games

> Of course language in general and concepts in particular often carry ideological implications. But as Wittgenstein puts it, in most cases the meaning of a word is its use. Used in different situations by different speakers, the word 'woman' takes on very different implications. If we want to combat sexism and heterosexism, we should examine what work words are made to do in different speech acts, not leap to the conclusion that the same word must mean the same oppressive thing every time it occurs, or that words oppress us simply by having determinate meanings, regardless of what those meanings are.
>
> (Moi, 1999: 45)

Moi is concerned to indicate that arguments that suggest that every usage of the term 'woman' is exclusionary are misplaced. Here she draws on Wittgenstein's (1958, s 43) dictum that 'For a *large* class of cases – though not for all – in which we employ the word "meaning" it can be defined thus: the meaning of a word is its use in the language.' Thus, Moi comments, 'In my view, all the cases in which feminists discuss the meaning of the words woman, sex and gender belong to the "large class of cases" Wittgenstein has in mind' (1999: 7). Her argument is that Wittgenstein proposes some convincing philosophical alternatives to certain post-Saussurean views of language.

Wittgenstein was concerned that any analysis of language should not be abstracted from the context of its usage. In this Wittgenstein was concerned that 'philosophy should not provide a theory of meaning at all: one should look at how words are actually used and explained, rather than construct elaborate fictions about how they must work' (Stern, 1995: 41). In this respect Wittgenstein's later concerns opposed his earlier work in the *Tractatus* that argued that language had a uniform logical structure that can be disclosed through philosophical analysis. Rather, in his *Philosophical Investigations* he thought that 'Language has no common essence, or at least, if it has one, it is a minimal one . . . connected . . . in a more elusive way, like games, or like the faces of people belonging to the same family' (Pears, 1971: 14).

For example, although a word may have a uniform appearance this does not mean that its meaning will be similarly uniform and from which we can make generalizations. Wittgenstein illustrated this point through an analysis of the word 'games'. When we use the word 'games' we might refer to board games, card games, ball games, Olympic games, and so forth. He comments that instead of saying because they are all games there must be something common to them we should '*look and see* whether there is anything common to all . . . To repeat: don't think, but look!' (Wittgenstein, 1958: s 66). For example, some ball games, such as tennis, involve winning and losing whereas some ball games, such as when a child throws a ball against a wall, do not. If we extend the analysis to games that do not use a ball we will find that again some are about winners and losers and others are not. For example, games such as ring-a-ring-a-roses are amusing but not competitive. Chess games are competitive. Overall 'the result of this examination is: we see a complicated network of similarities over-lapping and criss-crossing: sometimes overall similarities, sometimes similarities of detail' (ibid.). Wittgenstein called these relationships 'family resemblances' and argued that 'the line between what we are and are not prepared to call a game is likely (a) to be fuzzy and (b) to depend on our purposes in seeking such a definition' (Winch and Gingell, 1999: 58).

McGinn (1997: 43) comments that the conceptualization of language games brings 'into prominence the fact that language functions within the active, practical lives of speakers, that its use is inextricably bound up with the non-linguistic behaviour which constitutes its natural environment'. Thus an analysis of meaning has to be considered in relation to its usage rather than as an abstraction from its context. In this way Wittgenstein asks us to think through the taken-for-granted of everyday speech and to begin to notice that which we never notice. This includes both linguistic and non-linguistic features. As McGinn comments:

> Wittgenstein's concept of a language-game is clearly to be set over and against the idea of language as a system of meaningful signs that can be considered in abstraction from its actual employment. Instead of approaching language as a system of signs with meaning, we are prompted to think about it *in situ*, embedded in the lives of those who speak it. The tendency to isolate language, or abstract it from the context in which it ordinarily lives, is connected with our adopting a theoretical attitude towards it, and with our urge to explain how these mere signs (mere marks) can acquire their extraordinary power to mean or represent something. (1997: 44)

Thus Wittgenstein argued that we should look at the spatial and temporal phenomena of language rather than assuming 'a pure intermediary between the propositional signs and the facts' (McGinn, 1997: 94). In this way we would see that 'our forms of expression prevent us in all sorts of ways from seeing that nothing out of the ordinary is involved' (ibid.) and that 'everything lies open to view there is nothing to explain' (Wittgenstein, 1958: s 126).

In taking up these perspectives from Wittgenstein Moi applies this to the tendency within some poststructuralist writings to avoid any reference to biological facts because it would imply some form of essentialism. In order to avoid biological determinism some feminists 'go to the other extreme, placing biological facts under a kind of mental erasure' (Moi, 1999: 42). The theoretical reasons given for this are that '*political* exclusion is coded into the very concepts we use to make sense of the world' (ibid.: 43, emphasis in original). Thus it is argued that the word 'woman' is always ideological and '"woman" *must* mean "heterosexual, feminine and female"' (ibid., emphasis in original). When such terms such as 'woman' are used, poststructuralists take recourse in the slippery nature of meaning in order to construct an armoury of defence against accusations of essentialism. As Moi comments, this is to soften any implication of exclusion but such a position is misplaced and is based on the incorrect view that the term 'woman' actually does have only one meaning and that meaning is independent from the context of its use. If this were the case, we would be unable to envisage any alternative kind of meaning for 'woman'. Thus, Moi comments:

> The incessant poststructuralist invocations of the slippage, instability, and non-fixity of meaning are clearly intended as a way to soften the exclusionary blow of concepts, but unfortunately even concepts such as 'slippage' and 'instability' have fairly stable meanings in most contexts. It follows from the poststructuralists' own logic that if we were all mired in exclusionary politics just by having concepts, we would not be able to perceive the world in terms other than the ones laid out by our contaminated concepts. If oppressive social norms are embedded in our concepts, just because they are concepts, we would all be striving to preserve existing social norms. (ibid.: 44)

Moi is clear that her appeal that we should focus on the ordinary, everyday usage of terms is not to argue all meaning is neutral and devoid of power relations. Rather, she is indicating that any analysis of meaning has to take account of the speech acts within which it is placed. In different locations and used by different speakers the term 'woman' has a range of different meanings. One has to understand such location and to understand the world from the perspective of the speaker. Or as Luke (1996: 1) reminds us 'concepts and meanings . . . are products of historically and culturally situated social formations'.

In addition, in taking up Wittgenstein, Moi is not arguing for a defence of the status quo, the commonsensical or the dominant ideology. Rather, she is directing our attention to the everyday as a place of struggle over meaning. In this she comments, 'The very fact that there is continuous struggle over meaning (think of words such as *queer, woman, democracy, equality, freedom*) shows that different uses not only exist but sometimes give rise to violently conflicting meanings. If the meaning of a word is its use, such conflicts are part of the meaning of the word' (1999: 210). It is to the political struggle over meaning that I now turn.

Contests about Meaning

A common strategy in the management of concepts in social research is to take a technical approach. This requires the operationalization of a concept into key indicators. A classic statement in this regard would be 'Concepts are, by their nature, not directly observable. We cannot see social class, marital happiness, intelligence, etc. To use concepts in research we need to translate concepts into something observable – something we can measure. This involves defining and clarifying abstract concepts and developing indicators of them' (de Vaus, 2001: 24). It would be a mistake to believe that such concerns are primarily related to those who undertake forms of research that rely on hypothesis testing and quantification. Qualitative researchers who work with theory building and analysis from more 'grounded' approaches similarly recognize that the management and analysis of data require conceptual clarification. For example, Miles and Huberman (1994: 18) note that 'general constructs . . . subsume a mountain of particulars'. Miles and Huberman label these constructs 'intellectual "bins" containing many discrete events and behaviours' (ibid.). An intellectual 'bin' might, therefore, be labelled role conflict or cultural scene.

In the operationalization of concepts de Vaus (2001: 24) notes that one needs to descend 'the ladder of abstraction' and move from nominal definitions, such as, say, class, that simply convey a broad category and conclude our descent with operational definitions. For example, the operational definition of class may be occupation, salary and/or it may be the self-definition of the researched. These operational definitions, or indicators, would then form part of a questionnaire, interview or observation. Miles and Huberman suggest that however inductive in approach, any researcher 'knows which bins are likely to be in play in the study and what is likely to be in them. Bins comes from theory and experience and (often) from the general objectives of the study envisioned' (1994: 18). The researcher therefore needs to name the relevant 'bins', describe their contents and variables and consider their interrelationship with other 'bins' in order to build a conceptual framework.

As de Vaus makes clear, the importance of descending the ladder of abstraction is to ensure the validity of research. Validity here is con-cerned with 'whether your methods, approaches and techniques actually relate to, or measure, the issues you have been exploring' (Blaxter et al., 2001: 221). In this an adequate operationalization of a concept through the use of indicators enables researchers to sustain the claims that are made for research in terms of causality, warrantability or trustworthi-ness. In qualitative research working within designs that require pre-cision in naming and labelling conceptual 'bins' facilitates cross-case comparability and can enhance its confirmatory aspects (Miles and Huberman, 1994).

There is no doubt that issues of reliability, validity, warrantability and comparability are exceptionally important in the design and conduct of research. The processes that are required through which researchers delineate concepts into indicators or categorize conceptual 'bins' facilitate an important recognition of the complexity of the social world and this in turn facilitates clarity and focus. However, many textbooks that discuss the issue of concept-indicator linkages imply that this is primarily an issue of technical difficulty. This is because, as any initial introduction to social research will indicate, there are a host of indicators that could be applied to any concept. For example, in the field of social gerontology the collection in Peace (1990) indicates how concepts such as age, dependency and quality of life have varied indicators. Here Hughes (1990: 50) notes that the definitional problems that arise when conceptualizing 'quality of life' arise 'in part from the problem of integrating objective and subjective elements and indeed, of determining which elements ought to be included'. These would include occupation, material status, physical health, functional abilities, social contacts, activities of daily living, recreation, interests, and so forth. Hughes also notes that the complexity of these indicators is further compounded by the variables of 'race', gender and class. Hughes comments that there is, inevitably, disagreement about the 'correct' indicators that would designate quality of life. This appears to be particularly the case in terms of the importance given to subjective data. For example, how does one weight the feelings and views of research respondents about the quality of their life in comparison to what are seen to be more objective data such as income, housing conditions, and so forth? However, Hughes argues that one should not abandon the search for an integrated conceptualization that would combine subjective and objective data as this 'would be to deny gerontological research vital evidence' (ibid.: 51).

Such a statement implies that if all researchers in a field of enquiry could agree on a set of required components, indicators or variables the problem of validity would be solved. However, it is a mistake to assume that what are often portrayed as technical issues are devoid of the political and that the delineation of a concept into a set of indicators is primarily a neutral act. It would be a mistake also, therefore, to assume that the issue of validity is resolved by recall to some set of apolitical technical acts. This assumes that the function of such indicators is purely descriptive rather than that such descriptions ascribe values that license inferences about what is warrantable and permissible (Connolly, 1993; Tanesini, 1994). To explore this further I turn here to an analysis of the divergence of opinion that arises in academic, and other, debates about the 'correct' meaning of concepts.

Swanton (1985) describes the contestation over conceptual definitions in terms that:

- certain concepts admit to a variety of interpretations or uses;
- the proper use of a concept is disputable;
- varied conceptualizations are deployed 'both "aggressively and defensively" against rival conceptions'. (ibid.: 813)

The question is 'Why do such contestations arise?' Connolly (1993) indicates how the internal complexity of certain key concepts gives rise to contestability over meaning. This internal complexity arises because, as Henwood (1996) makes clear in her analysis of dualism, certain key concepts form a web of connections. Connolly refers to these as cluster concepts. For example if we ask 'What is "woman"?' we might respond that she is relational, caring, 'raced', classed, aged, embodied, and so forth. We are, therefore, required to consider 'woman' in respect of decisions about a further broad range of contestable terms. This is because the interpretation of any of these terms is relatively open. For example in deciding what 'woman' is we also have to decide what 'race', class, age and embodiment are. Thus what are our indicators if we take 'race' as our variable? There are certainly a whole array of terms: Black British, Women of Colour, Black African American, and so forth. Certainly some individuals with South Asian heritage have objected to being encompassed within the term 'Black' as they do not identify with such a conceptualization of their ethnicity. More recently issues of Whiteness have come to the fore as central to any conceptualization of 'race'. As a result it has been argued that ignoring issues of Whiteness does not do justice to a proper conceptualization of 'race'. Thus, as Connolly argues, a term's 'very characteristics as a cluster concept provide the space within which such contests [of meaning] emerge' (1993: 15).

Connolly also raises a further issue in this respect. He suggests that if the issue at stake is merely a question of technicalities, then it is within the realms of possibility that researchers could agree on a set of finite indicators and whenever they use a particular concept these would be used. Yet this does not happen. Indeed, he indicates that contests over meaning are not perceived simply as irksome and a problem arising from the technicalities of naming and defining. Rather, contests over meaning are seen to be highly important in academic debate. What, for example, does our omission to include Whiteness as a factor in the conceptualization of 'race' indicate in terms of the failure of our analyses? It is self-evidently true that this is a common descriptor of many women. The reply is that it to ignore Whiteness is to imply that 'race' issues are not the concern of White people when palpably they are.

In exploring the extent of debate over new forms of conceptualization Connolly suggests that two issues are at stake. The first is related to claims to validity. As we have seen, the use of indicators to give conceptual clarity is linked directly to the internal and external validity of a research study. Thus contestability arises because of the connection between the use of 'correct' indicators and what can be claimed for the findings of any research. If one has not used the appropriate indicators then, of course, one's research is invalid.

The second issue relates to the theoretical frameworks within which a research study is placed. Connolly notes that researchers often have intense attachment to particular theoretical fields as offering the most salient of explanations for particular phenomena. Contestation over meaning therefore also impacts on the truth claims for any theorization. As Connolly notes:

> The decision to make some elements 'part of' cluster concepts while excluding others invokes a complex set of judgements about the validity of claims central to the theory within which the concept moves . . . the multiple criteria of cluster concepts reflect the theory in which they are embedded, and a change in the criteria of any of these concepts is likely to involve a change in the theory itself. Conceptual disputes, then, are neither a mere prelude to inquiry nor peripheral to it, but when they involve the central concepts of a field of inquiry, they are surface manifestations of basic theoretical differences that reach to the core. The intensity of commitment to favored definitions reflects intensity of commitment to a general theoretical perspective; and revisions that follow conceptual debates involve a shift in the theory that has housed the concepts. (1993: 21)

These issues can be further illustrated through an exploration of the common distinction that is made between normative and descriptive meanings of a concept. For example, in the case of 'What is "woman"?' identity and postcolonial feminists have indicated that the normative meanings of woman in early second-wave feminism are those of White, Western and middle class. To use the word 'woman' therefore implies that you are invoking this meaning. However, the distinction between normative and descriptive claims for a concept is often confused (Connolly, 1993; Tanesini, 1994). In particular those who invoke descriptive claims as if they were either simple issues of fact or technicality ignore 'a fundamental feature of description: A description does not refer to data or elements that are bound together merely on the basis of similarities adhering in them, *but to describe is to characterize a situation from the vantage point of certain interests, purposes, or standards*' (Connolly, 1993: 22–3, emphasis in original). When claims are made that the 'woman' of early second-wave feminism is Western or White or middle class, the central issue is not one of empirical fact. The issue is one of values. To assert the empirical facts of the diversity of 'woman' is to make claims about the values that we attach to that concept. White, Western and middle class are not descriptors but are in themselves concepts imbued with a host of value-led meanings. Thus:

> Essentially contested concepts . . . are typically *appraisive* in that to call something a 'work of art' or a 'democracy' is both to describe it and to ascribe a value to it or express a commitment with respect to it. The connection within the concept itself of descriptive and normative dimensions helps to explain why such concepts are subject to intense and endless debate. (ibid.)

In this light we can see that contests over meaning are not technical issues. Rather, they arise because conceptualization has an inferential-justificatory role. To claim that a particular meaning of a concept is the only valid one is to license the future use of that particular meaning. This means that contests over meaning are accounts of how terms should be used which, if successful, impact upon practices and theorization. Tanesini comments here that:

> Meaning-claims then do not perform any explanatory role; their purpose in language is that of prescribing emendations or preservations of current practices. In particular, their function is not that of describing the inferential-justificatory role of any linguistic expression. That is, they do not explain the content of an expression. Instead, meaning-claims are proposals about emendation or preservation of the roles of expressions; these claims become prescriptive, if one is entitled to make them. As proposals for influencing the evolution of ongoing practices, meaning-claims are grounded in social practices. (1994: 207–8)

As we have seen in the case of 'What is "woman"?' feminists who do not want to be seen as either racist, classist, colonialist or essentialist may at minimum qualify the term by adding what Butler (1990) refers to as the 'embarrassed etceteras' of 'race', class, etc. etc. This has certainly functioned to add to the list of descriptors what we might mean by 'woman'.

However, Tanesini also notes that more recently the concern over 'What is "woman"?' has taken a new epistemological turn. The list of descriptors has encouraged a sense of fragmentation of the concept of woman so that it is now no longer a useful category. Tanesini comments:

> Gender sceptics claim that racist, heterosexist and classist biases are part of the logic of the concept of gender. In other words, they claim that it is conceptually impossible to use the notion of gender without engaging in exclusionary practices. They hold that, if one is attentive to differences of ethnic origin, sexual orientation and class, the notion of gender disintegrates into fragments and cannot be employed any more as a useful category. (1994: 205)

In Tanesini's view, we would not understand these arguments simply as part of developing our understandings of the impossibility of ever fully describing 'woman' because of the multitude of descriptive elements of which she is comprised. Rather, we would see these arguments as an intervention in a debate that seeks to justify future use, or indeed non-use, of a concept. The implication of the argument that the term 'woman' is inevitably normative and exclusionary is that we should cease using the term. We might even invent a new one in terms of a broader deconstructive strategy.

However, as part of a counter-debate about this essentially contested concept we might also intervene and argue that the term 'woman' should be retained. In this case Moi (1999) demonstrates how we might draw on an alternative theoretical framework as a way of interceding. In this we might argue that it is quite permissible to continue using the word 'woman' because our meanings should be clear from the context. If feminists take up Moi's position, then we might see a change in theoretical framework that, say, more fully incorporates Wittgensteinean theories. If feminists take up the claims of 'gender sceptics' then we might find new terms created for 'woman' or the use of the term ceasing altogether in feminist analysis. What this latter position might mean for feminist politics is, of course, a moot point.

Case Study 1: 'Progress' in Zimbabwe: Is 'It' a 'Woman'?

I have been concerned in this chapter to indicate something of multiple meaning and conceptual contestation. I have used the question 'What is "woman"?' at various points for exemplification. Sylvester (1999) is similarly concerned with the meanings and representations of 'woman' and her research explores this through the further problematic concept of progress. Specifically, Sylvester considers how, and if, we can conceptualize progress through women's lives and testimonies. The framework of Sylvester's paper is a deconstructive analysis of narratives of progression and its linkage to issues of identity. In this she notes: 'Progress is at once a very common, common notion, easily grasped by the modern mind, and something difficult to understand and make happen or to repudiate absolutely' (ibid.: 90). As Sylvester also notes, progress can be an embarrassing word for feminists as it reminds them of a one-for-all 1970s' marching feminism where progression was guaranteed once one could agree on the best route to utopia. Clinton exemplifies the ambivalence toward progress in contemporary feminist theorizing as 'Sex in the US White House humbles some feminists for whom that skulker in dark corridors has been a darling of progress for women' (ibid.). Thus, 'Progress exists/does not exist, is asserted/contested in many ways. How does one investigate the elusive relevant and irrelevant wanted and absent? How does one research trickster "progress" at this point in time?' (ibid.: 91).

Sylvester's response to these questions is to argue that what is vitally necessary is to 'refocus and look at the everyday social constitution of "progress"' (ibid.: 92). Her paper is therefore based on interviews that she conducted between 1988 and 1993 with women in Zimbabwe's commercial farming and factories. Here she is concerned to 'telescope' their descriptions of their daily work and their desires for what they do not have. This is because 'the usual ways of studying progress [e.g. through statistical and economic analyses] are not designed to take the concerns of local "women" into account' (ibid.). The questions that Sylvester asked included whether they found their work met their expectations or was satisfactory, what changes, if any, they would make in their workplaces and what they would do if they were the President of Zimbabwe. Most importantly, Sylvester adds, she asked 'Are you women?' and 'How do you know?' Sylvester threads this interview data with fictional representations of women from noted Zimbabwean literature produced in the 1980s and early 1990s.

Sylvester's research illustrates the connections between meanings of progress and meanings of 'woman' in varied ways. In fiction these connections include:

- woman as having progressed because she is 'freed from the fetters of loyalty to fixed and inherited places' (ibid.: 94);
- woman as in need of progress because she is 'the dregs of agricultural labor . . . the non-permanent, casual, . . . desperate' (ibid.: 94–5);
- woman *as* progress because she is the labour aristocracy.

Women's own accounts similarly illustrated these fictionalized elements and illustrated how women experienced sexual harassment and the common gendered inequalities in access to promotion, permanent work, equal pay and positions of power and influence in worker representation systems. Their testimonies also illustrated how women sought to circumvent and resist these imperatives to lack of progress. Sylvester indicates how '"Progress" existed in everyday narratives of effort and movement and in the counter-efforts of others to patch up problems and get on with progress' (ibid.: 111). The women that Sylvester interviewed also offered multiple meanings of woman. They noted that they could not speak for 'all' women, that some women may have different views and politics about 'progress'. Sometimes they could point to particular women as exemplars of progress. Nonetheless, 'Always [progress] was a desiring of movement around the usual rules for women at work. And just as always, the outcome would be ambiguous. Would the fiesty factory "women" be promoted? Would commercial farm "women" get women supervisors? Were the transgressions we noted powerful or just quick tricks?' (ibid.: 112). Sylvester's paper makes it clear that there are no easy answers to these questions. This is because in terms of its meanings and empirics, 'Progress is so tricky' (ibid.: 113).

Summary

As an opening chapter I have attempted to illustrate what has influenced my own thinking in framing this text. What follows explores key terms in feminist theory to illustrate their diverse conceptualization and their application in feminist research. In the concluding chapter I return to the issue of conceptual literacy. Here I am concerned to indicate ways in which conceptual literacy might be further developed.

FURTHER READING

Connolly, W. (1993) *The Terms of Political Discourse*. Oxford: Blackwell (Third Edition). This is a classic text on conceptual contestation. It is written primarily for politics students and draws on the term 'politics' for exemplification.

Plumwood, V. (1993) *Feminism and the Mastery of Nature*. London: Routledge. Plumwood does an excellent job in illustrating the distinctions between binaries and dualism. I have only had space here to draw attention to this issue and so would recommend much fuller consultation of her work.

Equality 2

An understanding of male and female as distinctly different and complementary to an understanding of male and female as equal was a radical shift in gender ideology.

(Munro, 1998: 52)

Evans (1994) suggests that there are three issues that are central to contemporary feminist conceptualizations of equality. The first is that the most common assumption made about the meaning of equality is that this must mean 'the same'. Thus feminists have argued that as we are all born equal we should be treated as equals. But, of course, this begs the question 'Equal to what?' The measure, or the normative standard, of that equality has been men's lives. Men had the vote, property rights and access to education and so these became spheres of early feminist campaigning. More recently, feminists have noted how men still maintain their positions at the top of employment hierarchies. As a result, feminist campaigns for equality have sought to break through the metaphorical glass ceiling that prevents access to higher positions.

It is true to say that some of the achievements of feminism have been in terms of accessing the public realms of social life. There are more women in the British Parliament and more women in managerial positions in organizations. In terms of legislative change, it is almost four decades ago that the Equal Pay Act (1963) was passed in the United States. In the UK it is just over three decades ago that the Equal Pay Act (1970) was passed and over a quarter of a century ago that the Sex Discrimination Act (1975) was passed. Despite these changes, parity with men in all of these arenas is yet to be achieved. And, internationally, it should be remembered that such legislation is not a global phenomenon.

However, it is women's responsibilities in terms of the family that appears to be the most resistant to change and this brings us to the second issue that Evans highlights as central to feminist conceptualizations of equality. This is that this has focused primarily on achieving equality based on entry into paid labour. A key problem with this is that it has left women's family responsibilities unchanged. Research has demonstrated how greater access to paid employment cannot be viewed simply as a liberating phenomena that leaves women less dependent on male partners and more fulfilled as individuals. Indeed, it is evident that women either have to manage as best they can the two greedy spheres of paid work and family and/or take part-time, flexible employment with its associated lower economic and social value. This has led to continuing lobbying for a range of policies such as childcare facilities, maternity and paternity leave, flexible working hours, and so forth.

Third, while equality has not disappeared, it has more recently been under sustained critique. For example, the assumption that equality means 'the same' has been explored in terms of its political and philosophical implications. The notion that women should view the masculine as the normative, that is as the goal to be achieved, is certainly not one that is ascribed to by all feminists. For example, cultural feminists have sought to valorize the feminine and have argued that women are indeed different to men. Their political goal is to have an equal value placed on women's difference.

Plumwood (1993) summarizes these positions within discussions of equality in terms of two models. One of these she calls 'the feminism of uncritical equality'. This is associated with models of feminism in the 1960s and 1970s that 'attempted to fit women uncritically into a masculine pattern of life and a masculine model of humanity and culture which was presented as gender-neutral' (Plumwood, 1993: 27). Although this position is mainly associated with liberal feminism, it should be noted that the masculine ideal of selfhood is also found in socialist and humanist-Marxist feminism when the emphasis is placed on the human as a producer or worker (Plumwood, 1993, see also Grosz, 1990b). The second model Plumwood calls 'the feminism of uncritical reversal'. This is where feminists are seeking to give a higher value to the female side of the female/male binary. This model is mainly associated with the maternalist stance of cultural feminists writing in the 1970s and early 1980s.

This chapter explores these issues and debates and their implications for conceptualizing equality in the following ways. The first two sections that follow are concerned to understand equality as 'sameness'. The first of these is concerned with the measure of sameness. What is this sameness that is being measured? How is it measured? The second of these is concerned with the legislative impact of liberal perspectives of equal rights. Here I outline measures for individual and group-based rights and the major critiques of these. In the third section of this chapter I turn to some of those feminists who argue that women's difference is the root of their equality. Here I distinguish between those who could be described as arguing that women are equal *but* different and those who are arguing that women are equal *and* different. In the case of the former I outline first- and second-wave theorizing about women's 'natural' calling and higher value as mothers. Here I also illustrate the impact that critiques of essentialism have had on feminist thought. In terms of the latter I outline aspects of Italian feminism.

My final conceptualization is concerned with material inequality. I note here how attention to issues of material inequality has been decreasing. Among other reasons this is because increasing theorization now focuses on aspects of identity and there is considerable recognition given to the complexity and multiplicity of social positioning. This has led to substantial critiques of earlier class-based conceptualizations of material inequality. I offer two examples of contemporary theorization (Fraser, 1995; Bradley, 2000) that attempt to take account of more recent aspects of feminist thought in relation to material inequalities.

The Measure of Equality

- Women and men have equal natures   *Axiom*
- So if women are given equal treatment with men   *Programme*
- The outcome will be equal performance   *Goal*

(Thornton, 1986: 78)

Feminist history tells us of the significant campaigns that have been undertaken to enable women to vote, to give them access to higher education and to equal pay and conditions in the workplace. The fundamental basis of these campaigns has been the argument that, as human beings, women are the same as men. Women therefore have a right to equal treatment. As a corollary to this, feminists have also argued that any differences we see between the sexes are the result of socialization or inequalities of treatment. Given that women and men are the same, women are equally capable of being scientists, astronauts and corporate executives of global companies. They are also equally entitled to the same pay for the same work and the same levels of access to education (Phillips, 1987; Evans, 1995).

The basic tenets of these kinds of sex equality arguments in terms of axiom, programme and goal have become something of a 'common-sense' view of sex equality. Moreover, the notion of equality as a universal concept, that is a set of rules, norms and principles that are equally applicable to everyone and can be recognized and acceptable to everyone, appears at first sight to be an attractive concept for feminism. Nonetheless, this fairly simple set of statements belies the complexity of philosophical, political and empirical issues upon which they draw.

Thornton (1986) notes that there are three elements to this standard argument for sex equality. These are: women's nature; the social treatment of women; and women's performance. Each of these issues raise considerable problems in terms of the concept of equality. Let us begin by noting that if we are to say that one thing is equal to another we need to have a workable, and agreed, measure:

> *Equality* is a concept that can only be applied to two (or more) things *in some specified respect*. There has to be a characteristic which both have in respect of which they are said to be equal. Two sticks might be equal *in length*, two persons equal *in height* (*equally long, equally tall*). But if I call my first stick *a* and my second stick *b*, I cannot meaningfully say simply that *a* is equal to *b*; nor can I meaningfully say to Les and Viv simply that Les is equal to Viv – not unless I specify, or at least presume, the particular respect in which they are equal. (Thornton, 1986: 77, emphasis in original)

A key criterion of equality is that of measurement. In terms of the stick that Thornton refers to, the criterion of length provides a readily accessible measure. Nonetheless, if we were interested in the aesthetic beauty of the bark on two sticks from different trees, what workable criterion would we draw on to give us an equal measure? There may be some agreed criteria for measuring the beauty or artistic worth of an object in terms of the density of the bark, the colour, diversity, and so forth. These would, often as not, call on 'expert' judgements and the qualitative and political nature of such criteria means that they will be subject to challenge, disagreement and change. The relative preciseness and agreement that occur when using length as a measure is lost when one extends the discussion to more heterogeneous characteristics. How, then, do we measure equality? What are the characteristics for 'sameness' that are drawn upon?

With respect to the standard sex equality argument set out above, the axiom that women and men have equal natures begs a whole host of political and philosophical questions about the 'nature' of humanity and how this might be measured. Feminist responses to these questions have argued that what masquerades as the universal human subject is masculinity. Indeed, we might qualify this further to say that in Western societies predominantly the yardstick is White, middle-class masculinity. This yardstick creates the standard against which we should measure our lives and the standard against which our lives are measured. It provides a model for our desires and our aspirations, our values and our politics. It means that one is always 'less than' if one does not measure up. A view of equality based on this form of 'sameness' means that the norms and ideals of a masculine value system, and its concomitant power, are unchallenged. Moreover, to achieve equality on the basis of this form of 'sameness', those aspects that distinguish women from men, for example, the fact that women give birth, must be minimized (Grosz, 1990b). And so, to fit this model of 'sameness' one has to deny difference.

When we turn to the programmatic elements of equal treatment, further problems arise. For example, does equal treatment mean identical treatment? Does it mean a more muted fairness and parity? Or does it require certain forms of professional or expert judgement that calls for variation of treatment? Evans (1995: 163) comments in this respect that 'We do not expect equal "amounts" of treatment, the same doses of drugs, identical types of medication, for different ills. Indeed, a doctor who treated differently diagnosed patients identically would be treating them *unequally*, in that there would be different results.' What, then, are the measures or criteria that are called on to ensure equal treatment? Certainly, legislative measures have sought to resolve some of the issues that arise from this question. Yet pertinently Bacchi (1990: 176) comments: 'People are not algebraic symbols and cannot simply be slotted into an equation.'

Finally, the assumed goal of the standard sex equality argument is that of equal performance or outcome. However, the assumption that equal treatment will produce equal results can be critiqued in terms that such an argument is both circular and speculative. Sevenhuijsen indicates such arguments are based on an assumption of a natural 'sameness' and they rely for evidence on the differences between us:

> Although the argument that equal treatment will produce equal results sounds quite plausible, in fact this is a circular and speculative mode of reasoning. Since it is hard empirically to prove a natural or original equality, evidence of its existence is largely based on difference in treatment. The implication is that it is because people are treated differently that

they depart from their natural sameness. The principles and objectives of equal treatment are thus conflated into an indivisible whole. (1998: 42)

Sevenhuijsen notes that this conflation means that when equality of treatment does not lead to equality of results, it is easier for people to claim that this is because of biological differences in terms of, say, genetics and hormones. In an interesting example of girls' greater achievement we can see how these issues are invoked. Education is considered to be an important site for the equalization of life chances. Accordingly, Orr (2000) reports on the curricular changes in the British school system since 1975. She notes how inspectors' reports commented that reading materials in the early years were more focused on boys' interests and how the subject separation of girls and boys operated at all stages of the curriculum. This was particularly the case in girls' and boys' experience of science after the age of 14. The introduction of the National Curriculum in 1988 is one piece of legislation that is cited as reducing the sex differentiation in the school curriculum up to the age of 16. However, recent attention to girls' higher achievements in examinations in the United Kingdom has led to considerable concerns about boys' relatively poorer performance. In consequence, 'Current discussions about equal opportunities generally focus on boys' underachievement' (Myers, 2000: 221). In particular, there has been concern that these examination results suggest that masculinity-is-in-crisis (Blackmore, 1997). This has resulted in a range of explanations for boys' under-achievement that include assumptions of innate biological differences between girls and boys (Raphael Reed, 1999). These in turn have given rise to calls for changes to examination processes and teaching techniques as ideas that female and male brains operate differently are used to suggest that current teaching methods favour girls rather than boys. For example, it is suggested that in comparison to women, men's brains do not deal well with tasks that call for the emotional reflexivity that current examinations require.

These problems associated with the 'measure' of equality are embedded in equal opportunities policies. As the term suggests, equality of opportunity is primarily concerned with enabling all individuals in a society to have equal access to the same life chances such as education and employability. Theoretically, equality of opportunity is not concerned with achieving sameness of outcome. However, it is usually outcomes that form the basis of evaluating whether equal opportunities policies have been achieved. This is the very circularity and conflation to which Sevenhuijsen alludes. It is to equal opportunities and other formal equality policies that I now turn.

Case Study 2: Gender Wage Inequalities in Taiwan

Income is one of those areas of equality where one might imagine it would be possible to develop agreed measures. Equal pay for equal work has certainly been an underpinning feature of equity campaigns. Nonetheless, the pay gap between women and men continues unabated. Thus Reskin and Padavic (1994: 109) comment: 'In every country in the world, men outearn women.' The reasons that economists have given for this range from differences between the sexes in their investment in human capital to differences in the productive capabilities of women and men. Feminists have critiqued these arguments and have pointed out that horizontal and vertical segregated labour markets operate to women's disadvantage as they are mainly employed in sectors that are devalued as 'women's work' and are also positioned at the bottom levels of organizational hierarchies. Feminist research has therefore illustrated how sex segregation in the labour market combines with a devaluation of women's work. This creates comparable-worth dis-crimination where 'employers underpay workers who are doing jobs that are different from predominantly male jobs but are of equal value' (ibid.: 119).

Berik (2000) offers an example of research into pay equity that takes account of a number of economic factors. Berik's framework of analysis draws on the impacts of globalization and technological change in gendered labour markets. For example, Taiwan has experienced sig-nificant restructuring of its economic base with growing overseas investment and success in export-oriented manufacturing. This has meant that in the manufacturing sector there has been a decline in opportunities for women's employment. The key question that Berik's research addresses is the effects of this restructuring, particularly that of export-oriented growth, on gender wage inequalities. Berik's metho-dological approach is a statistical analysis of secondary data provided through industry-level panel surveys. These include changes in women's share of manufacturing employment; trends in wage–salaried worker ratios; gender earnings ratios; and the varied characteristics of female-intensive and male-intensive industries. Berik uses statistical equations to calculate wage inequalities across a range of dependent and independent variables.

Berik's findings indicate the gendered and class-based effects of com-plex economic restructuring processes. At the aggregate level between 1984 and 1993 women wage workers in manufacturing experienced a disproportionate loss of opportunities for employment and growing wage inequality. However, an industry-level analysis gives a slightly different result. Here Berik 'examined the separate effects of export orientation, overseas investment by Taiwanese firms, job restructuring, and capital intensity, after controlling for female share of industry employment, female reserve labor supply, and average firm size' (ibid.: 19). Berik's findings suggest that a greater orientation toward export growth 'is a source of lower pay not only for women workers . . . but also for men' (ibid.). Finally, the shift from waged workers to salaried employees also had gendered effects as 'women wage workers were losers in absolute and relative terms' (ibid.).

The 'Liberal' Heritage: Equality Rights and the Law

The historical antecedents of the standard sex equality argument can be found in the work of seventeenth- and eighteenth-century political and philosophical liberal theory. This is a period commonly termed the Enlightenment, marked as it is by a European philosophical movement whose basic belief was the superiority of reason as a guide to knowledge and human behaviour. Liberal theory contested the divine right of monarchs to political rule. It argued that men of propertied classes should have equal rights of citizenship. These were: the right to vote and to hold political office and the right to hold property in one's own name.

Arising from this period the writings of Mary Wollstonecraft (*Thoughts on the Education of Daughters*, 1787, *A Vindication of the Rights of Woman*, 1792) and John Stuart Mill (*On The Subjection of Women*, 1869) are often cited as forming the cornerstone of early feminist campaigns for equality. The basis of these was to argue that the natural justice accorded to men should be extended to women. In building on liberal philosophy the main emphasis in such arguments was that of individual rights.

With its liberal heritage equal rights feminism or formal equality, the two most common terms used here, has been seen to be the most successful form of feminism. This has, for example, reversed a previous absence in public consciousness of the role of women in society and women's rights to citizenship and equality before the law (Bulbeck, 2000). Indeed, how many of us would now give up our right to vote or our right to an education? Equal rights feminism has, in particular, sought to achieve equality through legislative means in order to secure the rights of the individual. In this respect Ashiagbor identifies four types of equality that inform legal definitions and the processes of law:

> First, ontological equality or the fundamental equality of individuals wherein all human beings are considered equal; secondly, equality of opportunity, namely meritocratic access to opportunities such as employment which leaves initial starting points untouched; thirdly, equality of condition, where there is an attempt to make conditions of life equal for relevant social groups; and fourthly, equality of outcome or of result, which would require some form of legislative or other intervention to compensate for inequality in starting points. (1999: 150)

It is equality of opportunity that has been deployed most often in UK law (Ashiagbor, 1999; Belcher, 1999). For example, in the UK the Sex Discrimination Act, 1975 outlawed discrimination on the grounds of sex and marital status in the fields of education and employment and in the provision of goods, facilities and services. The Sex Discrimination Act also established the Equal Opportunities Commission (EOC) that describes its vision as follows:

> Our *vision* is for a society and an economy that enables women and men to fulfil their potential and have their contributions to work and home life equally valued and respected, free from assumptions based on their sex. We want a society that guarantees equality for women and for men. (http://www.eoc.org.uk/ emphasis in original, accessed 1 June 2001)

As the EOC vision makes clear, the promotion of equal opportunities assumes a 'no difference' 'sameness' view of the sexes. The language of equal opportunity also conveys its main purpose as the facilitation of a level playing field between women and men so that any individual potentials can be realized within a competitive system. Nonetheless, there are a number of critiques that surround formal equality models. For example, rights-based arguments do not necessarily always work in women's favour. The supposed gender neutrality of rights-based arguments means that men can argue for their rights as they perceive them to be diminished by feminist activism. The case outlined above of boys' under-achievement is one example. Smart (1989) also illustrates this issue through the fathers' rights movement 'Families need Fathers'. With increasing divorce and the awarding of child custody to mothers, 'Families need Fathers' have lobbied successfully that their paternal rights need protecting. As Grosz (1990b: 338) comments 'men . . . have been able to use anti-discrimination or equal opportunity regulations to secure their own positions as much as women have'.

These formal conceptualizations of equality also do not adequately challenge the existing social order in terms of its hierarchical and competitive basis. Indeed, they can be said to uphold it. This is not only the case in terms of comparisons between women and men, social classes, ethnic groups, and so forth. It is also the case in respect of women as a group or class. Meyers (1997: 64) summarizes critiques of liberal equality arguments by stating that 'Liberal feminism is primarily an instrument for the advancement of well-off, talented women.' Similarly, hooks notes the 'race' and class privileges in equal rights arguments:

> Most people in the United States think of feminism or the more commonly used term 'women's lib' as a movement that aims to make women the social equals of men. This broad definition, popularized by the media and mainstream segments of the movement, raises problematic questions. Since men are not equals in white supremacist, capitalist, patriarchal class structure, which men do women want to be equal to? Do women share a common vision of what equality means? Implicit in this simplistic definition of women's liberation is a dismissal of race and class as factors that, in conjunction with sexism, determine the extent to which an individual will be discriminated against, exploited, or oppressed. Bourgeois white women interested in women's rights issues have been satisfied with simple definitions for obvious reasons. Rhetorically placing themselves in the same social category as oppressed women, they were not anxious to call attention to race and class privilege. (hooks, 1997: 23)

It is certainly the case that equality of opportunity policies have not produced equality of outcome (see, for example, Figes, 1994). As Case Study 2 illustrates, there remain considerable disparities in the income levels of women and men despite, in some countries, equal pay legislation. Few women actually do run global corporations or nations. There are even fewer Black and minority ethnic women in such positions. These concerns have led some feminists to argue for more interventionist or targeted approaches that would go beyond the individualism of rights-based equality. For example, in a discussion of Black women as a group facing discrimination in the labour market Ashiagbor comments on the individualizing framework of equal opportunities:

> Not only are the concepts of equality which inform anti-discrimination law seemingly hostile to the idea of group rights and the recognition of black women as a discrete group within anti-discrimination discourse but the nature of enforcement further reinforces the individualised form of equality which the law sets out to achieve. (1999: 153)

Arguments for group rights are based on the need to recognize that members of particular groups in society, such as minority ethnic groups, disabled people and women, face particular forms of discrimination and disadvantage. Eisenberg outlines the significance of weighting individual rights over group rights as follows:

> The principle of equality serves individual well-being by equalizing the resources individuals have available to them to lead good lives. Group rights might be required because some types of resources are only available to individuals through the groups to which they belong. Some minority groups cannot enjoy the security required to build a meaningful and rich cultural context without the additional protection of rights. (2000: 397)

Group rights come under a range of terms that include affirmative action, positive discrimination or quotas. Their aim is to equalize the chances or outcomes between groups in society rather than individuals. Bacchi comments on the range of programmes that can be termed affirmative action:

> Affirmative action, a term which originated in the United States, refers to a range of programmes directed towards targeted groups to redress their inequality. Broadly it takes two forms: policies to alter the composition of the labour force, and/or policies to increase the representativeness of public committees, political parties, and educational institutions. (1996: 15)

There is considerable variation internationally in the take-up and implementation of affirmative and positive action policies, as with equal rights policies more generally. For example, 'positive discrimination' or 'affirmative action' is unlawful in the UK. Instead, the overall principle is that issues such as recruitment and promotion must be undertaken on merit and irrespective of sex (Belcher, 1999). Chalude et al. (1994) report on the legal measures that have been developed within the European Union to enhance women's professional equality. These include more attenuated positive action programmes to 'allow better access for women to jobs where they have been underrepresented, better career and training opportunities, better relationships with their family and enhanced career responsibilities' (ibid.: 291). Chalude et al. note, however, that the legal framework for positive action varies for each country of the European Union. In the UK 'positive action' is permissible and is 'directed at equalizing opportunities, in line with the liberal conception of equality' (Belcher, 1999: 45). For example, training bodies can provide women-only access to training only in sectors of employment where women are significantly under-represented.

Case Study 3: Equal Opportunities and Positive Action in the British National Health Service

Iganski et al. (2001) comment that there are two main arguments that are offered to support equal opportunities measures. The first is that of justice arguments around fairness and equity that have been forwarded by feminists and others. The second is termed the 'business case' and is distinguished by its call to utilitarian, pragmatic self-interest. It is the latter argument that has been most persuasive in Britain for encouraging the take-up of equal opportunities policies.

Iganski et al.'s research is concerned with an analysis of positive action policies that were implemented by the British National Health Service (NHS). Their particular sphere of concern is analysing the extent to which positive action policies facilitated the recruitment of minority ethnic groups into nursing and midwifery. Their methodological approach was to select eight case studies from 50 nurse education centres in England that were responsible for initial registration training. However, Iganski et al. were not primarily concerned to select a representative sample of case studies. Rather their approach was based on the critical case approach whereby 'the method adopted entailed deliberately seeking out circumstances most likely to be favourable to the development and implementation of equal opportunities and positive action provisions' (ibid.: 299). For this reason the case studies were selected on the basis of their location in areas with high levels of minority ethnic communities. Empirical data was then collected through 81 semi-structured interviews conducted in 1996 and 1997.

The findings from Iganski et al.'s research illustrate how legislative change is no guarantor of social change. Their findings therefore illustrate the variability of implementation, necessary resourcing, organizational commitment and indeed understanding of equal opportunities issues. In all of the case study nurse education centres that were selected

> few positive action provisions had been established which were adequately resourced, part of a systematic strategy of targeting minority ethnic communities, or informed by data on those communities and on the characteristics of applicants and student cohorts. Most of the measures encountered were inappropriately resourced and ad hoc and commonly relied on the initiative of particularly committed individuals. (ibid.: 312)

Iganski et al. suggest that the reasons why so few effective initiatives were in place were 'the availability/acceptance of a *rationale* for action, the availability of *information* about the ethnic composition of student populations and the local labour force, and the existence of a *strategy* for action' (ibid.). Overall, Iganski et al. argue that what is required is an effective national strategy that links the justice/moral case for equal opportunities with the business case.

Principally because of the assumption of 'no difference' in equality laws, the issue of group rights is one that has proved to be quite controversial. For example Bacchi (1996: 20) comments: 'Because antidiscrimination legislation is couched in race- and sex-neutral language, it has been possible to argue that legislation like affirmative action which targets "women" or "Blacks" is a kind of discrimination, albeit "reverse discrimination".' Bacchi goes on to say: 'The dominant current understanding, even among supporters of the reform [for affirmative action] is that affirmative action means "preferential" treatment to assist "disadvantaged" people to move into better jobs' (ibid.: 33). Similarly, Eisenberg (2000: 397) comments: 'the benefits to individual well-being of any system based on group rights must be weighted against the costs of potentially undermining social cohesion and essentializing group identity'.

More generally, Bacchi (1996) comments that anti-discrimination legislation is minimally interventionist. For example, such legislation is based on a foundational assumption that primarily society's rules are generally functioning quite fairly. It is only when 'discrimination' occurs that intervention is necessary. The form of intervention is also relatively minimalist as it is only activated when an individual draws attention to discriminatory action through court action. In addition, such legislation maintains a distinction between the private and the public by exempting, for example, private schools and single sex clubs. Finally, equal opportunity approaches are critiqued in terms of their relatively limited conception of equality. In particular, the denial of 'difference' is seen to present innumerable problems that restrict the potential meanings of equality. While these issues are more fully explored in the following chapter, I shall now indicate the centrality of motherhood to some conceptualizations of equality.

Equal *but* Different, Equal *and* Different: The Centrality of Motherhood

The ideology of the organised white, middle-class women's movement in nineteenth-century Britain, Australia, and America, was more of a piece than is often assumed. Concerning functional and metaphysical issues, feminists in this movement in the main shared a common vision. They believed that the maternal function was vitally important and that women were suited by nature for this role. They also believed that women were 'equal' to men in the sense that they shared a common human spirit. Women were equal, but different in their social function as childrearers and in their distinctive maternal character.

(Bacchi, 1990: 6)

Bacchi's analysis of eighteenth- and nineteenth-century feminism highlights how the issue of women's sameness and difference was perceived in terms of an equal *but* different view. The 'sameness' arguments are those outlined above. Women were viewed as having equal intellectual capabilities and their common humanity with men meant that they should be granted the same rights and freedoms. However, their maternal difference was such that they would naturally also be the homemakers and carers of children. The work of Mary Wollstonecraft illustrates this position well. As I have commented, Mary Wollstonecraft is commonly seen as the originator of the movement for women's rights. In particular, she argued strongly for women's access to education. Nevertheless, the basis of her argument was not only that education was a natural right for both sexes. Wollstonecraft argued that education would make women better wives and mothers as it would create the mental discipline necessary to ensure that they were not flighty or frivolous. It would also increase their sense of autonomy so that they would no longer be slaves to their emotions. In this, therefore, Wollstonecraft and those who initially followed her were not concerned with changing the social roles of women and men. Indeed, they believed that women were morally superior and the care of children was woman's highest calling. Thus, Mill and his contemporaries in the nineteenth century would have approved of women's primary roles as mothers because 'the hand that rocked the cradle belonged to the most elevating of all minds' (Robson and Robson, 1994: xxxiv). In so doing, women would have an equal but different place in the social order.

The 'rights'-based model of first-wave feminism did not, therefore, aim to challenge the ways in which social roles are gendered. Rather, it was assumed that individual rights would give women the right to choose between a public life in civic pursuits or a life as a wife and mother. It was also assumed that most women would choose motherhood (Robson and Robson, 1994). Indeed, first-wave feminists did not question the sanctity of motherhood but assumed that this was a woman's 'natural' calling. In part this is because in moral terms motherhood is often perceived as the epitome of selfless love. In societies that are heavily influenced by market capitalism with its individualistic and competitive values, motherhood is taken in a range of writings to metaphorically express an idealization of the many relationships and experiences to which a feminist world could aspire (Umansky, 1996).

The division between identifiable factions of 'sameness' and 'difference' arose, according to Bacchi, in the inter-war years when the question of whether or not married women should engage in paid employment came to the fore. These divisions were part of broader political divisions between *laissez-faire* individualism (*Gesellschaft*) and welfarism (*Gemeinschaft*). The ensuing debates were set between the idea that women should forego their maternal duties and engage in equal competition with men (i.e. 'sameness') or accept their traditional roles within the home (i.e. 'difference'). For example, early second-wave feminism is particularly noted for how it theorized motherhood as an oppressive institution. Such feminists focused on women's financial dependency in marriage, their overwhelming responsibilities for child-care and the isolation and ensuing depression that women felt when being at home alone caring for young children. In addition, the intransigence of the public worlds of paid employment and politics to the requirements of childcare left women with either choosing motherhood or paid employment or working the 'double shift'. In terms of what can be seen as a counter-discursive strategy within feminism to these critiques and as offering a political resolution of these problems, 'The "female as superior" construct was re-activated' (Bacchi, 1990: 87). This was particularly through the work of cultural and radical feminists.

'Cultural feminism spoke about the existence of a separate female or woman's culture based upon distinctively female characteristics such as nurturance, care and the ability to relate to others. These the characteristics traditionally assigned to women but now they were to be valued not denigrated' (ibid.: 86). Similarly, Bohan (1997: 32) comments that cultural feminism 'presents traits deemed distinctively women's as indeed different from but equal or even preferable to those that characterize men in general. Thus, difference is affirmed, but the customary valuation of difference is turned on its head; women's ways of being are revered rather than demeaned.' The work of Noddings (1984) and Ruddick (1980) are often cited as exemplars of this perspective. Noddings took up the argument of Gilligan (1982) that an expanded view of moral development was required which included women's ways of reasoning. Noddings saw the maternal relationship as the epitome of the virtuous relationship. Her work has been particularly influential in the field of education where it has been taken up in terms of classroom pedagogies and school management.

Ruddick recognizes the oppressive nature of motherhood that arises from women's sense of powerlessness and the intensity of mothering work. Nevertheless, she comments that 'to suggest that mothers are principally victims of a kind of crippling work is an egregiously inaccurate account of women's own experience as mothers and daughters' (Ruddick, 1997: 585). Ruddick puts love at the centre of her analysis of motherhood. Indeed, she comments on how a mother's love survives the most inhospitable conditions of poverty, social isolation and denigration. She also reflects on how important motherly love is to the development and well-being of the child. Thus love 'when realized, invigorate preservation and enable growth . . . the capacity of attention and the virtue of love is at once the foundation and the corrective of maternal thought' (ibid.: 595). Maternal thinking, Ruddick argues, should be extended to the public spheres of life.

The major critique made of these perspectives is that of essentialism. Bohan offers the following conceptualization:

> Essentialist views construe gender as resident within the individual, a quality or trait describing one's personality, cognitive process, moral judgement, etc. Thus, it is an essentialist stance to argue that 'relationality' or a 'morality of justice' is a quality possessed by the individual. Essentialist models, thus, portray gender in terms of fundamental attributes that are conceived as internal, persistent, and generally separate from the ongoing experience of interaction with the daily sociopolitical contexts of one's life. (1997: 32–3)

Essentialism has become a key word in policing feminist thought. To have one's work labelled as 'essentialist' is to be called to account. The charge of essentialism suggests that one's analysis has, for example, failed to acknowledge diversity, failed to take account of the historical, cultural and political locatedness of meanings and has implied that women do not have access to other modes of being (ibid.). In particular, essentialism is often compared with social constructionism, which Bohan defines as:

> By way of analogy, consider the difference between describing an individual as friendly and describing a conversation as friendly. In the former case, 'friendly' is construed as a trait of the person, an 'essential' component to her or his personality. In the latter, 'friendly' describes the nature of the interaction occurring between or among people. Friendly here has a particular meaning that is agreed upon by the participants, that

is compatible with its meaning to their social reference groups, and that is reaffirmed by the process of engaging in this interaction. Although the essentialist view of gender sees it as analogous to the friendly person, the constructionist sees gender as analogous to the friendly conversation. (ibid.: 33)

The intense debate that has ensued over the meanings and implications of essentialism has led to some rethinking about the relationship between the biological determinism of essentialism and social constructionism (see Schor and Weed, 1994). For example, Bulbeck (2000: 51) compares the problems of both perspectives in terms that 'Most of us know that essentialism is a "bad thing," simplifying a complex reality into a single cause; possibly politically reactive if it takes a form such as biological essentialism. Constructionism can, however, produce a claim that identities are totally fluid and just a matter of performance.' In an interview (Spivak with Rooney, 1994), Spivak reflects on how she has been attributed with arguing that essentialism is an important strategic tool in feminist politics. Spivak comments that the widespread take-up of her comments on essentialism has led her to slightly change her original view. In particular, she notes that there are dangers in an unreflexive assertion of strategic value as this 'gives a certain alibi to essentialism' (ibid.: 155). She cautions that it requires vigilance in order to build for difference.

The strength of critiques of essentialism should not be read as assuming that feminists have rejected the potential of exploring the 'feminine'. In a discussion of Italian feminist arguments that surround the concept of equality, Bock and James (1992) note that while there is a considerable amount of consensus with other feminist movements, there are a number of distinctive features that set it apart from both Anglo-American feminism and French feminism. For example, Italian theories and practices of sexual difference (*practica* and *pensiero della differenza sessuale*) are less deeply rooted in psychoanalytic theory that is a mark of French feminism. In addition, Italian feminists have drawn very strongly on their experiences with political movements such as the Christian Democrats, who could be described as traditional conservatives and the Communist Party who adhered to the view that the 'woman question' would be solved through class struggle. Bock and James note that this has meant that Italian feminists:

acquired an exceptionally concrete understanding of what the most 'progressive' forces on the male political spectrum understood by women's equality. To combat the prevalent conception of equality as sameness, as an invitation to join men on men's terms which feminists came to call 'emancipationism', they developed a sophisticated range of theoretical insights and political practices centred on their distinctive notion of female difference. (ibid.: 6)

According to Bock and James, these political experiences have led Italian feminists to argue more strongly than most that there is a male bias in *all* traditional discourses about women and equality. For example, while some North American analyses of domestic life have argued that the family is a site of both female oppression and power, Italian feminists argue that women are ruled by men in both the private and public domains. Thus, Bock and James note that:

> This conclusion contributes to the view, so central to *pensiero della differenza sessuale*, that a primary, originary female difference has, in all areas of social life, been homologized or assimilated to a male perspective which hides behind a mask of gender neutrality in order to subordinate women. The remedy for this state of affairs cannot lie in the traditional conception of women's difference, a conception which functions on male terms and has been used to keep women in their inferior place. Rather, so the Italian feminist movement insists, it lies in a new exploration of an autonomous *differenza sessuale*, understood as a basis for women's liberty. (ibid.)

In searching for an autonomous sexual difference that is not adapted to the needs of masculinity, Bock and James argue that Italian feminists have focused their attention on those areas of social life that have been the primary locus of women's domestication. These are maternity and women's body, language and subjectivity. Their aim is to shape these areas in terms of women's rather than men's interests. Nevertheless, lest it appears that such aims would accord with a maternalist stance that can be found in some North American feminism, Italian feminists are not concerned to identify a primary essence of womanhood (see de Lauretis, 1994, for a fuller discussion of Italian feminism and the issue of essentialism). Indeed, they would argue that it is as essentialist to assume that women are the same as men as it is to assume that they are different. Both positions assume some innate nature or essence of being. Rather, their position is one that argues that we cannot know what woman essentially is because this knowledge cannot be gained outside of the past and present conditions to which she is subjected. We can, however, know how womanhood is differentiated from, subordinated to, and shaped by masculinity. Thus, unless women shape these fields of knowledge and practice for themselves, they will remain homologized, that is made to correspond with masculine interests.

In terms of equality, this is expressed in terms of 'an equal liberty to shape oneself in accordance with whatever differences one finds significant' (Bock and James, 1992: 7). Or as Cavarero puts it, this means to be both equal *and* different:

> It is possible to be both different and equal, if each of the two different beings is free and if the kind of equality at stake radically abandons any foundation in the logic of abstract, serializing universalization of the male One. It is possible to be both different and equal if not only a new logical foundation of the concept of equality can be developed, but a new model of society and politics. (1992: 45)

Material Inequality

> There is a strange paradox about the current practice of social science. On the one hand, statistical evidence . . . shows that inequalities between social groups have been increasing . . . At the same time interest in material inequalities as a topic for social scientific analysis has been steadily diminishing, especially those forms of inequality . . . which were formerly explained in terms of relationships of class and capitalism.
>
> (Bradley, 2000: 476)

Clearly, equality is not a preserve of liberal or cultural feminist perspectives. Evans (1995: 109) notes how early socialist feminism had a radical concept of equality in that 'It demanded capitalism's overthrow; the expropriation of the property-holders, the abolition of private property, and the concomitant emancipation of the proletariat; a necessary preliminary to the liberation of women.' Within Marxism gender equality was based on the assumption that capitalism would increasingly draw women into the labour force and this would destroy the sexual division of labour (Hartmann, 1981). Marxist and socialist feminists have demanded rights to economic equality as well as political equality. Central to their position was that 'political liberalism was hollow without the economic means to realize it' (Eisenstein, 1984: xv). However, more recently there has been a retreat from the class-based politics that had their origins in Marxism and socialism (Skeggs, 1997). There has also been an associated retreat from a concern about material inequalities. Bradley (2000) notes how statistical evidence highlights growing inequalities between rich and poor families in Britain and

North America and between 'developed' and 'Third World' nations (see also O'Connell, 1996). She comments that 'if anything the world is becoming more rather than less unequal' (2000: 484). Bradley's analysis of the reasons for the lack of attention given to material inequalities includes the increasing recognition of the complexity of issues that surround social differentiation, such as class, gender, ethnicity, age, dis/ability and so forth. An appreciation of this complexity has been reinforced by postmodern social theory in terms that it was unlikely that any one single theory, such as Marxism, could account for and explain complex and pluralistic social groupings. Bradley (2000: 480) argues for a conceptualization of material inequality that takes account of what she terms '"fractured identities" in contemporary social life' that arise from increasing fragmentation and hybridity. She suggests that there are four sources of fragmentation:

1   Internal fragmentation that occurs within particular classed group-ings, for example, the divisions within the working class.
2   External fragmentation that arises because of the impact of variables such as 'race' and gender.
3   The impact of social change, for example, young women are able to take advantage of career opportunities that are not available to older women.
4   Increasing individualism as people are more socially and geographi-cally mobile.

Fraser (1995) explores the complexities of post-socialist political life with its decentring of class and the multi-axial, cross-cutting axes of difference through an analysis of the politics of recognition and the politics of redistribution. The politics of recognition is the term Fraser uses for the contemporary predominant focus on identity and cultural expression. This includes attempts to valorize groups in society who are devalued and despised on the basis of, for example, their sexuality, ethnicity, religion or sex. The politics of redistribution is concerned with the need to remain focused on inequalities of material wealth. She comments that 'Increasingly . . . identity-based claims tend to pre-dominate, as prospects for redistribution appear to recede. The result is a complex political field with little programmatic coherence' (ibid.: 70). For example, Fraser highlights how redistribution and recognition approaches contradict each other. Thus the aim of programmes such as affirmative action are to write out or obliterate any issues of cultural differentiation. This is the pursuit of sameness. On the other hand, those who argue for a revalidation of aspects of identity, such as Gay Pride or cultural feminists who extol the virtues of motherhood, are emphasizing and make more obvious cultural differentiation.

Fraser sees her task as developing 'a *critical* theory of recognition, one which identifies and defends only those versions of the cultural politics of difference than can be coherently combined with the social politics of equality' (ibid.: 69). This is because of the inter-relationship of material and cultural inequalities. For example, the low value placed on woman-hood is reflected in wage levels, career opportunities, educational path-ways, sexual exploitation, domestic violence, and so forth. To do this Fraser argues that it is necessary to conceptualize cultural recognition and social equality in ways that support rather than undermine one another. Her analysis indicates that 'redressing gender injustice requires changing both political economy and culture, so as to undo the vicious circle of economic and cultural subordination' (ibid.: 88). Fraser argues that the dilemma that arises from the inter-relationship of low cultural valuation and material inequality is both real and cannot be easily resolved. At present the task is to find ways that minimize the conflicts that arise from redistribution and recognition approaches to equality. Here she suggests that a combination of socialism and deconstruction is the most fruitful answer although she notes that this approach is not also without its problems:

> For both gender and 'race', the scenario that best finesses the redistribution–recognition dilemma is socialism in the economy plus deconstruction in the culture. But for this scenario to be psychologically and politically feasible requires that people be weaned from their attachment to current cultural constructions of their interests and identities. (ibid.: 91)

Case Study 4: Under-Educating Women

Brine (1999) offers an analysis of what she defines as the '"class ceiling" [these are] the structures and processes that prevent working-class women from getting out of the cellar' (ibid.: 2). In this her analysis focuses on European education and training policy. This is because education and training appear to offer a way out of poverty. Yet central to Brine's analysis is the assertion that working-class women and men are 'socially constructed as "low educated" – they are *under*educated' (ibid.). Education may increase opportunities for a few but competitive markets require the cheap, flexible labour provided by working-class individuals. Brine's research combines policy analysis with empirical, case study data. Her analytic framework focuses on the implications of globalization and draws on Foucaldian analyses of power and discourse. Here she explores conflict, collaboration and resistance in relation to regionalized and national state policies and practices through the work of training providers, femocrats, feminist educators and unemployed working-class women. Her intention is to explore the connections between different levels of policy and process.

Central to Brine's analysis of the continuation of material inequalities is a focus on the discourses of equality. Brine distinguishes between two forms of inequality. These are formal and material. Formal equality is concerned with an equalization of political and legal rights and this is dealt with through legislative means. To alleviate material inequality more radical policies are required that will redistribute the wealth and success of a society. Brine argues that the European Union only recognizes formal inequality. A consequence of this is that material inequalities can be maintained as well as reduced. One example is that of changing UK policy towards the employment of lone mothers. Because of their responsibilities for childcare lone parents had until recently been considered as legitimately excluded from the labour market. However lone mothers are now offered 'employment opportunities' and are encouraged to take these up through changes to state benefits. Underpinning this are persuasive equality arguments. Brine summarizes these as

> There is a widespread understanding that unemployed people need jobs, an understanding that we cannot be complacent about unemployment; that unemployment is linked to social exclusion and poverty, and conversely that employment is linked to self-esteem, greater economic independence, social inclusion and freedom of movement. The neoliberal equality discourse speaks of increasing opportunities for employment and removing barriers to employment; the discourse says 'why shouldn't lone mothers (or disabled people) have the opportunity to work, they need help with understanding the opportunities for training, for employment, that are open to them'. (ibid.: 148)

As Brine points out, while such a discourse may be highly persuasive, it requires the existence of enough employment opportunities. Thus she comments: 'The key point is that such employment opportunities do not exist – at least on the scale needed. Instead of employment opportunities we have *opportunities* for employment – a highly significant discursive difference' (ibid.). From this point of view, as Brine further notes, 'benefit-linked training programmes construct a falsehood of opportunity, and the discourse's compulsion disguises its punitive actions' (ibid.). Nevertheless Brine refuses a deterministic, and over-whelmingly pessimistic, reading of the implications of this. Here she draws attention to the possibilities for resistance and agency that are enacted by those committed to the politics of material inequalities.

Summary

This chapter has explored the varied meanings of equality by illustrating the particular predominance, and relative success, of liberalist rights-based arguments. Such arguments, summarized by Brine (1999) as formal equality, have been taken up in legislation that has argued for both individual and group rights through equal opportunities, affirma-tive and positive action policies. As this chapter has shown, equal rights are not the only conceptualization of equality that has been important to feminism nor have they been uncritically accepted. Rights-based arguments have been critiqued from a number of positions in terms of their propensity to maintain the hierarchical, competitive and indi-vidualizing organization of society. Deconstructive approaches to rights arguments by ethics of care feminists are further explored in Chapter 5.

This chapter has also drawn attention to the continuation of material inequalities. In this respect Skeggs (2001: 296) comments: 'Recognition politics has shifted the terrain in terms of who can make political representations and be recognised as worthy of public legitimation. This shift has also enabled discourses of inequality to be replaced with those of difference.' As a corollary to this, it should therefore be noted that an understanding of the varied meanings of equality cannot be fully appreciated without a similar exploration of conceptualizations of difference. These are considered in Chapter 3.

FURTHER READING

Bacchi, C. (1990) *Same Difference: Feminism and Sexual Difference*. St Leonards, NSW: Allen and Unwin.

Bacchi, C. (1996) *The Politics of Affirmative Action: 'Women', Equality and Category Politics*. London: Sage. The 1990 text by Bacchi offers an extremely useful historical analysis of feminist debates on equality. The 1996 text undertakes an analysis of the problematic nature of affirmative action policies for feminist politics. Together they provide an excellent foundation for an analysis of contemporary issues.

Phillips, A. (1987) *Feminism and Equality*. Oxford: Blackwell. Phillips' text provides a highly accessible introduction to a range of conceptualizations of equality and she links this to their implications for feminist politics.

Difference 3

Emblazoned on book covers, routinely invoked in intellectual
debates, 'difference' functions as an unassailable value in itself,
seemingly irrespective of its referent or context. Difference has
become doxa, a magic word of theory and politics radiant with
redemptive meanings.

(Felski, 1997: 1)

The centrality of difference within social and cultural theory has led
Moore (1994: 2) to remark that there is 'an obsessive concern with
issues of difference, and such is the malleability of the term that almost
anything can be subsumed under it'. Barrett (1987) uses the term
ubiquitous to portray the extent and frequency of difference in feminist
theorizing. Similarly, Evans (1995: 6) remarks: 'One oddity of "difference", both within the debate and elsewhere in feminist thought, is that
it would appear to be endlessly invoked, but again, often is not defined.'
Of course, this issue of definition has been taken up in a variety of ways.
For example, Moore explores this 'passion' for difference in terms of its
linkage to 'its unspoken and under-theorized pair, "the same" or
"sameness"' (1994: 1). Weedon (1999) undertakes a review of difference in terms of liberal, radical, lesbian, socialist, Black and postcolonial
feminisms. Hekman (1999) argues for a new approach to issues of
method and truth that will offer alternative theories of difference.

Despite this multiplicity of conceptualization and approach there is a
major narrative of difference in feminist theory. Indeed, this narrative
confirms Bacchi's (1990) concern with over-simplified views of feminist
history as it suggests a simple three-stage, linear progression that denies
the variety of perspectives existent at varied points in history. Felski
(1997) sets this out in the following terms. Felski notes that the origins
of feminism are commonly ascribed to the writings of Mary Wollstonecraft who set out to argue against the first difference. That is that there
is a difference between women and men. As we have seen, Wollstonecraft argued that women shared a common humanity with men. This

no-difference position was challenged by gynocentric second-wave feminism. This sought to reaffirm women's difference from men. In so doing it was claimed that the goal of equality upon which the first difference was based was illusory and masked a phallocentric logic. Nevertheless, poststructuralist and identity politics have since highlighted the political biases and exclusions of such gynocentricism or woman-centred feminism. This has critiqued feminism as mainly concerned with White, middle-class, Western issues. It has also called into question the notion of a unified subjectivity of womanhood.

Felski notes that this narrative is told on many occasions and in a number of ways. However, there are two main evaluations that are made about the story of difference in feminist theorizing. On the one hand, there are those who see this story as a narrative of progress away from essentialist and universalist ideals and towards more sophisticated understandings. Woman is no longer understood as a unified whole but as a process, as fragmented, as in flux and as multiple. On the other hand, there are those who see this story as contributing to the demise of feminism as a movement. This is because the attention that has been paid to deconstructing womanhood has left feminism without a unifying identity. If 'woman' ceases to exist, who are we fighting for?

This narrative is evident in the conceptual schema of difference set out by Barrett (1987) and Evans (1995) (see Table 3.1 and Table 3.2). Both Barrett and Evans suggest that there are three main categories of difference. However, while their categories share some similarities, there are also significant variations. These arise from the underpinning theoretical frameworks upon which Barrett's and Evans' categorizations rest. Evans' schema draws on particular schools of feminist thought, such as cultural, liberal and postmodern feminism. Barrett's schema also draws on these schools of thought but the basis of her delineation is located in the specificity of difference that she has identified. In particular, Barrett separates experiential, positional and sexual difference and locates these differences across the traditional schools of feminist thought. For example, sexual difference has been explored within cultural and poststructural feminist approaches.

Specifically, and for her purposes, Evans suggests that there are three schools of difference (see Table 3.1). These are:

1 Valuing woman's difference from man (the 'weak' and the 'strong' versions of cultural feminism).
2 Differences between groups of women (identity politics).
3 Différance or the difference within (postmodernism and poststructuralism).

Table 3.1 Evans' (1995) conceptual schema of difference

Issue of difference	Difference 1	Difference 2	Difference 3
Name of school of thought	Woman-centred school/ Cultural feminism/ Gynocentricism/ gynandry	Identity Politics	Postmodern/ Poststructural
Form of difference	Differences between women and men	Differences between groups of women in terms of sexual preference, 'race', ethnicity, country of birth, and so forth	Concerned to deconstruct dualisms and 'fixed' identities
Standpoint	Revalues women's difference from men but two main schools: (a) different but equal – women have complementary virtues to those of men (b) rebut, refuse, attack all that is man-made. Woman's difference is superior.	Feminism is based on an over-homogenized White women's experience	All views are equally good
Politics	Belief in some kind of universality or commonality of womanhood	Identity politics based on religious practice, ethnic identity, sexual preference, etc.	Group representation is a problem as it calls into question the category 'woman'
Illustrative feminists	Mary Daly, Adrienne Rich, Carol Gilligan	Iris Young	Judith Butler, Joan Scott

Table 3.2 Barrett's (1987) conceptual schema of difference

Issue of Difference	Difference 1	Difference 2	Difference 3
Name of school of thought	Difference as experiential diversity	Difference as positional meaning	Sexual difference
Form of difference	Differences between women *and* men. Differences between groups of women in terms of sexual preferences, class, 'race', and so forth	Linguistic difference, difference produced through discourse	The creation of gendered subjectivities accounts of sexual difference
Standpoint	Rests on a view of the unitary human subject who is an active and effective agent. Confidence in empirical methods and an ontological reality	Deconstruction of the unified subject of humanism. Rejection of *grands narratives*. Challenge to transcendental meaning. Dismantling of supposed certainty	The centrality of sexual difference to women's oppression
Politics	Recognition of diversity of social experience both between women and men and within groups of women	Textual and local	A reclaiming of the unconscious
Illustrative feminists	Mary Daly, Adrienne Rich, Andrea Dworkin, Dale Spender	Angela McRobbie	Juliet Mitchell, Luce Irigaray, Julia Kristeva, Melanie Klein, Nancy Chodorow

Barrett remarks that the variety of meanings attributed to 'difference' results in confusion. Because of this confusion Barrett argues that sexual difference, positional difference and experiential diversity are best identified separately. Barrett's first category of difference, that of difference as experiential diversity, is a combination of Evans' first two differences. This is because experiential diversity is central to why feminists have distinguished woman's difference from man and have found differences in terms of 'race', class, disability, and so forth between groups of women. Barrett's second category of positional difference concurs with Evans' postmodernist and poststructuralist difference. Barrett's third category, that of sexual difference, is not included in Evans' initial schema. This third category focuses on psychoanalytic theories. Thus, Barrett's schools of difference are: '(I) a sense of difference effectively to register diversity of situation and experience between women; (II) difference as an understanding of the positional rather than absolute character of meaning, particularly as developed in Derridean terms, and (III) modern psychoanalytic accounts of sexual difference' (1987: 30).

Maynard (1995: 262) comments: 'a rather obvious point to make about the way in which feminist thought has been classified is that there is no real consensus as to which categories are the most meaningful, how many there are and which writers are to be located within each'. Both Evans and Barrett note the difficulties and dilemmas that they experienced in constructing these frameworks. For example, Evans comments that her categories may be strait-jacketed positions that do not necessarily hold when applied to actual texts and may indeed split specific schools of thought. Barrett notes that her categories are in some ways artificial and indeed overlap. The difficulties that Evans and Barrett have experienced in terms of categorization and the potential overlaps and cross-cutting ties between their different 'differences' are also evident in the organization of this chapter. For example, it should be noted that some cultural difference, sexual difference, identity school and postcolonial theorists also use poststructuralist approaches. What is important to comment on here is that labelling of this kind should not be understood as an accurate representation of some kind of empirical reality that can be found in the literature. Rather, it operates as a heuristic device that allows us to explore and explicate particular issues and points.

This chapter explores and extends the categories of difference set out by Evans and Barrett. In particular I explore Evans' three differences and indicate the overlaps with Barrett. I then outline sexual difference. Finally, I explore conceptualizations of difference within postcolonial theorizing. Neither Barrett nor Evans deal directly with this form of difference. This comment is not made to criticize them. Rather, it is to draw attention to the importance of reading with the date of publication in mind. Postcolonial theorizing, while not 'new', has recently become more visible within broader discussions of feminist thought. Indeed, it is beginning to take on a 'received' narrative structure that I am conscious of replicating in this chapter!

Valuing Woman's Difference from Man

One of the interesting features of the first difference that Evans identifies is that she has decided to foreground difference rather than equality as the central concept for exploration of cultural feminism. This reinforces our understanding of the inter-relationship of meaning that is drawn from the dualistic pairing of difference–equality. Thus, although we first encountered these in Chapter 2 under the concept of equality, Evans refers to the variety of schools that are termed 'woman-centred', 'cultural', 'gynocentrism' and 'gynandry' as a form of difference. These schools of thought, as Barrett notes, draw on women's experiences of being different from men. This difference from men is not in terms of liberal feminism that argues that there are *no* important differences between the sexes that should stand in the way of equality. On the contrary, the difference that this school of thought argues for is that there *are* differences between women and men and the political task is to valorize these.

What is useful is that Evans extends our understanding of the equal *but* different school introduced in Chapter 2 by distinguishing between 'weak' and 'strong' versions of cultural feminism. Evans refers to 'weak' cultural feminism as 'woman's kindness'. 'Weak' cultural feminism would be arguing for woman's values to be incorporated into the public spheres of life. The 'good' traits of womanhood are not exclusive to women. They could, and importantly here should, also be developed by men. Evans explores the 'strong' school of cultural feminism through the work of Mary Daly, Andree Collard and Adrienne Rich. What they each have in common is that their work aims to revalue women's activities and traits that have been devalued by patriarchy. In comparison to 'weak' cultural feminists their strategy is more separatist as they do not see how woman can reclaim, retain and recreate her unique differences in patriarchal cultures.

Differences between Groups of Women: Identity Politics

In outlining her second category, that of identity politics, Evans focuses on Black feminist experiences and critiques of racism in the White women's movement. For example, Black women have illustrated how feminism has assumed Whiteness as a normative category (Carby, 1982). Evans comments that this critique of White feminism and later of the heterosexist nature of predominant feminist assumptions led to a broader 'move towards "identity politics", that is, basing an activism, a political viewpoint, and a sense of selfhood on, say, religious practice, ethnic identity, or sexual preference' (1995: 22). This new pluralism, Phillips notes:

> homes in on identity rather than interest groups; not those gathered together around some temporary unifying concern – to defend their neighbourhood against a major road development, to lobby their representatives against some proposed new law – but those linked by a common culture, a common experience, a common language. These links are often intensely felt, and, more important still, are often felt as opposition and exclusion. Identity groups frequently secure their identity precisely around their opposition to some 'other', focusing on a past experience of being excluded, and sometimes formulating a present determination to exclude. (1993: 146–7)

Evans' exploration of identity politics focuses on the relatively neglected issue of class through the work of Iris Young (1990). Evans regards Young as an exemplar of changes in socialist feminism where a faith in 'sameness' equality has been lost and has been replaced by an understanding of identity divisions and disadvantages based on issues of gender, 'race', class, sexuality and disability. To reinforce the point made in the introduction to this chapter, what is also significant is that Young's theoretical framework of difference is derived from the poststructural/modern theorizing of Derrida, Lyotard, Foucault and Kristeva. This is combined with Marxist critical theory and Black philosophy. Given that Evans' third category of difference is the postmodern/poststructural, this illustrates how the labelling and categorizing of a field of knowledge must function as an umbrella term within which there will be a variety of theoretical, philosophical and political positions.

One of the main critiques of identity politics is that the presentation of a unified identity can mask the differences within a particular group. As many feminists have noted (see, for example, Spelman, 1988), there will be many other axes of difference within groups designated by virtue of 'race', ethnicity, class, disability, sexuality, and so forth. For example, Brah (1990) summarizes critiques of the term 'Black' when it is used to define the experiences of South Asian and African-Caribbean groups in Britain. These include the charge of essentialism that the term 'Black' conveys a pre-given nature or identity and in addition that it is not a term with which all groups can identify. Indeed, it is this attention to the complexities of group analysis that is the primary reason why Evans categorizes Young's work as 'identity politics'.

Young's text is critical of individualist and sameness principles in the achievement of equality. Instead, Young argues for a politics of difference that accords with affirmative and positive action approaches to group rights that were introduced in Chapter 2. In this respect she argues that 'social policy should sometimes accord special treatment to groups' (1990: 158). However, Young does not see groups as homogenous entities that would parallel humanistic notions of the individual. Rather, she argues for a contextualized and relational understanding of difference where:

> Group differences will be more or less salient depending on the groups compared, the purposes of the comparison, and the point of view of the comparers. Such contextualized understandings of difference undermine essentialist assumptions. For example, in the context of athletics, health care, social service support, and so on, wheelchair-bound people are different from others, but they are not different in many other respects. Traditional treatment of the disabled entailed exclusion and segregation because the differences between the disabled and the able-bodied were conceptualized as extending to all or most capacities. In general, then, a relational understanding of group difference rejects exclusion. Difference no longer implies that groups lie outside one another. To say that there are differences among groups does not imply that there are not overlapping experiences, or that two groups have nothing in common. The assumption that real differences in affinity, culture, or privilege imply oppositional categorization must be challenged. Different groups are always similar in some respects, and always potentially share some attributes, experiences, and goals. (ibid.: 171)

As Young notes, one clearly needs to be attentive to the potential divisiveness of identity politics if one is seeking to work within a political framework that emphasizes difference rather than sameness. Thus, while Young seeks to validate difference, she argues that this has to be accomplished 'within a public arena that can encourage interaction and change' (Phillips, 1993: 151). In other words, what is required is a wider shift in the meanings of difference. This point is also taken up by some feminists who are discussed within postmodern and poststructural framings of difference.

Différance or the Difference Within: Postmodernism and Poststructuralism

In her assessment of the postmodern school of difference Evans remarks: 'Postmodernism is frequently regarded as a recipe for statis, if not indeed paralysis: and I believe that' (1995: 140). Although postmodernism is an umbrella term that covers a range of theoretical positions, it is certainly the case that postmodernism has been highly contentious within feminism. For example, the postmodern view does not see history as progressive but as cyclical. There are, therefore, no guarantees within postmodern theorizing that activism will bring about a hoped-for utopia or better world. Instead all we might hope for is something different. In addition, there are great concerns about postmodernism as a relativist creed whereby all views are considered equally valid. This issue of relativism is linked to a postmodern critique of metanarratives and in particular on how metanarratives act as forms of social legitimation. As Norris (2000: 28) notes: 'A metanarrative is a story that wants to be more than just a story, that is to say, one which claims to have achieved an omniscient standpoint above and beyond all the other stories that people have told so far.' In this respect, aspects of feminism can be regarded as a metanarrative because of the claims to 'truth' that are made about gender relations. Postmodern critiques note that there are as many claims to 'truth' as there are different language games and discourses. As we have seen above, early feminist claims to knowing the 'truth' about women's experiences have been shown to be the 'truth' of White, middle-class, Western feminists. Indeed, Lather (1991: 4) comments: 'postmodernism profoundly challenges the politics of emancipation'.

Weedon (1999) notes that much of the critique that has arisen within feminism over these issues is due, in part, to a conflation of postmodernism with poststructuralism. Issues of universality, subjectivity and power overlap in postmodernist and poststructuralist concerns. However, while postmodernism may be termed a 'position', Weedon comments that poststructuralism 'offers useful and important tools in the struggle for change' (ibid.: 180). In this Beasley (1999) suggests that one way of understanding the distinction between postmodernism and poststructuralism is to view poststructuralism as a sub-set of post-modernism. For example, Butler and Scott (1992) caution that poststructuralism is not a position such as socialist feminism, radical feminism, or liberal feminism commonly found within feminist theorizing. Rather, poststructuralism is 'a critical interrogation of the exclusionary operations by which "positions" are established' (Butler and Scott, 1992: xiv). As such, and of course marked by variety, poststructuralist deconstruction can be viewed as a methodology that is used to examine, for example, how commonly accepted 'facts' about women's lives come to be established and maintained. In this regard, Spivak comments:

> Deconstruction does not say there is no subject, there is no truth, there is no history. It simply questions the privileging of identity so that someone is believed to have the truth. It is not the exposure of error. It is constantly and persistently looking into how truths are produced. (2001)

It is with poststructuralist conceptions of deconstruction and différance that I am mainly concerned here. Barrett notes that poststructuralism is a response to critiques of Marxist certainties and the problems that are associated with finding adequate theories of ideology and subjectivity. Poststructuralist analyses seek to explore the relations between discourses, subjectivities and power. The conceptualization of subjectivity within poststructuralist writings owes much to the Derridean notion of différance and the processes of deconstruction that were discussed in Chapter 1. In addition, feminist poststructuralism draws on post-Lacanian psychoanalytic theories that I discuss more fully below, and Foucaldian analyses of power.

Chapter 1 illustrated how poststructuralist accounts argue that there is no fixed structure to language. Poststructuralist accounts also argue that language is central to the development of subjectivities. Here the argument suggests that as language is multiple and varied with no guarantees of the transference of intended meanings, so too, subjectivity is multiple, varied, contradictory and processual. For many feminist poststructuralists this view of the subject as process is a positive one. This is because it gives rise to the possibility of creating new gender discourses and, by implication, new subjectivities and ways of being and doing. Figure 3.1 summarizes these key aspects of poststructuralism.

There are four elements of Foucault's conceptualization of power which are essential to an understanding of the attention given to the significance of discourses. These four elements are: (a) power can be understood in terms of a matrix or capillary; (b) where there is power we will find resistance; (c) the operations of power, through disciplinary

1. The experience of being a person is captured in the notion of subjectivity. Subjectivity is constituted through those discourses in which the person is being positioned at any one time . . . One discourse that contradicts another does not undo one's constitution in terms of the original discourse. One's subjectivity is therefore necessarily contradictory.
2. The concepts of the individual and the collective are not understood in terms of a dualism but are constituted through the multiple discourses available.
3. One can only ever be what the various discourses make possible, and one's being shifts with the various discourses through which one is spoken into existence.
4. Fragmentation, contradiction and discontinuity, rather than continuity of identity are the focus. However, continuity is recognized as existing and is as yet inadequately theorized.

Source: Adapted from Davies, 1991: 43

Figure 3.1   Subjectivity within the poststructural

practices, regimes or techniques, give rise to self-surveillance or self-discipline; and, finally, (d) power is productive rather than repressive. Through the relations of discourse, subjectivity and power, poststructuralism facilitates a recognition of how power is exercised within groups as well as between them; how, for example, women exercise power over other women.

Evans' focus in delineating this school of difference is through the attention given to deconstruction and différance. In this her choice of an exemplar of deconstruction is Joan Scott (1988). The exemplar of différance is Judith Butler (1990). Scott's essay takes a deconstructive approach to conceptualizations of equality and difference. She comments on the difficulties for feminism that have arisen through these two terms:

> When equality and difference are paired dichotomously, they structure an impossible choice. If one opts for equality, one is forced to accept the notion that difference is antithetical to it. If one opts for difference, one admits that equality is unattainable . . . Feminists cannot give up 'difference'; it has been our most creative analytic tool. We cannot give up equality, at least as long as we want to speak to the principles and values of our political system. (Scott, 1988: 43)

Scott's response to this problem is to argue that feminism should not be forced into such a pre-existing dichotomy. In this, feminism needs to find a way that can both retain difference and also argue for equality. Scott does this through illustrating how equality and difference is a false dichotomy. Although equality and difference are usually paired, the correct opposite of equality is inequality and the correct opposite of difference is sameness. However, in terms of their dominant meanings in contemporary North American debates, equality relies on difference and difference relies on equality. For example, Scott notes that the aim of equality is to overcome particular differences. Thus: 'Demands for equality have rested on implicit and usually unrecognized arguments from difference: if individuals or groups were identical or the same there would be no need to ask for equality. Equality might well be defined as deliberate indifference to specified differences' (ibid.: 44). In terms of difference, Scott argues strongly for the importance of contextuality. She comments:

> There is nothing self-evident or transcendent about difference, even if the fact of difference – sexual difference, for example – seems apparent to the naked eye. The questions always ought to be: What qualities or aspects are being compared? What is the nature of the comparison? How is the meaning of difference being constructed? (ibid.).

Overall, therefore, Scott argues that feminists have to resist the false antithesis of equality–difference and instead insist on the multiple meanings of difference through continual deconstructive moves:

> Placing equality and difference in antithetical relationship has, then, a double effect. It denies the way in which difference has long figured in political notions of equality and it suggests that sameness is the only ground on which equality can be claimed. It thus puts feminists in an impossible position, for as long as we argue within the terms of a discourse set up by this opposition we grant the current conservative premise that because women cannot be identical to men in all respects, we cannot expect to be equal to them. The only alternative, it seems to me, is to refuse to oppose equality to difference and insist continually on differences – differences as the condition of individual and collective identities, differences as the constant challenge to the fixing of those identities, history as the repeated illustration of the play of differences, differences as the very meaning of equality itself. (ibid.: 46)

In turning more fully to différance, Evans draws on the work of Judith Butler (1990). Butler's work is viewed as the founding text of queer theory. As Butler comments in the Preface to her second edition, one of her concerns is to 'criticize a pervasive heterosexual assumption in feminist literary theory. I sought to counter those views that made presumptions about the limits and propriety of gender and restricted the meaning of gender to received notions of masculinity and femininity'

(1999: vii). In this regard Weedon notes:

> In theoretical terms queer theory is in many ways postmodern, since it renounces any fixed notions of difference; in particular, fixed distinctions between masculine and feminine, maleness and femaleness. Binary oppositions are replaced by a proliferation of differences which queer theory and politics refuses to hierarchize. Gender ceases to express anything fundamental about women and men. For some queer theorists, gender becomes a question of performance. Transgender practices, such as drag, are seen as fundamentally transgressive. As Judith Butler argues in *Gender Trouble*, once the centrality, obviousness and naturalness of heterosexuality are questioned it is no longer clear that gender has any natural meaning, and drag is one way of acting out this political point. (1999: 73–4)

The issue of gender as performativity is one that Butler (1999) further takes up in the Preface to her second edition of *Gender Trouble*. She notes how difficult it is to give a precise definition of performativity because her own views have changed over time. She comments:

> I originally took my clue on how to read the performativity of gender from Jacques Derrida's reading of Kafka's 'Before the Law'. There the one who waits for the law, sits before the door of the law, attributes a certain force to the law for which one waits. The anticipation of an authoritative disclosure of meaning is the means by which that authority is attributed and installed: the anticipation conjures its object. I wondered whether we do not labour under a similar expectation concerning gender, that it operates as an interior essence that might be disclosed, an expectation that ends up producing the very phenomenon that it anticipates. In the first instance, then, the performativity of gender revolves around this metalepsis, the way in which the anticipation of a gendered essence produces that which it posits as outside itself. Secondly, performativity is not a singular act, but a repetition and a ritual, which achieves its effects through its naturalization in the context of a body, understood, in part, as a culturally sustained temporal duration. (1999: xiv–xv)

Butler notes that this doctrine has raised a number of questions the most significant of which is:

> The view that gender is performative sought to show that what we take to be an internal essence of gender is manufactured through a sustained set of acts, posited through the gendered sytlization of the body. In this way, it showed that what we take to be an 'internal' feature of ourselves is one that we anticipate and produce through certain bodily acts, at an extreme, an hallucinatory effect of naturalized gestures. (ibid.: xv)

Butler's concern with overcoming the binaried relationship of internal and external and with finding ways through which theories of power and theories of the psyche are not polarized has led her to turn to psychoanalytic perspectives. For example, Butler comments that in addition to considering how Foucault and psychoanalysis can be brought together, she has

> also made use of psychoanalysis to curb the occasional voluntarism of my view of performativity without thereby undermining a more general theory of agency. *Gender Trouble* sometimes reads as if gender is simply a self-invention or that the psychic meaning of a gendered presentation might be read directly off its surface. Both of these postulates have had to be refined over time. (ibid.: xxv).

Indeed, it is psychoanalytic explanation that I now consider.

Case Study 5: Women Without Class

Although there had been something of a demise of interest in class analysis, more recently there has been a return to a focus on class through explanations that take account of the multiple nature and discursive constitution of class-based subjectivities. Because of their insistent attention to the structuring of class relations such accounts of class could be defined as materialist forms of poststructuralism. Thus Bettie (2000) comments that her title '"Women without Class" has multiple meanings' (ibid.: 3). These include a standard understanding of class in terms of low educational attainment, low income and little cultural capital and to signify that her paper is an intervention in theoretical debates that have marginalized class concerns. Bettie's research is therefore concerned with developing an understanding of the complex and contradictory ways through which young women understand class difference. Her goal was to 'explore the relationship between class symbolism and the formation of subjective class identity . . . in which class subjectivity is constructed in relationship to gender and racial/ethnic identity under late capitalism' (ibid.: 7). Bettie describes her methodological approach as ethnographic as she 'hung out' with working-class girls in a Californian high school with a high proportion of Mexican-American students. While Bettie is concerned to foreground issues of class she interweaves her account with issues of 'race' through, for example, a focus on 'acting white' and 'acting Mexican'.

Bettie's analysis considers the performativity of class through which she 'came to define students not only as working or middle class in origin but also as working- or middle-class *performers* [whereby] Girls who were passing, or metaphorically cross-dressing, had to negotiate their "inherited" identity from home with their "chosen" public identity at school' (ibid.: 10). In this way Bettie understood the gap between how their families looked and talked at home and how these students looked and talked at school as a way of conceptualizing class 'as not only a material location but also a performance' (ibid.). In this Bettie explores issues of class-based meanings of taste, success and authenticity and the enactment of working- and middle-class femininity. She concludes by arguing that the usefulness of conceptualizing class as performative is that it focuses attention on class identities as effects of social structure and as a sense of place (see also Skeggs, 1997). This 'helps explain why class struggle is often waged more over modes of identity expression than over explicit political ideologies' (Skeggs: 29).

Sexual Difference

Psychoanalysis is concerned first and foremost with the acquisition of what is assumed to be healthy, mature, gendered subjectivity. The basic psychoanalytic presupposition that gendered subjectivity is acquired rather than inborn accounts for much of the attraction of psychoanalytic theory for feminists.

(Weedon, 1999: 80)

Barrett begins her account of feminist theories of sexual difference by noting the ground-breaking work of Juliet Mitchell (1974). Mitchell used Freudian and Lacanian psychoanalysis to contribute to feminist developments in Marxist theory. Weedon (1999) also details the significance of Freud and Lacan in terms of feminist accounts of sexual difference. She notes, for example, the development of feminist object relations theory. A principal theorist here is Nancy Chodorow (1978) who emphasized the cultural and psychoanaltyic dimensions to mothering. More recently there has been considerable discussion of what is termed post-Lacanian feminism. Lacan integrated Freud's work on the unconscious and conscious into a linguistic framework. In this Lacan distinguished between the discourses of the unconscious and the discourses of consciousness:

> For Lacan, while consciousness is articulated by means of grammatical
> and syntactical organization, the unconscious is a system which does not
> obey these rules. Through repression, signs are reduced to signifers – ie
> they are quite literally robbed of their meaning, detached from their
> signifieds . . . The unconscious is thus unable to speak in its own voice and
> vocabulary. It can only speak through and by means of conscious
> discourse. It is not the smooth, continuous unfolding of meaning; rather, it
> is expressed as silence, verbal slips, stutterings, gaps, and puns. (Grosz,
> 1990a: 77)

It is this attention given to language in the construction of selfhood that
has made Lacan attractive to feminists (Grosz, 1990a). This is because
his analysis emphasizes a social, rather than biological, construction of
identity. Nevertheless 'For Lacan, meaning, and the symbolic order as a
whole, is fixed in relation to a primary, transcendental signifier which
Lacan calls the *phallus*, the signifier of sexual difference, which guarantees the patriarchal structure of the symbolic order' (Weedon, 1997:
51–2). Feminists have critiqued the status of the phallus as the central
signifier of meaning in that it leaves women with no direct access to the
symbolic order. Thus, while the attention given to language is important, Lacan's analysis of the phallocentric order of meaning has been
critically evaluated by post-Lacanian feminists. In this respect Weedon
notes:

> In post-Lacanian feminist theory attempts to rethink the symbolic order in
> non-patriarchal terms focus on the body of the mother and the maternal
> feminine. However, the focus of this work is radically different from
> Chodorow's theory of mother–child relations. Under patriarchy the
> maternal feminine is repressed by the processes of psycho-sexual develop-
> ment which enable the individual to enter the symbolic order as gendered
> subject. It is further marginalized by the structures of the patriarchal
> symbolic order which govern the Law, culture and sociality. It is exiled
> from the symbolic order – an order which women can only inhabit via a
> patriarchally defined femininity. Post-Lacanian feminists have identified
> the unconscious as the site of the repressed feminine which has its roots in
> the pre-Oedipal relationship with the mother, before the feminine takes on
> its patriarchal definition as lack. (1999: 86–7)

Irigaray, Kristeva and Cixous are regarded as central to the development
of theories of post-Lacanian sexual difference. Although both designa-
tions imply a false unity of position, they are variously referred to as
members of the 'French' school of feminism and the *écriture feminine*
school. This label is because of the attention they have paid to issues of
language and how this is conveyed through their styles of writing.
Beasley (1999: 72) notes that feminists within the school of *écriture*

feminine are concerned to question the Lacanian assumption 'that femininity can only be seen from the point of view of phallic culture (culture as masculine dominance) and argues for other possibilities'. For example, Irigaray has explored a philosophy of the feminine. This has put questions of sexual difference at the centre of her exploration of women's experiences of desire and subjectivity and the female body (Bainbridge, 2001). Because of the attention she has given in her work to the importance of the maternal function in the development of the individual, Kristeva is attributed with 'revolutionising the position and importance of the maternal function in psychoanalytic theory' (Oliver, 2001: 177).

Felski (1997) suggests that there is now a 'second generation' of feminist theorists of sexual difference writing in Europe, Australia and the United States. In this regard she names Braidotti, Grosz and Cornell respectively. Each of these theorists is striving to avoid problems of essentialism and naturalism in their work. They are also trying to avoid the problems of dematerializing women. For example, Braidotti (1994) offers the metaphor of 'nomad' as a way of conceiving a post-humanist utopian feminist subjectivity that is located within language and geo-political contexts but has given up all desire for fixity. Braidotti defines sexual difference in the following terms:

> sexual difference is neither an unproblematic nor an autonomous category; it is the name we give to a process by which diverse differences intersect and are activated alongside or against each other. It is the process by which subjectivity functions and should be the process by which an adequate form of politics is posited for it. (1997: 39)

Braidotti argues that central to understanding theories of sexual difference are two terms. These are paradox and contradiction. The key paradox is that: 'Sexual difference is based on one theoretical and practical paradox: it simultaneously produces and destablizes the category "woman"' (ibid.: 26). 'Woman' theories of sexual difference form part of a broader concern with the production of the individual in modernity. They also challenge the masculinity at the heart of humanism. Sexual difference theorists also destablize the category 'woman' through their deconstructive approaches. These deconstructive approaches can be seen in terms of a key contradiction that is at the heart of sexual difference theorization. This contradiction is the contradiction of subjectivity: 'Sexual difference brings into representation the play of multiple differences that structure the subject: these are neither harmonious nor homogenous, but rather internally differentiated and potentially contradictory. Therefore, sexual difference forces us to think of the simultaneity of potentially contradictory social, discursive and symbolic effects' (ibid.: 27).

Braidotti comments that her standpoint is that:

> sexual difference is primarily a political and intellectual strategy, not a philosophy. Neither *dogma* nor dominant *doxa*, it emerged mostly out of the political practice of Continental feminism in the 1970s as an attempt to move beyond some of the aporias and the dead ends of equality-minded, marxist-based feminism. (ibid.: 26, emphasis in original)

Cornell (1997) similarly offers a definition of sexual difference though her focus is to develop new conceptualizations of legal equality that focus on the female imaginary. She notes that 'the feminine within sexual difference must be affirmed rather than repudiated' (ibid.: 54). Cornell's definition confirms the political significance that is accorded to sexual difference for feminist activism and lays stress on the challenge to compulsory heterosexuality:

> What do I mean by sexual difference? First, I mean that who we are as sexed beings is symbolic, institutional; second, it is a way of being that claims one's own sex outside of the imposed norms of heterosexuality. The first is a point about how to understand gender. The second is a political aspiration that must reform our dreams of how we are to be sexed and to claim our personhood at the same time. (ibid.: 41)

Cornell opposes the assumption of 'neutered' personhood that lies at the heart of legal theories of equality. In contrast, she is concerned to develop a theory of legal equality that takes account of individuals as sexuate beings. This is because 'Sexed beings have a phenomenological existence that puts demands on them' (ibid.: 42). In other words, although legal theory might assume a 'no difference' view of the individual, this ignores the sexed, 'raced' and classed meanings that make life meaningful to individuals. For example, Cornell offers the example of hair braiding that some African-Americans undertake and which can cause discrimination or harassment. She notes that hair braiding is one way in which African-American women can continue to identify with African traditions. Yet under formal equality laws in the United States 'hair braiding is not an "immutable characteristic," and therefore it does not fall under the traditional understanding of race discrimination' (ibid.: 44). Because the law assumes a single axis of discrimination, in this case that of 'race', it is not possible to sue. Within Cornell's expanded definition:

The theory of equality gives to women of all nationalities and 'races' the right to represent their own meaning of their racial, national, and sexual identification. The symbolic aspect of feminism implicates renaming and reshaping our form of life . . . I not only recognize but also insist on a feminist analysis that clearly sees that any actual specificity that is given to feminine sexual difference is inherently and necessarily racialized, nationalized, and linguistically conditioned. (ibid.: 53)

Grosz's (1990b) comments in respect of the implications of difference in the work of Irigaray, Gallop and Cixous may therefore also be applicable to Cornell. She comments:

The notion of difference affects not only women's definitions of themselves, but also of the world. This implies that not only must social practices be subjected to feminist critique and reorganisation, but also that the very structures of representation, meaning, and knowledge must be subjected to a thoroughgoing transformation of their patriarchal alignments. A politics of difference implies the right to define oneself, others, and the world according to one's own interests. (1990b: 340).

Postcolonial Differences

As with all the terms in this text, the meanings of postcolonialism are contested. The most basic contestation relates to the term 'post'. In common with other assumptions surrounding this term, some readings suggest that postcolonialism refers chronologically to the period after colonialism. Other readings imply that postcolonialist writing is that which is opposed to and resists colonialism. The difficulties that inhere from this contestation are mainly concerned with the political nature of postcolonial writing. In respect of the first definition, we cannot assume that all writing produced after colonial rule is politically resistant. In respect of the second definition, we cannot assume that all resistance writing will be concerned with anti-colonial experiences or cultural practices. This is because 'Not all of it will be concerned with colonial power issues such as establishing identity and, in the case of women's post-colonial writing, family/kinship, motherlands and mother tongue' (Wisker, 2000: 13). These issues of political definition are significant to understanding the issue of difference in feminist postcolonialist perspectives. In this respect I shall highlight three issues (see also Table 3.3):

Table 3.3 Postcolonial differences

Name of school of thought	Postcolonial, 'Third World', Post-National, Global
Form of difference	Multi-axial, e.g. differences between 'Third World' and Western Women, differences between diasporic and migratory communities
Standpoint	Critiques Western 'Othering' and imperialism of Western cultures. Retains a concern with the political and cultural usefulness of some aspects of a unified identity
Politics	Specific and local
Illustrative feminists	Chandra Mohanty, Gayorvati Spivak, Avtar Brah

1 The critique of colonialist modes of representation in Western feminist work and related issues of voice.
2 An emphasis on multiple differences, complex diversities and locationality arising from issues of cultural hybridity and diasporic experiences.
3 A cautionary retention of the importance of a unified political identity.

In respect of modes of representation Wohl (2001) illustrates how the colonialist nature of British Victorian popular literature and science portrayed Irish, Black and working-class people as unreasonable, irrational, childlike, believing in superstition, criminal, excessively sexual, filthy and inhabitants of 'dark' lands. These pervasive and extensive assumptions of Victorian superiority throw into sharp relief Weedon's (1999) remarks in respect of Western feminist writings on Third World women. Weedon comments that they 'share a marked tendency to view women from other societies through a Eurocentric gaze which privileges Western notions of liberation and progress and portrays Third World women primarily as victims of ignorance and restrictive cultures and religions' (ibid.: 188).

A classic example of a critique of this form of representation is Mohanty's (1991) discussion of how the concept of the 'Third World Woman' has been authorized through Western discourses. This 'Third World Woman' was represented as passive, oppressed and the victim of 'traditional' religions and cultures. Narayan's (1998) focus on feminist critiques of masculine epistemology also illustrates how these overlook the concerns of non-Western women. For example Western feminism has been critical of the individualism of positivism because this concurs with a political emphasis on individualistic liberal rights. However, Narayan notes how concepts such as individual rights are highly useful for fighting problems rooted in 'traditional' cultures. In this respect Narayan (1998: 83) comments that 'different cultural contexts and political agendas may caste a very different light on both the "idols" and the "enemies" of knowledge as they have characteristically been typed in western feminist epistemology'. Central to a critique of the imperialistic nature of Western feminism is, therefore, its attempts to 'speak for' others. Ang (1997: 57) comments in this regard that there is a 'profound suspicion of any hegemonizing, homogenizing, universalizing representation of "us" and . . . a strong resistance against modes of political mobilization on the basis of such representations, especially among those who used to be silenced or rendered invisible by them'. Drawing on the idea of multiple subjectivities postcolonial analyses have also challenged Western binary oppositions through a focus on cultural hybridity and diasporic experiences that give rise to multiple differences. Thus:

> Against nativist visions of autonomous racial or cultural difference, post-colonial theorists are likely to note that such distinctions are no longer feasible in an era of pervasive migration, media globalization, and trans-national information flow. The colonized's fashioning of an insurgent counteridentity is inevitably shaped by the experience of colonization; the colonizer's culture is irrevocably altered by contact with the native. As a result, a conception of distinct, singular, internally homogenous groupings gives way to a model of metissage, of borrowing and lending across porous cultural boundaries. (Felski, 1997: 12)

In this respect, Barkan and Shelton (1998: 5) suggest that the political significance of diaspora is the creation of a '"nonnormative" intellectual community'. Such a community is considered able to provide a critical, though ambivalent and fragmented, voice that may contribute to dismantling the relations of colonialism. Wisker (2000: 16) refers to this as colonization in reverse and she makes the point that 'Post-colonial migrants both unsettle and enrich what was thought of as the centre of imperial powers.' The theoretical and political response to these issues has been a call for the acknowledgement of the multi-axial cultural, historical, temporal and locational specificity of subjectivities. For example, Brah provides a possible future through multi-locationality and dia-synchronic relationality:

> What I wish to stress is that the study of diasporic formations . . . calls for a concept of diaspora in which different historical and contemporary elements are understood, not in tandem, but *in their dia-synchronic relationality*. Such analyses entail engagement with complex arrays of

> contiguities and contradictions; of changing multi-locationality across
> time and space. (1996: 190, emphasis in original)

In terms of politics this leads to a complex project. This entails a variety
of concrete practices designed to undermine the relations of power at
the economic, political and cultural levels while at the same time
remaining 'vigilant of the circumstances under which affirmation of a
particular collective experience becomes an essentialist assertion of
difference' (Brah, 1990: 143). For example, Brah's concerns are to
'critique discourses of fixed origins while also seeking to reconstruct a
space of identity from which a different kind of subject might speak and
act' (Gedalof, 2000: 344). Thus, in an interview with Brah, Davis and
Lutz suggest that for her:

> identity is about hierarchies which are constantly in flux and need to be
> seen in context . . . She finds any politics constituted around the primacy
> of one axis of differentiation (gender, race or class) over all others limited
> in its ability to do justice to the everyday experiences of most individuals
> who – like herself – have mixed allegiances and move in and out of
> different identities. (2000: 369–70)

The notion of mixed allegiances and the moving in and out of identities
and on the specific and local is foregrounded in Tripp's (2000) analysis
of the women's movement in several African countries. In this respect,
Tripp comments: 'There are enormous disjunctures between Western
feminist discourses of difference and how the idea of difference has been
articulated in women's movements in Israel, Northern Ireland, the
former Yugoslavia, or India – that is, places where difference has
mattered "too much"' (ibid.: 649). Her analysis illustrates how the
women's movement in Sudan, Uganda, South Africa, Nigeria and Kenya
has been able to bridge extensive ethnic, racial and religious differences.

   In particular, the concept of locationality has been a significant aspect
to postcolonial theorizing. Wisker (2000) offers a useful conceptualization that illustrates that location is both a matter of culture, history or
geography and a place of values, ideology and spirituality:

> 'Location' as a notion and phenomenographical whole is much richer
> merely than that of the cultural, historical and geographical context of
> writing and reading, which it includes. Location and the 'loci of enunci-
> ation' are the places or contexts from which we experience and speak,
> where we place ourselves ideologically, spiritually, imaginatively. In
> everyday language, it answers the question 'where are you coming from?'
> and so gives us, as readers, a sense of the differences we need to negotiate,
> the information and feelings we need to find out about in order to gain a

better understanding of writing by those who come from and speak from contexts different from our own. (ibid.: 7–8)

The materiality of location should also be stressed. Issues of location are imbued with the politics of identity, nationhood and geography. These restrict and facilitate our movement and operate to 'place' us and be 'placed', to 'name' and be 'named'. For example, Mohanty reflects on how she was constructed as an illigitimate outsider through the visa requirements that were necessary to visit the Netherlands:

> leaving for the Netherlands, I discovered a visa was required to enter the country. I am an Indian citizen and a permanent resident of the United States. Procuring a visa involved a substantial fee ($60); a letter from my employer (the letter of invitation from NOISE was inadequate) indicating that I have a permanent job in the US; that I was going to Utrecht for a professional conference; and that my employer would be financially responsible for me while I was in the Netherlands; and finally, a notarized copy of my green card, the 'proof' of my permanent residency in the United States. I never leave home without this card. (1997: xi)

Moreover, Beasley comments:

> despite the interest of [postcolonial] feminists developing a cultural politics of difference in the postmodern agenda of destabilizing identity, they generally do not display as unreserved a determination to demonstrate the fluidity of identity, especially of identities linked to race/ethnicity. Additionally, they often express doubts about the extent to which social relations can be described in postmodern terms. (1999: 115)

In this sense postcolonial feminists seek to reaffirm the connections between difference and hierarchy (Felski, 1997). Thus, while postcolonial theorists might want to avoid the fetishization and Orientalism of Western assumptions of difference, they are also wary of those who urge that old divisions are being replaced with new alliances and that the fragmentation of modernism is creating similarities rather than differences. In this respect Beasley (1999: 115) notes: 'Reservations regarding this plurality appear to be linked to concern that it may imitate a form of cultural genocide.' Smith's commentary on those who speak of progress, independence, development and decolonization illustrates how the significance of power relations and identity are central to the postcolonialist project:

> Is this imperialism? No, we are told, this is post-colonialism. This is globalization. This is economic independence. This is tribal development. This is progress. Others tell us that this is the end of modernism, and

therefore the end of imperialism as we have known it. That business is now over, and so are all its associated project such as decolonization. People now live in a world which is fragmented with multiple and shifting identities, that the oppressed and the colonized are so deeply implicated in their own oppressions that they are no more nor less authentic than anyone else. While the West might be experiencing fragmentation, the process of fragmentation known under its older guise of colonization is well known to indigenous peoples. We can talk about the fragmentation of lands and cultures. We know what it is like to have our identities regulated by laws and our languages and customs removed from our lives. Fragmentation is not an indigenous project, it is something we are recovering from. While shifts are occurring in the ways in which indigenous peoples put ourselves back together again, the greater project is about recentring indigenous identities on a larger scale. (Smith, 1999: 97)

Case Study 6: The Colonial *Flâneuse*

Wollacott (2000) offers an historicized account of postcolonial perspectives through her research into the reasons why large numbers of white Australian women came to live in London in the early years of the twentieth century. In 1911 there were 13,000 Australian-born women living in England and Wales. Standard accounts of colonialism tend to portray colonization as a one-way process through which the imperialist culture is left relatively unchanged. Wollacott points out how the significance of this historical analysis not only enables us to understand the fluidity and diversity of the modern city of the early twentieth century but also how such diasporic movements as those of Australian women bring change and influence to the imperial society.

Wollacott's analysis draws on the work of feminist geographers, historical sources and fictional accounts. She explores how living in the imperial metropolis enabled White colonial women to appropriate 'new possibilities for physical and social mobility, including new professional and career opportunities, as women remade their subjectivities, lives, and spaces' (ibid.: 762). Wollacott's theoretical framework can broadly be described as postcolonial. Here she draws on two concepts. These are hybridity and *flâneuse*. By hybridity Wollacott is rejecting the binaried nature of, for example, colonizer and colonized. Rather, she is concerned to explore the 'complexities and interstitialities of colonial regimes . . . as a means of capturing the slippages of colonialism, colonized peoples' subversion of categories imposed by colonial states, and the racial and cultural mixing that colonialism has inescapably instigated' (ibid.: 763). Her use of the term *flâneuse* is designed to offer an insight into, particularly middle-class, 'women's historic encroachment on autonomous movement around the city . . . their ability to inhabit public space on their own without harm to either their bodies or their reputations and to feel that they belonged in that space and could possess it in a leisurely fashion' (ibid.: 765).

Wollacott notes that because of their Whiteness Australian colonial women were not visibly distinctive or seen as racially inferior. She also argues that their status as outsiders gave them greater freedom that was combined with 'their culturally based self-definition as confident and capable' (ibid.: 766). Wollacott's findings therefore illustrate how travelling to London opened new careers and educational possibilities for women in newly emergent fields of social work and state administration and in the theatres, stages, music halls, agents offices, publishing and newspaper houses, art schools and nursing colleges. In this respect Wollacott comments:

> Women training and performing as professional musicians, scraping together a living by hawking manuscripts to Fleet Street editors, or combing the streets of outcast London in the name of social work were all claiming the right to work and be seen in the public domain, to have publicly professional careers, and to be both recognized and paid for them while retaining complete respectability. (ibid.: 769)

Overall, Wollacott argues:

> The consciousness of another life and other places, combined with their sense of belonging in London as the center of their empire and their in-between status as white colonials (not quite truly British and at the top of the imperial hierarchy but white and therefore positioned as more privileged than and superior to colonial people of color), all facilitated Australian women's ability to claim public space in London. (ibid.: 783)

In these ways they were 'important agents in women's encroachment on the public domain at the same time that they were part of the modernity and the colonialism transforming the city' (ibid.: 784).

Summary

This chapter has explored five conceptualizations of difference. These are different-but-equal and identity differences; poststructural and postmodern difference; sexual difference and postcolonial difference. While these are relatively standard distinctions in the feminist literature, there are considerable overlaps between the positions that individual theorists may take up within each of these distinctions with consequent implications for the application of these labels. The organization and labelling of knowledge fields are political acts that are in consequence highly contestable. In addition, this chapter has demonstrated the tyranny of dualism in that when we seek to discuss difference we are constantly drawn to explore issues of equality.

FURTHER READING

Mongia, P. (ed.) (1997) *Contemporary Postcolonial Theory: A Reader*. London: Arnold. An excellent resource, this text contains reprinted articles from key postcolonial theorists.

Weedon, C. (1999) *Feminism, Theory and the Politics of Difference*. Oxford: Blackwell. Weedon offers a very accessible, comprehensive and up-to-date review of the range of differences within feminism. Her text includes a discussion of class, 'race', ethnicity, sexual orientation and age. It also explores the critiques of difference in terms of the politics of feminism.

Choice   4

How do individuals define their self-interest? How are people's desires socially constructed? Do conventional definitions of a separate 'self' reflect a masculine view of the world? Some feminists of post-modern persuasion have argued that rational choice is simply an interpretive fiction. Others insist that we need a theory of individual choice that retains at least some emphasis on rationality broadly construed as reasonable, purposeful behaviour.

(Folbre, 1994: 17–18)

The term 'choice' conjures up strong ideas of human agency. The individual is free to select whatever action she or he desires or may discriminate between different available options and pick the most suitable. These ideas extend from purchasing food to selecting a life-style. As Plummer (2000: 432) comments: 'the idea that we are auto-nomous human beings who can choose the kind of personal life we wish to live has become a deeply entrenched one'. Indicating that how choice is conceptualized and experienced as a lived reality is historically specific, Giddens (1991) suggests that these aspects to choice are bound up with the conditions of late-modernity. For Giddens (ibid.: 2) choice forms part of the 'new mechanism of self-identity'.

Giddens identifies four influences that give rise to a diversity of choices. First, the signposts of how to act that are commonly found in traditional societies are no longer present. Late modernity is characterized not only by a plurality of choices but also by no guidance as to which choices should be made. Second, late-modern societies contain diverse, seg-mented lifeworlds. Individuals are surrounded by, and have knowledge of, alternative ways of living. This is, third, reinforced through a global media that brings to the individual an even greater array of milieux. Fourth, in marked contrast to the reasoned certainty of the Enlight-enment, the reflexive nature of late modernity is marked by doubt.

Choice is, of course, also entwined with the individualism, rights and freedoms of liberalism. This can be seen in the language of choice that has come to prominence in recent years in political discourses and policies. For example, the 'individual's right to choose' has been an important aspect of British educational policy. This is evidenced in the development of educational markets and the rhetoric of parental choice (see, for example, Gewirtz et al., 1995). Feminism is no exception in taking up the liberalist discourses of choice. Eisenstein (1993: xiii, emphasis in original) makes this point in relation to feminist theorizing when she comments: 'Although differences still exist . . . the more interesting point is that significant similarities exist as well. And at the core of *all* the differences remains "the" liberal feminist recognition of woman as an individual with "rights" to freedom of choice.'

This emphasis on the freedoms and agency of choice has been heavily criticized for not taking enough account of issues of social structure. Walsh (1998: 33) defines structure as a 'recurring pattern of behaviour [that] has a constraining effect'. Structural issues therefore impact on the autonomy of choice. For example, while a purely agentic account of career choice would suggest that individuals are able to select any form of employment they desire, a structuralist account would highlight how career choices are constrained, for example, by the gendering of women's and men's work. The extent to which anyone is absolutely free to choose is therefore called into question. Anderson (1998) provides an example of this from research into the psychology of career choice. She comments:

> In couching the issue of occupational behaviour within a choice frame-work, there is an inherent assumption that all people have to do is choose a particular job or career from a whole array of different options. To operate from this assumption simplifies the issue and implies some kind of deficiency on the part of those who appear to restrict their selection to specific fields . . . educational and occupational choice is a complex process that is significantly influenced by environmental variables. Consequently, the current terminology and framework of choice . . . is inappropriate. (1998: 145)

Anderson offers the term 'occupational fate' as a way of conveying the structuring of choice and to imply that in many cases 'choice' is absent.

Nevertheless, structural accounts present the opposite problem to those of autonomy and agency. They are critiqued for being overly deterministic as they give primacy to the power of structural forces that reduce an individual's freedom of manoeuvre. This, then, leaves us with a problem. This is how we might avoid an analysis that rests within the dichotomy of agency–structure. McNay (2000: 10) comments that feminist attempts to create a balanced account have highlighted how women's 'experiences attest to the capacity for autonomous action in the face of often overwhelming cultural sanctions and structural inequalities'. However, she also comments that feminist theorization has replicated the agency–structure dualism of mainstream social theory. This is because theorization has either mainly focused on micro-sociological accounts of agency or, alternatively, deterministic accounts of structure. Jones (1997: 262) describes social theorists' attempts to avoid either an overly optimistic account of human agency or an overly deterministic account of social structure as an 'endless ping-pong'.

The concept of choice is clearly a useful area in which to explore these broader issues of agency–structure. For this reason I shall detail two quite distinct conceptualizations. The first is that of rational choice theory. Rational choice is the central theorization of economics. It privileges the autonomous agent who pursues her or his self-interest. Rational choice accords with many everyday perceptions of choice. Within assumptions of rational choice one has a list of options and carefully selects the most appropriate within the ordinary constraints that exist of, say, time, money or insufficient information. Feminist critiques of rational choice theory offer an excellent example of the problems of agentic accounts of choice. Yet many of these critiques do not appear to go beyond the 'ping-pong' identified by Jones.

In contrast, the second conceptualization of choice that is explored is that of the poststructuralist 'choosing subject'. One of the perceived strengths of poststructuralism is that it offers a way out of the 'ping-pong' impasse. In particular, poststructuralism is seen to provide an explanation for resistance and contradiction. An exploration of the 'choosing subject' enables us to consider how this is achieved.

Rational Choice: Choice as an Act of Technical Rationality

Central to rational choice theory is a particular conception of the individual. Specifically, the individual is perceived to be 'utility maximizing' and, as the terminology implies, to act rationally in their choices. Scott (2000: 126) defines rational choice theory as 'the idea that all action is fundamentally "rational" in character and that people calculate the likely costs and benefits of any action before deciding what to do'. Within rational choice theory, therefore, the individual is conceptualized as primarily motivated by the rewards and costs of their actions and the likely profit they can make.

This conceptualization of the rational behaviour of the 'utility-maximizing' individual assumes that choice is predicated on the following three stages:

1   Possibilities are identified and separated out as 'different' and distinctive from one another.
2   Information is acquired about each different option, so that they can be evaluated one against another, and against previously held criteria.
3   This rational appraisal leads to the selection of one option as the 'choice'.
    (David et al., 1997: 399)

In addition, rational choice theory is based on an approach termed 'methodological individualism'. Implicit within methodological individualism is a particular conceptualization of society. This rests on the centrality in neo-classical economic thought that is given to markets as regulators of human behaviour. Thus, choices arise from free trade, competitiveness and individualism. These elements can be seen in Becker's (1991: ix) comments that rational choice 'assumes that individuals maximize their utility from basic preferences that do not change rapidly over time, and that the behaviour of different individuals is coordinated by explicit and implicit markets'. As Scott notes, central to rational choice theory is the idea that complex social phenomena can be explained as the result of the actions, and interactions, of individuals. In rational choice theory the individual is taken as the elementary unit of social life and 'social explanations [are] based entirely on trade between rational individuals' (Gardiner, 1997: 150). Figure 4.1 summarizes these elements of neo-classical economics. While such an approach *may* hold good for understanding why people choose one particular consumer product over another, such a theory has posed a number of problems for economists in analysing choices where more complex information is required or where there are uncertainties or misinformation. In response to these issues Fine and Green (2001) note how new theoretical developments in economics during the 1970s took account of the differential effects that imperfect information had on markets. In consequence, the development of these new theoretical and econometric directions enabled the discipline of economics to extend its analyses beyond its traditional spheres of financially based market relations. One such area is that termed New Home Economics.

Gardiner (1997) notes that the development of New Home Economics arose from what neo-classical economists saw as a paradox. That

1   Economics is about the alternative uses of scarce resources.
2   Economics is about the exchange of goods and services, normally for money.
3   Economics is about the market mechanism: the role of price in bringing about a balance between supply (sellers) and demand (buyers).
4   The market is a democratic institution in which buyers and sellers have equal status.
5   The primary economic agent is the individual; households and firms act as if they were individual agents.
6   Economics has universal applicability and can be applied to different societies and historical periods.
7   The main purpose of economics is to make valid predictions on how individuals and economies will behave.
8   Economic theory suggests that the economic role of the state should be minimal and that markets should be given the greatest possible freedom to allocate resources.

Source: Gardiner, 1997: 12

Figure 4.1   Neo-classical economics

is that there were increasing numbers of women in employment in the context of rising real incomes. Why, it was asked, should women choose to work when their husbands' incomes were more than sufficient? The sphere of New Home Economics introduced 'the notion of the household as a maximising unit' (ibid.: 37). This means that the household was assumed to function in a unified, rational and ahistorical way.

Two illustrations from Becker (1991) will illustrate how neo-classical economists have confronted, first, the problem of imperfect information and, second, have assumed the household can be analysed as a unity. Becker is a key proponent of rational choice theory and has applied this to an analysis of family life. Through mathematical models, Becker's treatise on the family explores a number of issues including the division of household labour, marriage, divorce, fertility and employment. The following extract indicates a rational choice theory perspective of utility maximization as it is applied to choice of marriage partner. According to Becker, longer searches may increase the likelihood of finding the perfect partner but they are more expensive. The 'rational person' will find the optimum point between initial costs and eventual returns.

Increased search and better information raise the utility expected from marriage by improving the quality of marital choices. However, time, effort, and other costly resources must be spent on search, and the longer the search, the longer gains from marriage are delayed. A rational person would continue to search on both the 'extensive margins' of additional prospects and the 'intensive margin' of additional information about serious prospects until the marginal cost and marginal benefit on each margin are equal. In particular, rational persons marry even when certain of eventually finding better prospects with additional search, for the cost of additional search exceeds the expected benefits from better prospects. (Becker, 1991: 325)

Becker argues that the common indicators of a good 'choice' such as family background, educational level, religion, income, and so forth are only proxies for the traits desired of a good marriage partner. Because they are proxies they constitute imperfect information. The real business of getting to know your partner occurs in the first few years of marriage or cohabitation. The problem of 'imperfect information' is, in consequence, the reason for high divorce rates in the early years of marriage. Thus:

> I suggest that marriages fail early primarily because of imperfect information in marriage markets and the accumulation of better information during marriage . . . Women who divorced early in their marriage report that 'difficult' spouses and value conflicts were major sources of their discontent, presumably because these traits are much better assessed after a few years of marriage. (ibid.: 328)

The view that the household is a unified decision-making unit is illustrated in Becker's analysis of altruism. As Gardiner (1997) notes in the public world of employment, production and consumerism neo-classical economists argue that the market acts as a coordinating mechanism that will regulate excessive behaviour. This coordinating mechanism is absent in the household. Becker resolved this through his discussion of altruism and selfishness. In Becker's treatise altruism can be located in the head of the household to whom Becker gave the male pronoun. The female pronoun was given to the one who acts selfishly. This altruist will be a 'benevolent dictator' and act in the best interests of the household. He (*sic*) will control the resources and make decisions. In this way, therefore, the economic analysis of the household can proceed as if it were an individual.

The application of rational choice theory can also be found in debates about human and social capital. Human capital, again strongly associated with Becker, is commonly related to the extent to which education and training constitute investments in individuals that give rise to increased productivity or an increased economic yield. This relationship gives rise to studies which measure, for example, the national economic returns to education in terms of Gross Domestic Product or the impact of training on company profits. It is also used to explain differential incomes on the basis that investment in initial education and training will produce higher incomes (see Tight, 1996, for a useful summary and critique).

Gardiner (1997: 37) comments: 'Whilst individual maximising behaviour has normally been used to explain male economic behaviour, such as the supply of labour to the market, the notion of the household as a maximising unit has usually been introduced where there is a need to explain female economic behaviour.' Thus, in response to explanations for women's lower earnings economists turn to the household. For example, human capital theorists argue that women's lower earnings can be explained by their lack of investment in human capital. Such explanations have suggested that because young women know that as adults they will be primary carers of their families, they make rational choices not to invest in initial education and training. More recently, women's increasing participation in paid labour and their higher investments in education have produced alternative 'choice' explanations. In relation to the high proportion of women in part-time paid employment, for example, such explanations argue that women choose employment that requires less energy and time because this compensates for the greater time they will have to spend on domestic work. Overall, as Gardiner (1997: 49) comments: 'Gender differences in employment patterns are explained as the result of the cumulative effects of men and women individually and in household units responding rationally to the way the market signals their comparative advantage in the different spheres of production.'

The general criticisms of rational choice theory focus primarily on the absence of a recognition of the many problematical aspects of the social world. Fine and Green (2001: 78) note that neoclassical economics is both ahistorical and excessively formalistic: 'Because it is constructed on the foundation of methodological individualism, its concepts are timeless, universal and not infused with real history.' Scott (2000) cites three main areas where rational choice theory is problematic:

- in respect of explanations for collective action as rational choice theory cannot explain why individuals join different kinds of groups and associations;
- in terms of the origins of social norms such as trust, altruism and reciprocity;
- in respect of the impact of social structures. Within rational choice theory primary emphasis is placed on the actions or agency of individuals.

Conceptualizations of social capital have been heralded as adding an important social dimension to economic theories and in this way contributing to what is seen as a major weakness of economic theories of rational choice. This has been particularly through the work of Coleman (1987; 1988a; 1988b). Coleman is associated with forms of methodological individualism developed by scholars in the Department of Sociology at the University of Chicago (Fine, 1999). He is, as Fine points out, the intellectual partner to Becker. Working within theories of functionalism and individualism, Coleman saw his work in terms of a convergence between economics and sociology that was underpinned by a rational choice model of human action. In this he sought to develop human capital theory by recognizing the role of social relationships.

In economic terms social capital is:

> the network of social and community relations which underpin people's ability to engage in education, training and work and to sustain a healthy civic community. Key conditions for the nurturance of social capital include reciprocity and trust, the imposition of sanctions when these fail, the existence of horizontal, not vertical, mechanisms for the exchange of information and support and the willingness of the community to take on responsibility for the provision of as many social services as possible. (Riddell et al., 1999: 55)

This perspective can be seen in the work of Coleman whose main concerns were to demonstrate how an individual's attainment of human capital, say, in the levels of their examination and scholarly successes, were influenced by family and inter-family relations.

Coleman suggested that social capital is generated in two ways. These are within the household and between households. For example, an important source of social capital is the amount of time that parents spend with their children and one another. In this way, Coleman offered an explanation of why parents rich in human capital themselves might not pass this advantage to their children. Their engagement in paid work, for example, meant that they had limited contact with their children and with each other. The result is a lack of necessary invest-ment of time and energy in their children's potential human capital. In another example, Coleman (1988a) recounts a situation in Asian immi-grant households in the USA where mothers purchase copies of school textbooks in order to help their children. Here Coleman argues that the social capital available for the child's education is extremely high while their human capital is low. This social capital, according to Coleman, is converted into human capital in the form of educational qualifications.

By recognizing the significance of family and household the explanatory framework that Coleman develops does take more account of the influences of social structures than is found in the explicit individualism of Becker's earlier work on human capital. Nevertheless, it is a muted development of an individualistic discourse that still relies on exchange relations between rational individuals for its primary explanatory framework. Using the language of trust, reciprocity, mutuality, support and community, the literature on social capital conveys a rosy glow of social relations as it posits exchange relations as beneficent and democratic (Blaxter and Hughes, 2000).

There are several critiques of these conceptualizations of rational choice that I wish to draw attention to and shall expand upon below. Overall it is hard to avoid the implication of this theorizing that neo-classical economists believe that if we were all to act as maximizing, atomistic, exchange-focused individuals the problems of social life would cease. However, how adequate is this framework both in terms of a representation of the realities of social relations and in terms of an appropriate moral and ethical framework? And, what does this mean in terms of the development of policy frameworks that encourage a greater extension of rational choice market-based economics? Certainly, feminism has had some responses to these questions.

Case Study 7: Girls in the Education Market

Since the late 1980s British educational policy has embraced the market through its concern with parental choice and encouraging competition between educational institutions. Rational choice theory provides the centre-piece of this as it is assumed that parents will select the school that is most appropriate to their child's needs through a rational appraisal of how these are matched through the school's ethos and results. Ball and Gewirtz (1997) offer an analysis of how single-sex schools for girls are responding to their market position and how parents and their daughters choose between single-sex and mixed schools. Their research is based on interviews with parents and case studies of the schools in question. Their analytic framework seeks to explore both the demand and supply side of the market in girls' education.

Ball and Gewirtz illustrate how schools position themselves in the market place through, for example, careful consideration of the images they present. These include changes to uniforms to ensure they represent a 'respectable' status and producing brochures that extol the benefits of all-girl schools. In these ways senior managers in schools juggle between professional and entrepreneurial interests and discourses. Parental approaches to choice certainly include a careful perusal of the documentation and other published information such as school league tables. They also visit schools on open days. However, Ball and Gewirtz comment that 'both making choices and choices made is far from the rational calculus conjured up by some market theorists. While material class interests and concerns about the life opportunities available to girls clearly inform and underlie choice-making these are realised through a "fuzzy" and sometimes misguided logic' (ibid.: 219). Thus 'personal prejudices derived from their own school experiences, vague and uncertain grasp of received wisdom and reputational gossip acquired from local social networks and media hype . . . [together with] . . . powerful affective responses, positive or negative, from parents and daughters' (ibid.) consequent upon visits to schools all impact on choice.

Feminist Critiques of Rational Choice Theory

> Economics in the twentieth century became increasingly restricted to a theory of rational choice in the context of scarcity . . . Feminist economists have been key critics of the individualism and absence of an ethical dimension within mainstream economics.
>
> (Gardiner, 1997: 38)

Becker and Coleman's work evidence something more than gender-blindness. They evidence a political reassertion that the worthy individual is based within a subjectivity of White, middle-class, masculine rationality. Generally, therefore, feminist critiques draw specific attention to the inherent assumptions of gender, class, 'race' and sexuality that are present in rational choice models. For example, Folbre (1994) draws attention to the masculinity within neo-classical economics through her euphemism 'Mr Rational Economic Man'. R. Williams (1993) notes the dualistic thinking in much theorizing by feminist economists that retain the stable and unified assumptions of the female/male binary. She calls for a deconstructive approach that racializes theories of gender. Overall, there are three areas where feminist economists focus specific critique. As I shall illustrate, these draw more generally on the feminist literature and are concerned with the gendering of self-interest, rationality and individualism.

As we have seen, an aspect of the subject at the heart of rational choice theory is that of the utility-maximizing individual. Gardiner (1997: 55) thus comments that neo-classical economics has been constructed around the idea of 'self-interested, self-supporting economic agents who are faced with an array of options from which to choose within the limits of the resources available to them'. This means that self-interest provides the major element, not only for motivating choices but also for the efficient maintenance of the market and indeed for the 'good' of all. However, feminist economists point out that within economics the issues of self-interest, individualism and competitiveness are primarily equated with the public economy and market. In terms of individuals in the private economy of the household, the assumption is that these relationships are more harmonious and cooperative (England, 1993; Gardiner, 1997).

In particular, feminists point to Becker's analysis of altruism as evidence for this. Becker's choice of the masculine pronoun for the altruist and the feminine pronoun for the beneficiary of this altruism is a stark illustration of the more gendered assumptions underpinning his work. Becker's depiction of the family 'calls up a picture of a benign group of generous individuals, banded together in happy union . . . however, [the family in Becker] is more accurately characterized as 'The Present-Giving Male Dictator and His Selfish Wife' (Bergmann, 1995: 146). Strassman (1993) points out that Becker's model contains two old economic fables. These are the story of the benevolent patriarch and the story of the woman of leisure. Thus, the patriarch is engaged in paid work and acts as the necessary regulatory force of the household. As economically inactive, the wife is assumed to be unproductive.

There are two key points that feminist economists draw attention to in this respect. The first is the dualistic framework of public/private that is called upon. The economic model of rational choice assumes that market and household behaviour are essentially different. In the public market people behave competitively. In the private sphere of the home people behave cooperatively. Nevertheless, this suggests a uniform and unique set of behaviours characterized across a clear public/private binary. In the everyday of social relations such a binary falls down. Gardiner (1997: 236) comments in this respect: 'Economic life, whether in private companies, public sector organisations or households is pervaded by combinations of self-interested behaviour and cooperative endeavour, by conflict and altruism.'

In response to this feminist economists have called for greater consideration to be given to what goes on in families (Cantillon and Nolan, 2001). The 'benevolent patriarch' of Becker's model suggests that

'Although family members may have conflicting needs, the good provider dispassionately and rationally makes decisions that are in the best interests of the family' (Strassman, 1993: 58). Issues of power relations are therefore relegated to a model of 'free choice'. In particular, feminists draw attention to the asymmetrical power relations of households. These asymmetric power relations not only impact on who does what in the household division of labour. They also affect the distribution of other resources, such as food, clothes, access to private health care, and so forth.

The second issue associated with the notion of the utility-maximizing individual is that no account is taken of the gendered construction of self-interest. For example, women who assert their self-interest risk transgressing norms of femininity. They may therefore find themselves in a contradictory position when faced with the need to pursue self-interest, for example, in relation to employment careers or in terms of their health. In respect of the division of resources within the family, ideologies of motherhood require women to put their children first. Not to do so can reap severe sanctions.

In addition, the linkage of self-interest and rationality is also called into question. Folbre (1994) comments that in economics the term selfishness is often used in such a way as to imply that it is more rational than, say, altruism. Utility-maximization is linked to the individualism and competitiveness of markets. Such an argument would say that given that this is how markets are, it is only rational to behave in ways that will protect and enhance one's self-interest. In this way, selfishness asserts and confirms, rather than questions, the primacy of the market as a regulator of behaviour. So long as we can be sure that everyone is acting in terms of their utility-maximization, we can ensure the efficiency of the distributive mechanisms of the market.

Such a social system also assumes a notion of rationality as being conceptualized as dispassionate and objective. Here, there is no room for passion and subjective feelings but for a cool analysis of the 'facts'. For feminists this conceptualization of rationality is equated with the masculine side of the binary where it is contrasted with the association that women are more emotional and subjective. Lloyd (1996) charts women's changing relationship to conceptualizations of rationality from Aristotle to the present day. She notes how rationality was the mark of distinctiveness that separated humanity from animals. Women as fellow (*sic*) human beings could not, therefore, logically be excluded from having reason. Nonetheless, up until the seventeenth century, woman's reason was regarded as inferior to that of men as she was perceived to be more emotional or more impulsive.

It was with the development of Cartesian conceptualizations of rationality in the seventeenth century that woman was fully cast out, so to speak. Descartes developed a conception of rationality that was based on a systematized and orderly method. In so doing, he separated mind from body and reason from emotion. This formulation of rationality as an act of the mind and distinctive from emotion reified the possibilities of polarization:

> The search for the 'clear and distinct,' the separating out of the emotional, the sensuous, the imaginative, now makes possible polarizations of previously existing contrasts – intellect versus the emotions; reason versus imagination; mind versus matter . . . the claim that women are somehow lacking in respect of rationality, that they are more impulsive, more emotional, than men is by no means a seventeenth century innovation. But these contrasts were previously contrasts *within* the rational. What ought to be dominated by reason had not previously been so sharply delineated from the intellectual. The conjunction of Cartesian down-grading of the sensuous with the use of the mind-matter distinction to establish the discrete character of Cartesian ideas introduces possibilities of polarization that were not there before. (Lloyd, 1996: 154, emphasis in original)

It is important to note that many feminist responses do not reject the notion of a rational consciousness that forms the essence of the humanist subject (Weedon, 1997). For example, Walkerdine (1990) and Lloyd (1996) illustrate how we can understand the development of feminist activism as a response to this polarization. Thus, given it was necessary to be trained in reason, liberal feminist responses are such that access to reason through education and training, should be opened up to women. Alternatively, some feminists argue that reason needs to be imbued with feminine values and our conceptualizations of reason should include feelings and intuition. Hekman (1994) summarizes feminist critiques of rationality as being unified with postmodernists in terms of a concern with language and discourse. As 'Concepts formed from the male point of view create a male reality; both the real and the rational are defined in exclusively male terms' (Hekman, 1994: 52). For Hekman this means that the root cause of women's oppression 'is rooted in male-dominated language and a male definition of reality' (ibid.: 53).

These responses to the *Man of Reason* are present in feminist economists' arguments. For example, England (1993: 49) refers to rationality as 'the most "sacred" neoclassical assumption of all'. In addition, the assumption that competitive individualism and utility-maximization are rational ways of being in the world has been questioned from a moral and ethical viewpoint. England argues for an extended meaning to be given to rationality that includes issues of connection as well as separation. Nelson (1993) calls for economics to use the tools of 'imaginative rationality'. She suggests that this form of rationality would neither be masculine nor feminine but would be centred on how individuals, in interaction with others and their environment, provide for their survival and health.

Finally, feminists have highlighted how problematic the notion of methodological individualism is. Rational choice theory places considerable emphasis on the agency or autonomy of individuals with a consequent neglect of the structuring of choice. When it comes to issues of social structure, rational choice theorists presume that 'Those features of social life that are conventionally called "social structures" are . . . simply chains of interconnected individual actions' (Scott, 2000: 135). This means that explanations for social structures within rational choice theory are based on the cumulative results of individual processes at the micro level. At the group level, the family or firm for example, the group is taken as an agent, or individual, in its own right. Strassman (1993: 60) comments in this respect that the hidden assumptions of the 'free choice' model are: '(1) people are independent agents and unique selves, taking only their own needs and wishes into account; (2) people are able and responsible for taking care of their own needs'. Strassman notes that economists do not deny that these assumptions are problematic but they also view them as fairly benign. She remarks that these assumptions may fit the experiences of adult, White, male, middle-class American economists but they do not fit the economic realities of many others. Thus 'Economic theory's conception of selfhood and individual agency is located in Western cultural traditions as well as being distinctly androcentric. Economic man is the Western romantic hero, a transcendent individual able to make choices and attain goals' (ibid.: 61).

Folbre (1994: 51) uses the term 'structures of constraint' to critique the reductive nature of methodological individualism. These structures of constraint are related to issues of 'race', class, age, gender and ability and together they 'form a complex social edifice in which individuals and groups operate' (ibid.: 53). Folbre argues that the term 'rational choice' should be replaced with the term 'purposeful choice'. She argues that this change of language would mark a departure away from strict rationalist assumptions and would avoid the dichotomy of rational/non-rational. It would also encourage economists to focus on how people define and pursue their desires.

These agency–structure issues that are central to feminist critiques of rational choice theory are more fully explored in poststructuralist perspectives of the 'choosing' subject. It is to these that I now turn.

Case Study 8: WISE Choices?

Early feminist research and campaigning aimed to increase women's participation in scientific and technological areas of work. One campaign was called Women into Science and Engineering (WISE). This was based on equal opportunities discourses and assumed that the reasons why young women were not choosing scientific careers was because of a lack of relevant information and their masculine images. Action research initiatives in schools (see, for example, Kelly, 1987) were also set up. These used interventions such as curriculum changes that would more readily illustrate the relevancy of science to women's and girls' everyday lives and provide women scientists as role models to alter pupils' perceptions and to allow them to make more informed choices.

Henwood (1996) is critical of the narrow conceptualization of choice that she perceives in WISE initiatives. In particular she argues that it is not the masculine image that is problematic but the masculine culture of scientific work that impacts on decision-making. Henwood's research is based on interviews with two groups of students who were attending a college of technology in South-East England in the mid-1980s. One group of students were taking a 'traditional' women's course to become personal assistants. The second group of students were taking a 'non-traditional' course in Software Engineering. Henwood is concerned to analyse the reasons for these different occupational choices. Her framework for doing this is a discursive analysis of WISE intiatives.

Henwood's research illustrates that although they may not have detailed information, young women do have some important knowledge about different careers that impacts on choice. One of the primary reasons why young women chose the personal assistants course was because of their concern about the hostility they would face if they entered scientific or technological professions. These young women also knew that their chosen occupation had less status and financial reward. Henwood comments in this respect that this left them 'feeling most ambivalent about the work for which they had elected' (ibid.: 211). The expected hostility is confirmed in the accounts of those young women who were taking the Software Engineering course who encountered sexism and antagonism. Nevertheless, they also felt pride in entering a 'man's world' and were aware of its higher status and reward.

Central to Henwood's analysis is how predominant discourses that are found in initiatives such as WISE structure the perceptions and practices of both these groups of women and on what is sayable and unsayable. Thus for the personal assistants:

> WISE's liberal ideology of equal opportunities works to prevent a clear articulation of the conflicts and contradictions they experience in making decisions about this future work. WISE says 'opportunities exist' and women have only to 'give themselves a chance'. Thus, if these women are in traditional women's work, it follows that they must have chosen freely to be there. (ibid.: 212)

In this therefore they only have themselves to blame for their lower status and income. For the software engineers equal opportunities discourses of 'same as men' silence women in a slightly different way. Here they cannot speak out about their difficulties because 'this only serves to highlight their difference and, in dominant discourse, their inferiority and lack of suitability for this work' (ibid.). Henwood also notes that what is completely absent from WISE initiatives and discourses is the threat to men's sense of superiority and status that the entry of women represents. Henwood argues that what is needed is greater attention being given to the construction of masculine cultures in the workplace and how these construct 'choice'.

The Poststructuralist 'Choosing' Subject

> Post-structuralist conceptions of the subject have appealed to many because they seem to offer a way through an apparent tension in notions of 'social construction': how do we speak about people as constructions of the social order on the one hand, and as constructing agents or actors on the other, without erring on either side? Those 'social constructionist' accounts of schooling and socialisation which accentuated the determining effects of the social structure and ideology had been unattractive not only due to their inherent pessimism, but also for the ways in which they seemed to obliterate the 'real' thinking person who can choose to resist, change, and 'make a difference'. On the other hand, accounts which emphasised 'agency' and change were too often voluntarist, in danger of assuming an individual able to act and think independently of the social structure and its ideologies.
>
> (Jones, 1997: 262)

We have seen that a major critique of rational choice theory is that it privileges a voluntarist account of human agency. It suggests that individuals are relatively free to choose with no account taken of power relations or the structuring of advantage and disadvantage. Feminist critiques of rational choice theory certainly highlight issues of structure as entirely salient to understanding how choices are made. Yet structural accounts can be critiqued because they privilege a certain determinism. In this way they can appear to suggest that one has 'no choice'. In addition, the agency–structure dichotomy remains firmly in place as social theorists simply place themselves at varying points between its two polarizations.

Poststructuralist conceptions are offered as a way of going beyond such binary opposition. Jones comments on how poststructuralism has facilitated a questioning of simplistic accounts of socialization that would suggest that we are born into the world as 'blank slates on which an appropriate and uniform gender is more or less successfully inscribed' (ibid.: 262). A poststructuralist explanation would encourage us to recognize that we do not all turn out to be the same. It would enable us to know that when we invoke the terms girl or woman we know this in terms of aspects of difference. It would also encourage us to understand that, as much as we might take up particular discursive positions, we can also resist them. This is because one of the main features of poststructuralism is that it stresses: 'The doubled sense of "subject" (subject/ed *to* and subject *of* action) . . . [which] allows for an individual who is socially produced, *and* "multiply positioned" – neither determined nor free, but both simultaneously' (Jones, 1997: 263). This analysis of being both subject/ed to and subject of action can be seen in Walkerdine's (1990: 28) description of a school staffroom: 'The staffroom is full of women eating cottage cheese or grapefruit. Each of them knows about diet and eating and sexuality. They are willing and happy to talk about these, caught inside what they are: the unique combination of worker and woman, dependent and independent, free and trapped' (Walkerdine, 1990: 28).

In particular, poststructuralist accounts of agency draw on a critique of humanism. Davies (1991: 43) compares choice within a humanist framework and within a poststructuralist framework (see Figure 4.2). As Davies makes clear within humanist theorizing, strong connections are made between the ways that individuals make choices and our assumptions about them as people. Making choices in the prescribed rationality of weighing up the options and making an informed choice is seen to confirm that the individual is a coherent, orderly, rational and, indeed, sane person. Not to make choices in this way is to be regarded as faulty or lacking in this respect. Whereas within humanist theorizing choice is seen to be an act of consciousness and deliberateness in comparison conceptualizations of choice within poststructural

---

Humanistic
The choices that the individual makes are based on rational thought and are thus coherent choices that signal the coherence and rationality of the individual. People who do not make choices on this basis are regarded as faulty or lacking in some essential aspect of their humanness.

Poststructural
The choices that the individual makes may be based on rational analysis, but desire may subvert rationality. Desires are integral to the various discourses through which each person is constituted and are not necessarily amenable to change through rational analysis. Subject positions which individuals may take up are made available through a variety of discourses. One subject position, more often made available to white middle-class males than to others, is of the agentic person who can make rational choices and act upon them.

Source: Davies, 1991: 43

Figure 4.2   A comparison between humanistic and poststructural frameworks of conceptualizations of choice

perspectives view it as an aspect of subjectivity. The consciousness and deliberateness of 'rationality' might be subverted by both conscious and unconscious desire.

Desire is constituted through discourses through which one is subject of and subject to. Not all subject positions are equally available. Individuals have differential access to particular discursive positions. Discourses therefore have different gendered, 'raced' and class implications and we can only 'pick up the tools that are lying there'. In this way choices are understood as contextualized within the specific regulatory discourses to which we have access. As Davies notes, the subject position of the humanist subject, that is as experiencing oneself as 'continuous, unified, rational and coherent' (1991: 43) is mainly available to White middle-class males. Therefore the subjectivity of the rational humanist subject is more likely and more achievable for such individuals. For example, Walkerdine (1990) notes how modern conceptions of child development configure children as enquiring and active. These qualities are, moreover, strongly associated with the masculine side of the female/masculine binary. Thus, 'By definition, active childhood and passive femininity exist at the intersection of competing discourses. For girls, therefore their position as children must remain shaky and partial, continually played across by their position as feminine. Conversely, for boys masculinity and childhood work to prohibit passivity. And in both cases passion and irrationality are constantly displaced' (Walkerdine, 1990: 34). This means, as Davies (1991) notes, that men have greater access to discourses of autonomy. For women the achievement of autonomy is both tenuous and ambivalent. Walkerdine (1994) notes from her research into the achievement levels of children at school that no matter how poorly boys were doing, they were always judged as 'having potential'. This possibility was never claimed for girls.

One of the issues that poststructuralist theorizing has explored in relation to choice is its illusory nature. One may feel autonomous and free to choose. But the power of regulatory discourses means that such choice is both 'forced' and of false appearance. This is because 'the subject's positioning within particular discourses make the "chosen" line of action the only possible action, not because there are no other lines of action but because one has been subjectively constituted through one's placement within that discourse to *want* that line of action' (Davies, 1991: 46, emphasis in original). Two examples illustrate the illusory nature of choice. Walkerdine (1990) discusses the illusion of choice in relation to psychological perspectives of 'good' child rearing. She reflects on how discourses of child rearing urge parents to avoid humiliating a 'naughty' child through overt threats and sanctions as this will damage the child's growing sense of being an autonomous being. Rather, parents are encouraged to offer a child a 'choice' of different behavioural options whilst conveying to the child that there are, of course, 'right' and 'wrong' choices that can be made.

Laws and Davies (2000) explore how schooling regulates the possible choices that children have about their behaviour. Children at school are similarly encouraged to make the 'right' choices. For example, to be recognized as a good or competent student the child has to know how to learn, when to speak and when to be silent, when to work and when to be creative. These forms of regulation of children's behaviour are understood as central to creating the appropriate conditions for teachers to teach. The child who refuses to make these 'right' choices or does not recognize their import risks being viewed as unintelligent or difficult and so forth. In this respect Laws and Davies draw attention to the connections between 'choice' and 'consequences' and the agency of the individual:

> Both 'choice' and the closely related concept 'consequences' are central to the 'good school behaviour' discourse. They are used by teachers and students to 'manage' classroom order. But this management of order cannot be achieved by teachers' efforts alone. Students must take up as their own a desire for the sort of order the teacher wants. (ibid.: 209)

Within poststructuralist accounts agency is perceived to be the simultaneous act of free will and submitting to the regulatory order. In the act of 'choosing' and experiencing this choice as an individual act of will we are submitting to the requirements of particular regulatory discourses. This can be contrasted with humanism where an opposition is set up between autonomy and submission. Within humanism, one is either autonomous or submissive. Thus, one is either acting freely or one is forced to do something one would choose not to do.

One of the ways that poststructuralism seeks to demonstrate the paradoxical point that issues of agency and structure inhabit the same act can be seen through the attention that has been given to the twinning of mastery and submission. Butler (1995: 45–6) notes in this regard:

> The more a practice is mastered, the more fully subjection is achieved. Submission and mastery take place simultaneously, and it is this paradoxical simultaneity that constitutes the ambivalence of subjection. Where one might expect submission to consist in a yielding to an externally imposed dominant order, and to be marked by a loss of control and mastery, it is paradoxically marked by mastery itself . . . the simultaneity of submission as mastery, and mastery as submission, is the condition of possibility for the subject itself.

These processes of regulation that one submits to become internalized in terms of self-regulation. For example, the desire to be good means that one must master (*sic*) the subject position of the 'good' child or student. This is achieved through repetition. The more we repeat a practice or an action, the greater our mastery of it. Mastery, itself experienced as the achievement of the humanist self, is the ultimate self-regulation of our actions and behaviours. Thus, we take up our pen and form our hand-writing in uniform shapes. Or, as a child we might think 'my mother needs me to be quiet' and so we are quiet. We have in these moments accomplished key aspects of humanist discourses – individuality, choice, a recognition of the consequences of one's actions, autonomy and responsibility (Davies et al., 2001). Davies et al. explore this in relation to their experiences as pupils who had been 'successful in "getting the goodies" of formal schooling' (ibid.: 180–1). They describe how learning to be successful was experienced ambivalently but included acquiring the signifiers that would evidence that they were competent and good. This included subordinating the body to the mind, to love what it is the teacher teaches and producing the clean script. Their collective biography illustrates how:

> We have been able to show the hard work of becoming appropriate(d) – both its necessity and its risky fragility. There is no guarantee that even

the most conscientious schoolgirl will be able, repeatedly, to produce herself as that which she has come to desire for herself. Her knowledge of herself as acceptable depends on both a tight disciplining of the body, and a capacity to disattend the body and its needs. It depends on a capacity to read what the teacher wants and to produce it, but more than that, to want it for herself. At the same time, it depends on a capacity to distance herself from the Others, on whose approving gaze she is dependent, and to know herself *in contrast* to them. She must, paradoxically, find these points of contrast at the same time as she takes herself up as recognisable through the very same discourses through which she and they are constituted. (ibid.)

Finally, it should be noted that the point of a poststructuralist political project is not to set up a new binary of humanist subject and anti-humanist subject. To do so would simply reinforce the binary oppositions that poststructuralism seeks to move beyond. The point of poststructuralism is to 'show how the humanist self is so convincingly achieved' (Davies, 1997b: 272). As Davies et al. state:

The idea and the ideal of autonomy, which our theorising recognises as fictional, is nevertheless the conceptual and practical lynchpin of the appropriate(d) subject. The subject submits to the fictions of the self and gains mastery through them. And that mastery – of language, of the body – provides the conditions of possibility for investing something new, of seeing afresh, of creatively moving beyond the already known. (2001: 181)

Case Study 9: The Rush to Motherhood

Meyers (2001) comments that the choice of whether or not to have children has the most profound impact on women's lives. Such choices impact centrally on women's identity (see also McMahon, 1995) as either mothers or non-mothers. They condition people's judgements about oneself. They involve legal and social ties. And 'Through motherhood decisions . . . women assume an indelible moral identity and incur or disavow various caregiving obligations' (2001: 735). Meyers illustrates how feminist concerns around motherhood and abortion have focused on women's right to choice through rhetoric that portrays decisions as highly voluntaristic. Meyers' analysis seeks to illustrate how 'autonomous people have well-developed, well-coordinated repertories of agentic skills and call on them routinely as they reflect on themselves and their lives and as they reach decisions about how best to go on' (ibid.: 742). In addition, Meyers' starting point for such a subject is 'the socially situated, divided self . . . an evolving subject – a subject who is in charge of her life within the limits of imperfect introspective decipherability and welcome, though in some ways intrusive (or downright harmful), social relations' (ibid.: 744). Meyers' methodological approach is through an analysis of maternalist discourses and a review of previously published empirical research.

Meyers' principal concerns are to set out and argue for the development of the skills that she believes are central to an analysis and exercise of autonomy. Meyers argues that any assessment of an individual's autonomy requires an accurate analysis of their adeptness at using agentic skills. These are introspection, communication, memory/recall, imagination, analysis/reasoning, volition and interpersonal skills. A key concept that Meyers uses in her analysis is that of matrigyno-idolatory. By this Meyers is referring to celebratory, pro-natalist discourses that promote imperatives of procreation as the key/only route to womanhood and femininity. Such discourses could be summed up in terms that state 'A woman is not a woman until she has had a child'. Here Meyers notes that, given that some women actually do reject motherhood, it would be 'misleading to claim that this discourse determines women's choices' (ibid.: 762). Rather, her point is that such a discourse stifles 'women's voices by insinuating pronatalist imperatives into their self-portraits and self-narratives' (ibid.: 763). For example, it is virtually impossible to extol the benefits of non-motherhood and those women who reject motherhood speak defensively or aggressively about their decisions because they are put in such a counter-discursive position (see, for example, Letherby, 2001).

Although her focus is on skill development, Meyers' response to the overwhelming impact of matrigyno-idolatory discourses on autonomous subjectivity bears some strong similarities to those who argue for the development of critical literacies (see for example, Davies, 1997a; Hughes, 2002; Searle, 1998; Young, 1997). Meyers argues that what is necessary is the concerted development of autonomy skills through pedagogic methods. Thus, Meyers comments:

> To democratize women's autonomy, caregivers and educators must modify their practices and actively promote skills that enable women to discern the detrimental impact of matrigynist figurations on their lives, to envisage dissident figurations, and to entrust their lives to those figurations that augment their fulfilment and enhance their self-esteem. (ibid.: 767–8)

Summary

I have explored two conceptualizations of choice in this chapter. The first is rational choice theory that is both the most everyday under- standing of choice and the one that underpins much economic theory. The second conceptualization draws on poststructural theorizing and is referred to as the choosing subject. I have framed these conceptual- izations of choice within debates about agency and structure. Feminist economists have illustrated how rational choice theory puts too much weight on issues of agency and autonomy and too little weight on the structural issues associated with life chances and choices. Poststructur- alist accounts seek to avoid the 'choice' of either agentic or structural accounts by holding both agency and structure in simultaneous relation.

FURTHER READING

Becker, G. (1991) *A Treatise on the Family*. Cambridge, MA: Harvard University Press. There is no better way to gain an understanding of rational choice theory and the implications of arguing for a framework of atomistic exchange behaviour as the most significant basis for understanding social relations. It might be salutary to remember the accord given to Becker's work as Nobel Prize Winner of Economics in 1992. Who said we were in a post-feminist age?

Gardiner, J. (1997) *Gender, Care and Economics*. Basingstoke: Macmillan. An excellent review of neo-classical, political economy and feminist perspectives.

Hewitson, G. (1999) *Feminist Economics: Interrogating the Masculinity of Rational Economic Man*. Cheltenham: Edward Elgar. The Becker reading should be immedi- ately followed by Gillian Hewitson's text. Hewitson takes feminist economics fully into poststructural perspectives.

Care   5

The meaning of care is usually taken as given and often presented as comprehensive in its coverage of caring activity, when in fact the concepts of care employed are partial representations, or segments, of the totality of caring. Definitions of care are constructed such that boundaries are differentially drawn around what constitutes care, with the effect of excluding or including sets of social relations in definitions of caring relationships. In particular, concepts of care tend to be presented as generic when they are actually specific to, and within, either the private or the public domain.

(Thomas, 1993: 649)

Thomas (1993) questions whether care is a theoretical category or whether care should be primarily understood in terms of empirical entities that require analysis in terms of other theoretical categories. Her comments highlight the variety of meanings of care which are quite often divided into its physical and emotional aspects. Thomas's analysis here illustrates some important technical concerns. This is the translation of a term into a series of indicators and variables. Indeed, there appears to be little debate within the feminist literature in terms of which indicators might be appropriately included or excluded as constituting care. These empirical categories include cooking, cleaning, shopping, building and maintaining relationships, feeling concern, and so forth. The domains within which analyses of care have been located are similarly diverse. Although these domains are commonly divided into public and private spheres, they include the family, the office, the hospital and the community home.

Thomas's point about the status of care as a theoretical category is also an important one because it draws attention to the frameworks that are drawn upon to give meaning to a particular concept. In this respect she comments: 'Within different social relations of production, care takes on a variety of forms . . . "care" is an empirical category, not a theoretical one. Forms of care, and the relationship between them, remain to be theorised in terms of other theoretical categories' (ibid.: 666, 668). Certainly, research into care has drawn on a range of theoretical frameworks within sociology, psychology and philosophy. This has included Marxist analyses of production and reproduction, dual systems theorizing of patriarchal relations within capitalism, poststructural analyses of identity, psychological frameworks of the development of the self and justice frameworks of morality.

I begin by setting out three frameworks that illustrate something of the range of issues that are associated with the term 'care'. The first of these is that of Tronto (1993) who offers four meanings of care. Her analysis is significant because she draws attention to the values associated with care and the gendered hierarchies within which care is conducted. I next turn to an analysis by F. Williams (1993). Williams is primarily concerned with community care. However, the issues she highlights apply to all the spheres within which care is carried out. In addition, Williams signals how analyses of care include issues of feelings, motivation and social mores. I finally outline Thomas's (1993) seven key variables that she suggests are applicable to all analyses of care.

Although there is a diversity of meanings, indicators and variables associated with care, there are two areas where there has been some greater consistency in respect of the issue of care. The first of these has been in terms of feminist analyses of the gendered identity of those who are primary care givers. Although of course there are variations, research in this field has made explicit that it is women who undertake and are perceived to be mainly responsible for the physical and emotional work of care giving. This statement applies to all institutional settings from the diverse forms of family to the international corporation (see, for example, Corti et al., 1994; Cotterill, 1994; Hochschild, 1983; Lewis et al., 1992). The second area of consistency within sociological theorizing has been the naming of care as work.

In respect of these two issues, the second section of this chapter illustrates how meaning is derived from particular theoretical frameworks. Specifically I focus on how conceptualizations of care as work have drawn attention to its economic character that has particular implications for women. The economic character of care has been portrayed through analyses that focused on its unpaid and paid nature. These analyses have indicated how, for example, although unpaid, women's care of family members has important economic effects in terms of its contribution to the reproduction and maintenance of the labour force. The inter-connections and the structuring effects of women's responsibilities for care, in both the family and the labour force, have also been the foci of research and have indicated the cumulative economic disadvantages that women face. The discussion in this section also focuses on feminist responses to these issues in respect of linking issues of care to rights campaigns.

I continue to give attention to the contextualization of meaning through an analysis of what Connolly (1993) terms cluster concepts. My purpose here is to illustrate two issues. The first is how the meanings of care are drawn from other concepts that are invoked in its analysis. Indeed, as I illustrate, in the case of care, it is clear that there are chains of concepts and so chains of meaning that are involved. The second point is to indicate the domain-specificity of some meanings. Thus, although one of the predominant understandings of care in the family has been its oppressive qualities within the sphere of employment, some forms of care have been viewed as liberatory and progressive.

Overall, care holds a contradictory and ambiguous place in feminist theorizing. For example, it is both posited as a hallmark of woman's difference and it is viewed as an entrapment of subservience from which woman must escape. Ethics of care feminists argue that care is a higher order trait that should be celebrated and nurtured. This is because care offers an alternative to the hegemonies of individualism and atomism. Nonetheless, ethics of care feminists are critiqued not only for their perceived propensity to essentialism but also for the ways in which they offer rather sanitized conceptualizations of the connection and relatedness that lie at the heart of care (Flax, 1997). In the final section of this chapter I turn to the conceptualization of care as an ethical value. The discussion here indicates that, despite critiques, care is conceptualized as a higher order trait based in the relationality of womanhood. Specifically, ethics of care feminists argue that ethical reasoning based on care offers a useful alternative to rights-based justice discourses and policies.

Conceptualizations of Care

Tronto (1993) offers an analysis of care that illustrates how the values we associate with care are gendered, hierarchical and cross the public/private binary. Tronto conceptualizes care in four ways (see also Fisher and Tronto, 1990) (see Table 5.1). The first stage of caring is *caring about*. This is the initial recognition of a care need. Tronto notes that

Table 5.1   Four forms of care

	Who cares?	Value
Caring About		
Issues of state and the economy	Politicians and statesmen	High
One's children	Fathers	High
One's children	Mothers	Low
Taking Care of		
The homeless, the world's poor, etc.	Paid employees in the public sector	High
The diet of one's children or partner	Mothers	Low
The family income	Fathers	High
Care Giving		
Building houses for the homeless	Volunteer builders	High
Cleaning the toilets in a care home	Cleaners	Low
Operating on a cancer patient	Doctors	High
Checking a patient's blood pressure	Nurse	Low
Care Receiving		
The Chief Executive who needs his travel tickets booked	Personal assistant	High
The husband who is sick	Wife	Low
The wife who is sick	Husband	High

Source: Developed from Fisher and Tronto, 1990; Tronto, 1993

there is a perceived link between what it is that we care about and what sort of person we are. In addition, the division between what we care about and who has the responsibility for this initial recognition is crucial. For example, if we are responsible for caring about the public issues of state and economy, we are within the spheres of the most powerful. As those who care about such issues are accorded high value, so these activities are similarly given a high valuation. Conversely, caring about one's children or one's partner are primarily the spheres of the least powerful. Caring about these issues, and those who undertake this care are, in consequence, of low value.

The second stage of care is that of *taking care of*. This draws on ideas of agency and responsibility. This means that one has taken responsibility for a need and has decided how to respond to it. For example, we may decide that we will take care of Third World debt by lobbying parliament and we may decide that we shall take care of the dietary needs of our sick parent by consulting a dietician. What we find here are the same divisions in terms of value and power. When taking care of is associated with the public spheres of life, it is viewed as relatively prestigious. When it is associated with the private realm, it is viewed as relatively trivial. Moreover, the form through which we take care of influences our judgement of its importance. Men take care of their families through being in paid employment. Women take care of their families through, for example, housework.

The third phase in the process of care is that of *care giving*. This is the direct meeting of care needs and involves physical work and coming into contact with those who need care. This is the work of cleaning, dusting and cooking, of giving medicine to the sick and of counselling students. Tronto notes that primarily the giving of care is the work of slaves, servants and women. When men do undertake this work, we find a pattern of exceptionalism. Doctors have higher status than nurses and men who enter the caring professions, such as social work and teaching, are more likely to reach the top of them.

Care receiving is the final stage and this is where care needs are met. This has the lowest status of all because the acknowledgement that one has care needs is a threat to one's sense of autonomy. To receive care is to place oneself in a position of dependency and those with most needs are perceived to be the most dependent. In addition, we are either pitying or disdainful of those who need care. Importantly, Tronto notes that those with most power are able to define their needs in ways that maintain rather than undermine their privilege. In these ways the identification that to have care needs is to be less autonomous, to be disdained or to be pitied is avoided. This is accomplished in two main ways. First, their care needs are met by those who are in positions of greater dependency than they are. Second, their care needs are redefined in terms of freedom to pursue higher order activities. Thus, men's needs for care of themselves and their children are primarily met through the invisible and unpaid work of women. In the sphere of paid work, managers delegate care needs to others in order that they have more time to manage and senior consultants delegate the lower care needs of patients to junior doctors and nurses.

Tronto's depiction of the four phases of care illustrates something of the range of activities that come to describe care. In the field of community care F. Williams (1993) depicts this range in terms of five groupings. These are:

1   *Process of care*: for example, the day-to-day experiences of those who are involved in caring for someone.
2   *Context of care*: for example, domestic service, institutional care, mothering, neighbouring, caring for a gay partner. These contexts would demonstrate the varied historical, cultural and social sites and relations of care.

3   *Struggles of care*: for example, a focus on the difficulties and problems that arise in situations in which the person caring and the person cared for find themselves.
4   *Dilemmas of care*: for example, the conflicts and constraints facing those who seek to provide the best possible care.
5   *Rights of care*: for example, voicing the right that those in need of care can determine the kind of support they need.

Williams's depiction of these groups demonstrates that those who use the term care are referring to process, context, struggle, dilemma and rights. In this respect we can extend Williams's analysis to say that these issues are relevant to care in any setting. In each of these groupings a further wide range of features would also be significant and would draw on a host of values and other concepts. For example, Williams points out that care should not only be considered in terms of 'different contexts and relationships, but as a manifestation of different feelings and motivations: control, responsibility, obligation, altruism, love and solidarity' (ibid.: 81).

Thomas (1993) explores the broad nature of care through a consideration of seven key variables that impact on the different ways in which care is conceptualized. These are:

1   The social identity of the carer.
2   The social identity of the care recipient.
3   The inter-personal relationships between the carer and the care recipient.
4   The nature of care.
5   The social domain within which the caring relationship is located.
6   The economic character of the care relationship.
7   The institutional setting in which care is delivered.

Thomas argues that these seven dimensions are the building blocks that interlock to make up the total concept of care. For Thomas, therefore, 'the variable definitions at the level of these seven dimensions which, in combination, result in quite different concepts of care' (ibid.: 651). However, Thomas points out that although we might contrive to include every variable as part of our total construct of care, without adequate theorization we are left at the level of empirics and description. For example, we could certainly argue that 'care is both paid and unpaid provision of support involving work activities and feeling states. It is provided mainly, but not exclusively, by women to both able-bodied and dependent adults and children in either the public or domestic spheres, and in a variety of institutional settings' (ibid.: 665). This may be a useful working description but it does not explain why, for example, it is mainly women who undertake care work. It is to the realm of explanation that I now turn.

Case Study 10: Who Prepares Dinner Tonight?

Min (1999: 140) remarks: 'It is universally acknowledged that the kitchen is the world of women.' Her research is focused on the changing role of women in twentieth-century China. Her methodology is comprised of a narrative enquiry based on interviews with women from four generations of one Chinese family. These are: 'Ms Li, a housewife, aged 90 years, who had completed primary school . . . Ms Zhang, aged 69 years, a retired doctor . . . Ms Wang . . . a 40 year old mother and University Lecturer . . . Lian Lian, aged 10 years . . . a primary-school student' (ibid.).

Min's findings illustrate the considerable differences of time spent in the kitchen by these women. Thus Ms Li spends about ten hours a day on housework, Ms Zhang spends less than an hour per day and Ms Wang spends about two hours. Min comments that 'Apart from reasons such as diminishing family size, help by older family members, and employment, an essential factor that has influenced women's activity in the kitchen is the changing attitudes of women towards housework, across the three generations' (ibid.: 143). For example, for Ms Li who was born at the beginning of the twentieth century, there were only two ways in which women could demonstrate their worth. This was through bearing a son and through caring for their families. Ms Zhang lived in an age when equality in terms of sameness was stressed and women were expected to engage in paid work in the same ways as men. Ms Wang was born at a time when there was strong questioning of 'sameness' equality and where 'a woman of good qualities should not merely seek success in her career, but should also aspire to being a good wife and mother at home' (ibid.: 145).

While women across these generations spend different times in the kitchen, this does not mean that caring is no longer women's work. As Min notes, there is 'no indication that the well-entrenched sex-role patterns will become history in the 21st Century' (ibid.: 152). The reduced time in the kitchen that are features of the lives of Ms Zhang and Ms Wang was due to buying in help or through the use of female family members. For example, Ms Li takes on the housework for Ms Zhang. In this regard it is pertinent to note that the toy that the child in the family, Lian Lian, prizes most is the plastic kitchen that her father bought her for her fifth birthday. And as an epilogue to the study Min notes that at the close of her research Ms Wang moved to a new house with a kitchen that was twice the size of her previous one. In addition she has spent 'ten times her and her husband's salaries for a month' (ibid.: 154) on refurbishing the kitchen.

Care is Women's Work: Issues of Inter-Connection

As I have indicated, feminist research on the social identity of the person who undertakes and is perceived to be primarily responsible for care in society has, unsurprisingly, focused on its gendered character. In particular, it is women who are the primary care givers. In addition, one of the major landmarks of feminist research into care has been the recognition and naming of care as work, whether paid or unpaid. However, as Thomas (1993) notes, it should not be assumed that paid and unpaid care can be separated into the public and private domains respectively. Paid care occurs in family settings and unpaid care occurs in paid employment contexts. For example, Black feminist research has drawn attention to the 'race' and class dimensions of care. The role of Black women as care workers in the households of White middle-class women has both highlighted issues of class and 'race' power relations and challenged any assumptions that care in the household is always unpaid. The greater numbers of women in the workforce has led to an expansion in the employment of nannies and nursery workers.

The significance of conceptualizing care as work impacts on the kinds of theoretical frameworks that are drawn upon to explain care as a social phenomena and the nature of political change that is thought to be required. The economic character of care can be seen in explanations that have been put forward to explain why the needs of care fall disproportionately on women. Charles (1993) suggests that there have been four main sociological explanations why women have the major responsibilities for family care in capitalist societies. The economic nature of these is illustrated in terms of the attention paid to issues of industrialization, capitalism, production and reproduction and dual-systems theorizing. These explanations also illustrate how the domains of private and public are inter-connected. The four explanations are:

1 *Industrialization*: This focuses on how processes of industrialization removed the site of economic activity from the home to the factory. Prior to industrialization families worked collectively in, for example, agricultural and craft work. Factory production made it difficult for women to combine their domestic care work with paid work.

2 *The capitalist mode of production*: This focuses on the separation of waged labour from unwaged, domestic, labour. Marxist analyses highlight how labour is a commodity to be bought and sold in the market. Feminists took up the issue of surplus value that arises from the purchase of waged labour in the Wages for Housework debate. In contrast to Marxist analyses that domestic labour was unproductive, Wages for Housework feminists argued that domestic labour produces surplus value. This is because it produces goods, such as food, clothes and health care, that otherwise would have to be bought in the market. This lowers the value of labour and keeps wages down.

3 *Patriarchy*: The focus here is on male dominance of all women or the dominance of older men over women and younger men. Charles notes that analyses that explain gender divisions through the concept of patriarchy often offer a 'dual systems' explanation. This is because of the attention that is paid to the relationship and inter-connections of patriarchy and capitalism.

4 *Social reproduction*: Charles notes that there are varying conceptualizations of reproduction. Her discussion points out that the reproduction of labour power requires individuals to be literate, be sufficiently healthy and accept the values of a capitalist society. Feminists have highlighted how women's unpaid domestic labour contributes to the necessary maintenance of family members and, along with education, the media, health and social care services and so forth, they contribute to the socialization process. In addition, women's paid labour undertakes similar reproductive work.

In turning to the disproportionate numbers of women who work in the 'care' sectors of paid employment, sociological explanations have drawn attention to the processes of gendered labour market stratification. The labour market is stratified both horizontally and vertically. Horizontal segregation refers to how women and men work in different jobs or sectors of the economy. Hatt (1997) reports that in the mid-1990s women outnumbered men by four to one in hairdressing, clothing manufacture and medical and other health services. On the other hand, men constituted 80 per cent of employees in coal extraction, metal manufacturing and railways. Wilson (1999) also comments on how women are more likely to be employed in the lower-status caring professions such as nursing, teaching and social work than higher-status worlds of global financial capital.

Vertical segregation refers to how women occupy the lower positions in an organizational hierarchy and men occupy the higher positions. Despite claims that women are enjoying remarkable career success, research into 'glass' (Porter, 1995), 'concrete' and 'bedpan' (Lane, 2000) ceilings demonstrates the intransigence of masculine organizational cultures to women's entry at higher levels. Hatt (1997) notes that gender segregation is a feature of most developed countries in the world and endures even when women have high rates of labour market participation. For example, Bryson's (1998) analysis of Israel illustrates how employment patterns are highly gendered for all ethnic groups. Women are over-represented in caring and service work, in part-time and low status employment. Men have a near monopoly of top positions in the public and private sectors.

These features of the labour market are interconnected. For example, when men are employed in predominantly female sectors such as primary school teaching, nursing or social work they are also more likely to be occupying the senior positions in these sectors. In addition, Blackwell (2001) reports that women's part-time work is not only more gender-segregated than women's full-time work but also part-time jobs tend to be at the bottom of the occupational hierarchy.

The focus of research on gender segregation in terms of domestic care and in terms of paid employment primarily gives a pessimistic picture of progress in respect of greater equality between the sexes. Although there is some evidence in lesbian households of greater equality in the share of domestic work (see, for example, Dunne, 1997), changes in women's participation in paid employment and greater recognition of equal rights between the sexes have not led to significant changes in the domestic division of labour. Women in heterosexual relationships continue to undertake the major share of domestic and family care (Press and Townsley, 1998; Pilcher, 1999). As paid employees, care work is also seen to fix women into low paid and low skill sectors of the economy.

The connections between the public and private spheres have illustrated how women's responsibilities for care create mutually reinforcing structures. For example, Parker (1993) considers how inequalities in pay and the gendered nature of public policies reinforce the economic dependence of women in relation to spousal caring relationships. Parker's research has focused on the material and subjective meanings of being cared for. This adds further weight to arguments that women are in a disadvantaged position in relation to care through an analysis of the gendered implications of being cared for as a disabled woman:

> The evidence of this study adds support to the growing recognition that women can be *more* disabled than men in comparable circumstances. If they remain in the labour market, as women they have lower incomes anyway. If they are not in the labour market, indirect discrimination in the state benefits system means that they are likely to receive lower levels of benefits. Their need for help and support may be seen as less important, and their desire to retain control over domestic arrangements may be over-ridden by the provision of services which serve to replace, rather than enable, their role. Women who become disabled after marriage are also affected by the pre-existing dynamics of the relationship. In marriages where power is particularly unequal, disabled women find themselves very constrained in their ability to assert their needs. Even where power is not so unequal, women's general reluctance to assert their needs before those of other family members may find disabled women doing things they would rather not (like entering respite care) or not doing things that they would rather (for example, retaining control over domestic arrangements). (Parker, 1993: 125)

The inter-conections between women's caring responsibilities in both paid and unpaid work have also been assessed in terms of women's career progression and employability. Reviewing the careers of women in educational management in Europe Wilson summarizes the barriers that women face in terms of career advancement and progression as:

> The presence of young children in a family, the uneven distribution of domestic responsibilities between male and female partners, career breaks, the psychological status of combining the dual role of parenthood and teaching . . . The absence of family leave to care for young children, inadequate provision of childcare facilities for preschool children and differing levels of maternity/paternity leave are also significant variables. (1997: 213)

Hasibuan-Sedyono's (1998) analysis of women managers in Indonesia also illustrates how strong regulatory effects of assumptions about mothers' responsibilities for care impact on women's careers. Hasibuan-Sedyono comments: 'Indonesian society still insists that women have not completed their mission in life until they have married and brought up children' (ibid.: 88). Women managers in Indonesia therefore risk losing respect because they are thought to be giving less attention to their families and, unsurprisingly, these assumptions impact on their chances of further promotion. In addition, responsibilities for family care impact on the choices women make in terms of employment. For example,

Sullivan and Lewis' (2001) research indicates how fitting paid employment with childcare responsibilities was a major motivation for women to undertake telework. This was not the case for men who undertook this form of working arrangement.

Women's access to company-based childcare support is also limited. Reskin and Padavic (1994) note that it is normally large companies who provide such benefits. However, most people are employed by small companies. Thus, the number of women who benefit from family-friendly employer-provided policies are relatively small. In addition, the polarization of core–periphery working (Atkinson, 1985, for a critique see Pollert, 1991) that is being evidenced in the labour market between core workers who are higher status professionals and peripheral workers who are employed on part-time, casual or temporary bases is another division. Employer-provided benefits are normally restricted to those who form part of the core, full-time, permanent labour force.

One of the key responses arising from these research findings and analyses of the inter-connections between women's responsibilities for domestic care and their employment prospects in the labour market has been to lobby for childcare as a social right. Charles comments in this respect that: 'Feminism . . . defines child care as a social right and exposes the gendered nature of care work, arguing that the whole organisation of child care in advanced capitalist societies needs to be transformed in the direction of greater parity between women and men in both the private and public spheres' (Charles, 2000: 20).

The issue of rights in respect of care has also been more broadly linked to issues of citizenship. In this respect feminists have raised two main critiques with regard to the assumptions of the universality of citizenship (Bryson, 1998). First, claims of universality ignore the particular needs and circumstances of women. For example, it is necessary to be employed full-time to gain the economic security, social welfare and other resources for political participation. However, many women are either full-time carers or part-time workers. In addition, issues of nationality are significant because, as Charles (2000: 23) notes, 'even though black women are more likely than their white counterparts to be in full-time employment, this does not guarantee their access to citizenship rights which are limited by racialised definitions of national identity'.

Second, conceptualizations of citizenship emphasize its nature as a public activity. This ignores the essential work that women do within the home and the inequalities in family life. Bryson (1998: 128) argues for 'a reconceptualisation of citizenship based on a recognition of the social necessity of caring work and an analysis of the private bases of public activities and inequalities'. In this respect Bryson suggests there are three main areas in which policy demands are made:

1   The first of these concerns the caring needs of society and women's domestic work. Reforms advocated here are intended to provide state support for women's caring responsibilities, to enable these to be combined with employment and to facilitate and encourage greater domestic involvement on the part of men. They include parental leave, shorter working weeks and affordable, good quality childcare.
2   The second set of reforms rests upon the belief that personal economic dependency is incompatible with full citizenship. It seeks to provide economic independence for women by improving their employment prospects, securing greater rights for part-time workers and giving women independent access to state welfare benefits.
3   The final area is defined in narrower political terms and includes a demand for electoral reform and the introduction of quotas, in the belief that these will facilitate an increase in the political representation of women.

Cluster Concepts of Care

> In this context of fluid and changing definitions of families, a basic core remains which refers to the sharing of resources, caring, responsibilities and obligations. What a family is appears intrinsically related to what it does. All the studies in this book suggest that while there are new family forms emerging, alongside new normative guidelines about family relationships, this does not mean that values of caring and obligation are abandoned. On the contrary, these are central issues which continue to bind people together.
>
> (Silva and Smart, 1999: 7)

Silva and Smart's comments about caring and obligation illustrate an important feature of contextualizing the meanings of care. Care should not be understood only in terms of a number of variables such as the social identity of the carer or its economic character or only in terms of a number of indicators, such as housework, caring for the sick or lobbying for environmental change. Care invokes a host of cluster concepts. In addition to obligation these include dependency, responsibility, friendship, duty, reciprocity and trust.

A classic example of this is the research into family care undertaken by Finch (1989) and Finch and Mason (1993). Their analyses draw on issues of reciprocity, obligation, inter-dependency and responsibility. For example, Finch and Mason emphasize the importance of recognizing that taking on responsibilities for care rests on a range of negotiating factors that are part of reciprocal relations. These develop over time as part of a two-way process that attempts to balance the giving and receiving of support. It is important that one party does not become over-dependent on the other. Rather, the aim is to achieve a mutuality of inter-dependence. In addition, Finch and Mason stress that it is the interweaving of the material and moral dimensions of family life which are significant in understanding the meanings of responsibility for care. In particular, they draw on the connection between moral values and identity through the ways in which people understand what it means to be a good mother, a caring sister or a kind son. Through the negotiations of giving and receiving care, reputations as a 'good' person are at stake. In these enactments of responsibility, therefore, people are constructed as moral beings. Moreover, reputations are public property, shared, though not necessarily consensually, with members of their kin group and can impact on negotiations at later points in time.

Research into being cared for also illustrates the conceptual partnering of care. For example, research that has been concerned with the experiences of receiving care has given close attention to the relationship between autonomy and caring. This linkage has not only been important in terms of an analysis of the material and subjective experiences of receiving care but also in terms of the broader politics associated with the field of care. This is because being self-sufficient and socially independent when one is receiving care has been an important strand in rights arguments (see, for example, Morris, 1993).

As these examples illustrate, cluster concepts form a chain with other concepts (see Figure 5.1). At its most simple level one might connect care and responsibility. Thus, as we have seen, feminists have highlighted how women are vested with the major responsibilities for care work in both the public and private domains. Yet this in turn relies on further concepts. For example, feminist research into responsibilities for care in the family has illustrated how this structures women's dependence either on a male partner or the state. When dependency is invoked, the most immediate companion concept in this chain that we should be aware of is its opposite in the binary, that of independence. Thus the politics that arise from this awareness of women's dependency

Figure 5.1   Care: an illustrative chain of cluster concepts

focuses on ways through which women can be more independent. This may be through lobbying for childcare rights, the greater provision of workplace nurseries, increasing childcare benefits, and so forth.

A further complication is that the meanings of these companion concepts will also vary. Through a review of dependency as a key word in US welfare policy, Fraser and Gordon (1994) indicate that it has four registers of meaning. The first meaning is economic, when one depends on another person or institution for subsistence. The second meaning denotes socio-legal status as in the case of married women's access to independent welfare rights. The third meaning relates to being subjected to an external ruling power. This may be expressed, for example, through theories of patriarchy or capital. Moral and psychological meanings form the fourth category where the individual is judged to be excessively needy or lacks willpower and where she is deemed to be over-dependent.

A similar case can be made for other concepts (see, for example, Hughes, 2001). For example, Figure 5.2 sets out a range of meanings invoked through the phrase 'responsible for' (see Piper, 1993, for a discussion of this usage in relation to divorce and mediation). As this illustrates, responsibility can be conceptualized as an act of agency when, for example, it is related to concepts of choice. It can also be conceptualized as oppressive when choice of whether to have responsibility or not is absent. Responsibility may be conceptualized as empowering when

Responsibility and choice: agentic meanings	Take responsibility for Exercise responsibility for
Responsibility and lack of choice: oppressive meanings	Not relieved of responsibility for Too much responsibility for
Responsibility and status enhancement: empowering meanings	Given responsibility for
Responsibility and desire: aspirational meanings	Acquire/achieve/seek responsibility for

Figure 5.2   Responsible for: some common meanings

it is linked to status enhancement. It may be conceptualized as aspirational when it is linked with a desire for sought-after status.

Although meanings vary, they can be quite domain-specific. Within the low-status spheres of the family, greater attention is given to the oppressive meanings of responsibility in terms of 'not relieved of' or 'too much responsibility for'. Within the higher-status spheres of employment responsibility can mean higher status and financial rewards. In this way responsibility may be viewed as more empowering in terms of 'given responsibility for'. Perhaps to reinforce this point, Tronto (1993) comments that within employment markets caring labour is not conceptualized under the terminology of care. It is conceptualized as service, support and assistance. Thus, even the terminology will vary within each domain.

Fisher and Tronto (1990) link issues of domain with three main ways in which caring is conceptualized and organized in modern capitalist societies. These are through the household/community, through the market and through a bureaucracy. Their analysis of each sphere illustrates how care draws on domain-specific meanings. Fisher and Tronto argue that because caring about, taking care of and care giving constitute shared values and shared activities amongst women household/community care:

> caring also embodies a sort of justice and inspires a type of trust. Caring is seen as just when it refers to a shared standard by which each gives and receives her 'due.' Trust results because these standards are shared, and one can count on other community members to maintain them. (ibid.: 46)

This can be contrasted to care in the market place where care is a commodity and reduced to exchange relations. Within bureaucracies care giving is separated from taking care of. This means that care becomes a standardized routine and that those who receive care are mainly required to fit in with the demands of the bureaucracy.

The importance of the domain-specific meanings and varied terminology of care can be seen in Franzway's (2000) exploration of trade union work. This illustrates how service is predicated on care within relations of exchange-based masculine cultures. Franzway begins by noting that there is a distinction between feminine and masculine interpretations of the meanings of the trade union ethic of 'service to members'. This is translated in masculine terms as defending wages and conditions. It is enacted through '"toughness" understood as dedication and commitment combined with a hard, assertive personal style' (ibid.: 266). As women, women officials are therefore positioned within a complex array of discursive meanings and practices. If they are too tough, then they are perceived to be 'waspish'. If they are not tough enough, they are perceived to be 'wimpish'. Franzway's analysis indicates how women officials negotiate this terrain. Specifically, 'From throwing themselves into a wholehearted but unrestrained care, they report shifts into a more discriminating, perhaps instrumental, or utilitarian exercise of care . . . Overall, the women officials construe taking care in terms of empowerment rather than of helping' (ibid.: 266–7). Similarly, Thornley's (1996) analysis of care in nursing illustrates how care is divided into important skill distinctions. Recent changes in the training of nurses has given much greater emphasis on higher education qualifications as a means of restricting entry to, and enhancing the status of, nursing. Such entry qualifications neither value nor recognize prior caring experiences in terms of the caring for one's children or parents. In addition, this approach to the training of nurses places cure above care through a focus on the acquisition of technical rather than communicative knowledge.

Although the predominant meanings of *care giving* in family research have focused on its oppressive and unrelenting nature, in employment contexts certain forms of care have more recently been seen as an opportunity for women. This is because there has been a shift from what has been termed 'hard' discourses of human resource management to 'soft' discourses (Legge, 1995) 'Hard' discourses considered employees as passive repositories of the orders of their superiors. The emphasis was on forms of management that were autocratic and authoritarian. The discourses of 'soft' human resource management use terms such as empowerment and teamwork to convey a liberatory and egalitarian backdrop to these new management techniques. The core skills of care at the centre of 'soft' human resource discourses are those associated with relationality. Often termed 'people management skills', they include listening, discussing, taking an interest in and facilitating. As a discourse that is designed to fit with flatter organizational structures and so to some extent challenge traditional hierarchical relations between managers and workers, further skills that are required are those of subordinating one's ego and needs to those of others. These are important in order to facilitate the team working that has formed part of more recent managerial responses to gaining competitive advantage. In addition, the management of emotions whereby 'the employee is paid to smile, laugh, be polite, deferential or caring' (Forseth and Dahl-Jorgensen, 2001) are increasingly viewed as important corporate assets (see also Hochschild, 1983; Fineman, 1993; Blackmore, 1999).

These aspects of caring have been analysed in research on women's leadership (see, for example, Coleman, 2000; Ozga and Deem, 2000).

This has illustrated how women have a more relational style. Ozga and Walker (1995) comment that in contrast to masculine models of authoritative or consultative leadership, research has found that women prefer a participative style. Meehan (1999) distinguishes between those that assume there are internal factors that have given rise to feminine–masculine differences in management styles and those that focus on external factors. Those that focus on internal factors highlight issues such as early socialization and gender identity formation. Those that focus on external factors focus more strongly on organizational features such as company cultures. It is perhaps no surprise therefore that caring, when conceptualized as skills of relationality, should be viewed as an opportunity for women's advancement.

Nevertheless, it has also been important in feminist research to distinguish between women's styles of leading and approaches to leadership that accord more broadly with feminist politics. Strachan (1999) suggests that there are two aspects that distinguish women managers from feminist managers. One of these is a commitment to social justice. The other is the development of one's own and others' practices of caring. Ozga and Walker (1995) suggest that it is feminism's rejection of authoritarian and hierarchical organization, its recognition of the masculine inherent in such structures and its politics of emancipation that create the value context for this. In this framework, feminist management is considered to be the *doing* of feminism 'in such a way that it challenges and changes hegemonic institutional practices. This emancipatory practice is also imbued with an ethic of care in order that a sense of belonging, of being cared for, is built into organisational practices' (Tanton and Hughes, 1999: 248). It is more broadly to conceptualizing care as an ethic that I now consider.

Case Study 11: The Case of 'Taking Care'

Schreuder (1999) has undertaken a policy analysis of the introduction into the curriculum for secondary education in the Netherlands of the subject 'taking care'. This subject has been introduced because it is assumed in the Netherlands that everyone from the age of 18 years of age has to be self-supporting.

That is: everyone should either have a job, try to find a job or go to school of some kind. One of the main consequences of this policy is that neither parents, nor girls nor women can say that they (girls and women) do not really need an education because they will get married and have children. (ibid.: 200)

Another consequence is that 'boys too need to be prepared for a future in which gender roles are no longer what they used to be' (ibid.). A central question of Schreuder's research is whether or not the introduction of 'taking care' will contribute to greater gender equality.

Schreuder's analysis illustrates some significant changes to the educational aims of 'taking care' from its first introduction in 1993 to its revision in 1996. In 1993 the aims were primarily focused on domestic care. This received a lot of criticism both in schools and in the media because 'A very common opinion is that "taking care" is not a "real" school subject because pupils learn how to clean the bathroom and how to cook eggs. In other words, valuable time in school is wasted upon the trivial and unnecessary' (ibid.: 201). Schreuder notes that the revisions, enacted in 1996, 'show a different concept of care and care-taking, as well as different educational ideas' (ibid.). In particular, care is conceptualized as including the public as well as the private sphere. This has meant that there is a shift in emphasis away from 'practical skills and correct behaviour toward a notion of "care" in which knowledge, judgement and action are treated in coherence' (ibid.: 202). Overall, this has meant that 'Not only are pupils taught what to do, they are now also encouraged . . . to make reasonable and responsible decisions related to questions of care' (ibid.). For example:

> Pupils have to learn to think about different aspects and different faces of care, in order to make them more conscious of the importance of care (in a broad sense) for their own lives now and in the future . . . The apolitical casualness of care in the domestic sphere is now made into a subject for conversation, discussion and critical reflection. Care and care-taking are no longer part of the private domain only, but are made an integral part of the cognitive, rational, public and political domain. (ibid.)

Schreuder argues that these features of 'taking care' do suggest that it could contribute to greater gender equality. In particular, the inclusion of so-called masculine values of reasoned argument and the incorporation of the public sphere have led to a serious acknowledgement of care and care-taking as an important area of learning for all pupils. Thus, while Schreuder is cautious in claiming that such a course that is a small part of the overall curriculum will make an enormous difference to gendered responsibilities for care, she does argue that this course has made care a visible public policy issue.

Care as an Ethic

> Relationality is the key element of the American approach to the psychology of women. It distinguishes a uniquely female connected-ness that contrasts with male individuality and separateness.
>
> (Kaplan, 1992: 198)

The foundational bases of conceptualizations of an ethics of care can be found in psychology and philosophy. In particular, the conceptualiza-tion of care as an ethical position draws on Gilligan's (1982) work on women's moral development. In this respect Paechter (2000: 17) comments that Gilligan's work is 'an important example of the way the gendering of power/knowledge relations relates to the androcentric nature of Western thought'. Gilligan's research was focused on the reasoning women undertook when making decisions about abortion. In particular, Gilligan was concerned to demonstrate that the philosophical and psychological literature on moral development was systematically biased. Gilligan argued that not only were men the primary producers of these systems of thought but also theories of moral development were based on research into men's lives. This masculine predominance meant that women who failed to live out these normative theories were per-ceived to be morally under-developed. Brabeck (1993: 34) summarizes the common theme of these theories as suggesting that 'Men develop a rational moral attitude based on an understanding of alternative con-ceptions and a commitment to a universal abstraction. Women develop less of a concern for these abstractions, are more embedded in particular concerns about individuals, more feeling than thinking, less committed, and thus, more morally labile.'

Specifically, Gilligan drew on the work of her former teacher, Kohlberg. Gilligan argued that the moral development evidenced in the work of Kohlberg rested in a rights model that sought universal solu-tions to ethical dilemmas. In such a model these dilemmas would be resolved through recourse to a set of rules or practices that could be logically deduced. Such an ethical system can be seen in the work of Rawls whom Sevenhuijsen (1998: 51) describes as 'the most important spokesman of the paradigm of distributive justice and rational choice' (see Figure 5.3).

Placed within psychoanalytic theories of separation and attachment, Gilligan argued that women's processes of decision-making in relation to moral issues such as abortion differed from that of the masculine

- Citizens are addressed as disinterested and impartial persons.
- Rules have to follow rationalist argument in accordance with two key principles of justice.
- The first principle of justice is that everybody has an equal right to certain basic freedoms, such as freedom of conscience and opinion, freedom of association and assembly, and freedom of suffrage.
- The second principle of justice is that rules have to be developed that enable a choice to be made between equal and unequal treatment. Unequal social and economic treatment is justified if it favours those who are less well-off and is part of a wider meritocratic system of open competition for social goods.

Source: Adapted from Sevenhuijsen, 1998

Figure 5.3   A rights-based ethical system

rights-based model. Her research findings indicated that a sense of connection is fundamental to understanding how responsibility to others is integral to women's identity. It is this issue of relationality that Kaplan (1992) remarks is central to psychological perspectives of womanhood in North America and is summarized by Josselson (1996: 1) as a 'web of connection to others [whereby] [l]ife unfolds as a kaleidoscope of relationships'.

Gilligan's research illustrated how women see conflicting responsibilities as a moral dilemma. At the centre of this dilemma is the question of responsibility to oneself. The ideal goal is to meet obligations and responsibilities to others without sacrificing our own needs. However, achieving this resolution is particularly difficult as, according to Gilligan, women adopt a conventional interpretation of responsibility. This is one of being responsive to others. This interpretation, Gilligan indicates, has two effects. One is that it impedes women's sense of themselves as autonomous or independent subjects. The other is that it renders responsibility to oneself as an act of selfishness.

Despite criticisms of essentialism, ethics of care feminists have been unwilling to rescind their view that an ethic of care is preferable to the predominant ethical systems based on rights models (see, for example, Gilligan, 1993). This is in part because care is conceptualized as a higher order trait as Witherall and Noddings make clear in respect of the place of care in school teaching:

> The notion of caring is especially useful in education because it empha-
> sizes the relational nature of human interaction and of all moral life. The
> word can be used to describe a virtue or constellation of virtues – as in,
> 'She is a caring person' – but it is more powerfully used to characterize a

Table 5.2   A comparison of Gilligan's morality of care with Kohlberg's morality of justice

	Morality of care and responsibility (Gilligan)	Morality of justice (Kohlberg)
Primary moral imperative	Nonviolence/care	Justice
Components of morality	Relationships	Sanctity of the individual
	Responsibility for self and others	Rights of self and others
	Care	Reciprocity
	Harmony	Respect
	Compassion Selflessness/self-sacrifice	Rules/legalities
Nature of moral dilemma	Threats to harmony and relationships	Conflicting rights
Determinants of moral obligation	Relationships	Principles
Cognitive processes for resolving dilemmas	Inductive thinking	Logical-deductive thinking
View of self as moral agent	Connected, attached	Separate, individual
Philosophical orientation	Phenomenological (contextual relativism)	Rational (universal principle of justice)

Source: Adapted from Brabeck, 1993: 37

> special kind of relation. The one-caring, or carer, comes with a certain attitude, and the cared-for recognizes and responds to this attitude. The relation provides a foundation of trust for teaching and counseling alike. (1991: 3)

Similarly, Sevenhuijsen (1998: 70) defines an ethics of care as a focus on values such as 'attentiveness to the need for care, willingness to accept responsibility for others as well as for the results of actions, and responsiveness'. This concern to present an ethics of care as a counter-discourse to an ethics of rights has led to feminists in this field taking up a more deconstructive approach to the binary oppositions that give rise to essentialist assumptions. Contemporary ethics of care feminists have, therefore, been concerned to both expose, and overcome, the binary oppositions that were implicit within Gilligan's thesis. These binary oppositions are set out in Table 5.2.

The concern to deconstruct the binaries between care and justice ethical models has led Gilligan (1998) to distinguish between a feminine ethic of care and a feminist ethic of care. A feminine ethic of care accepts the patriarchal social order as it is. This includes an acceptance that the ideal psychological developmental state is that of autonomy and masculine rationality. A feminist ethic of care seeks to expose the problematic nature of such an idealization as evidence of patriarchal relations and as creating a false conception of the human world:

> Care as a feminine ethic is an ethic of special obligations and interpersonal relationships. Selflessness or self-sacrifice is built into the very definition of care when caring is premised on an opposition between relationships and self-development. A feminine ethic of care is an ethic of the relational world as that world appears within a patriarchal social order: that is, as a world apart, separated politically and psychologically from a realm of individual autonomy and freedom which is the realm of justice and contractual obligation. A feminist ethic of care begins with connection, theorized as primary and seen as fundamental in human life. People live in connection with one another; human lives are interwoven in a myriad of subtle and not so subtle ways. A feminist ethic of care reveals the discon-nections in a feminine ethic of care as problems of relationships. From this standpoint, the conception of a separate self appears intrinsically prob-lematic, conjuring up the image of rational man, acting out a relationship with the inner and outer world. Such autonomy, rather than being the bedrock for solving psychological and moral problems itself becomes the problem, signifying a disconnection from emotions and a blindness to relationships which set the stage for psychological and political trouble. This reframing of psychology in terms of connection changes the conception of the human world; in doing so, it establishes the ground for a different philosophy, a different political theory, a change in ethics and legal theory. (Gilligan, 1998: 342)

Tronto (1995) notes how distinguishing between a feminine and a feminist ethic of care is not a simple exercise. Indeed, they may overlap. Broadly, however, Tronto suggests that feminine analyses of caring assume that the traditional script about caring is correct. A feminist analysis would call for a revision of the political contexts within which caring is situated. In this respect Friedman (1993) draws attention to how the distinctive moralization of the two genders implied by these binaries creates a division of moral labour. Nevertheless, in practice there is considerable overlap between the two positions in that 'morally adequate care involves considerations of justice' (ibid.: 259). Overall, Friedman argues for a de-moralization of the genders that will no longer disassociate justice from care. This, she argues, will enlarge 'the sym-bolic access of each gender to all available conceptual and social resources for the sustenance and enrichment of our collective moral life' (ibid.: 271). In a similar vein, Young (1990: 121) argues that 'justice cannot stand opposed to personal need, feeling, and desire, but names the institutional conditions that enable people to meet their needs and express their desires'.

Summary

Thomas (1993) suggests that care is an empirical rather than a theoretical concept. Certainly the empirical aspects of care have been well documented in feminist research. This has overwhelmingly illustrated that care is women's work. This chapter has explored these features of care by illustrating how the frameworks for the sociological analysis of care have built on conceptualizations of care as paid work. This has drawn attention to the inter-relations between the private and the public. In addition I have illustrated how care operates as a cluster concept through its connections to issues of dependency, responsibility and autonomy. I have also drawn attention to the feminist politics of care in respect of issues of citizenship. My final concern has been to focus on the moral conceptualizations of care and how feminist care ethicists have sought to counterpose care to the individualism of rights-based discourses.

FURTHER READING

Held, V. (1995) *Justice and Care: Essential Readings in Feminist Ethics.* Boulder, CO: Westview Press. This text comprises an anthology of mainly previously published articles concerned with an ethics of care. An excellent overview and introduction to key debates.

Time 6

There is no single time, only a multitude of times which inter-penetrate and permeate our daily lives. Most of these times are implicit, taken for granted, and seldom brought into relation with each other, the times of consciousness, memory and anticipation are rarely discussed with reference to situations dominated by schedules and deadlines. The times expressed through everyday language tend to remain isolated from the various parameters and boundaries through which we live *in* time. Matters of timing, sequencing and prioritizing stay disconnected from collective time structures, and these in turn from the rhythms, the transience and the recursiveness of daily existence.

(Adam, 1995: 12, emphasis in original)

If we reflect for a moment we will find a myriad of phrases and words that register temporality. I'm late; you're early; time is running out; I haven't got enough time; rhythms; changes; what's the time? clocking-on; retirement; how old are you? development; progress; waiting; part-time; full-time; future; past; contemporary; slow down; doing time; deadline; life's too short; free time; maturation; life cycle; there's not enough minutes in the day; annual leave; flexibility; how long have you got? stages; was; is; might; dead time; juggling; synchronize; pay day; life; death; history; memory; educate; learn; facilitate; I didn't have time; formation; the working week; habits; stability; construct; tell me your life story; my biological clock is ticking; becoming; not in my time; measure; generation; timetable; time off; school years; modern; post-modern; ancient; career; speed; too old; too young; time to go; I must manage my time better; you must manage your time better . . .

Temporality, as Klein (1994) states, is a basic category of our experience and cognition. The very essence of communicating with each other means that our languages contain a rich array of temporal expressions. There is no doubt also that time is commonly drawn upon to analyse or draw conclusions about a range of social phenomena. Indeed, Nowotny (1992) suggests that there are some common patterns that can be discerned from her analysis of time in empirical studies. These include:

- Time as a problem and as a scarce resource in 'time-compact' societies (see, for example, Blaxter and Tight, 1994; Hochschild, 1997).
- Changing patterns of working and leisure time (see, for example, Negrey, 1993).
- Specific areas where time has been central to the analysis include unemployment where the temporal experience is regarded as distinctive; doctor–patient relationships where time is a crucial negotiable variable (see, for example, Graham, 1990); education and organizations as significant institutional sites of temporal experience (see, for example, Blaxter and Tight, 1995) and of the management of time (see, for example, Blyton et al., 1989; Coffey, 1994).

Indeed, Nowotny notes that a further theme that has arisen from her analysis of empirical research is that time in relation to gender has superseded that of time in respect of social class. There is, indeed, plenty of evidence for this attention to time and gender as these following few examples will indicate.

Descriptions and analyses of feminism are littered with time motifs. Revolutions (Brownmiller, 1999) in feminist thought are often described in terms of first, second and third waves. These waves are also fixed at specific time periods. Such significations convey the linearity of calendar time and, often mistakenly, convey a linearity of development in feminist theorizing and politics. The term 'post' also indicates linearity and in particular something that comes immediately after something else. And, together with social thought more generally, feminist analyses are littered with the time signifiers of the linguistic and textual 'turns'.

In terms of more specific attention to feminist perspectives of time Forman (1989) offers a critique of the philosophical relationship between being and time. Time and being have been extensively explored in Heidegger's work (1977; 1980) to the extent that 'Being and time nearly coalesce' (Stambaugh, 1977: xi). Heidegger's approach illuminates how birth and death are the time frames through which we live. In this regard time is 'the boundary to life' (Adam, 1990: 30). Nonetheless, feminist perspectives have been drawn upon to critique the emphasis on mortality in Heidegger's work. This is because this offers no entry point for women (Forman, 1989) and, while Heidegger might illuminate aspects of living *in* time, he does not articulate the *giving* of time. In this respect Forman comments that 'women do not only live in time (from birth to death), they also give time and that act makes a radical difference to Being-in-the World' (ibid.: 7).

Research into employment has focused on time in a number of ways. For example, feminist research illustrates how the linearity of the masculine career model that assumes full-time, continuous paid work does not fit the reality of women's lives as they take breaks for child and elder care (Evetts, 1994; Nicolson, 1996). Many women's lives are, therefore, lived *out of time* in respect of this predominant model. There is also a considerable body of work that considers women's patterns of working time in terms of full-time, part-time, flexible, temporary, and so forth. Fagan (2001: 239) indicates that much of the ensuing debate in this field 'is based upon conjecture or inadequate indicators, often drawing oppositional models of gender differences in preferences which neglect the similarities between the sexes'. And, of course, research in this field has explored the changing balance of time between women's paid and unpaid work responsibilities (Hewitt, 1993). In the field of higher education Edwards (1993) offers an analysis of the experiences of women 'returners' who have to combine study with family responsibilities. Edwards reflects on the limitations of linear analyses that arise from the predominance of clock time. She notes that the multiplicity of tasks that women undertake while combining study with the care of their families means that 'Neither clock nor task-defined time capture the allocation of psychic or mental time, nor do they address the forms of consciousness required within different allocations of mental time' (ibid.: 64). In relation to research on the time implications of caring and motherhood, Ribbens (1994) remarks on the relationship between space and time. Her research evidences how 'Caring for children' was defined in terms of 'being there'. 'Part of the belief about time, then, seemed to centre not just on "spending time" on children, but on "being there", so that mothers are available when their children need them' (ibid.: 170–1). Research into the identity meanings of motherhood also point to the significance of time. While there has been considerable discussion about the implications of linear time in terms of women's age and the biological clock, feminist research has also highlighted the less recognized classed and 'raced' meanings of the 'right time' to have a child (Phoenix, 1991; McMahon, 1995).

Indeed, Nowotny (1992: 441) comments: 'The extremely rich gamut of temporal themes in social science research could be pursued beyond the mere listing I can offer here . . . one can certainly not claim that "time is neglected" in the social sciences.' Nonetheless, a wider consciousness and integration of the centrality of time to the development of social theorization are surprisingly absent (Adam, 1990; 1995). This may be because 'social scientists study a social world which they themselves inhabit, it can be a considerable effort to challenge and confront the taken-for-granted aspects of that social world. Few things exemplify this better than the concept of time' (Bechhofer and Paterson, 2000: 104). The seeming invisibility of time as an important theoretical framing and explanation of social life, Nowotny suggests, is because 'it is recalcitrantly transdisciplinary and refuses to be placed under the intellectual monopoly of any discipline' (1992: 441). Nowotny argues that because 'time' refuses to be fixed within one discipline it is a highly productive vehicle for the development of interdisciplinary and indeed transdisciplinary perspectives. Given that interdisciplinarity and trans-disciplinarity have been central rationales for the development of women's studies time would appear as a key concept awaiting significant further development. In this respect Adam (1989: 458) forcefully argues that time offers feminist social theory the opportunity to transcend the 'pervasive vision of the "founding fathers"'. Adam illustrates her point through an analysis of the multitude of times that exist in a single moment. She argues that the recognition of such multiplicity and complexity allows for a firm grounding of the analysis of experience. In addition, a feminist theorization of time would facilitate a move away from dualistic thinking (see also Adam, 1995).

To date, that theorization is still waiting to happen. Broadly, the majority of feminist research that has used time as a key concept has stayed within dualistic framings of what Davies (1990) refers to as 'male time' and Knights and Odih (1995) refer to as 'female time'. This is the counterposing of 'male' linear, commodified, clock time with 'female' cyclical, reproductive time. And although, as I shall illustrate, there are exceptions analyses that focus on the complexity of time to which Adam (1989) refers are relatively few. In this regard, I would agree with McNay (2000: 111) when she comments:

> In feminist work on time, this complexity [that Adam (1989) refers to] is often reduced to a dualism where feminine experience tends to be located in the level of everyday temporality understood as cyclical, reproductive and expressive and which falls in the shadow of a masculine temporality understood as progressive, standardized and instrumental (Ermath, 1989). However, such dualist notions of time do not capture adequately the variable effects of detraditionalization and globalization upon women's lives.

Male Time and Female Time

> The linear conception of time – where we see time as unfolding in a straight and unbroken line, unidirectional and heading towards an

unlimited horizon – is the time that has preponderance today. On a concrete level, this time consciousness is mirrored in our time reckoning where atomically measured seconds flow into minutes and hours and days and ultimately years. Years that linearly follow each other into an unending future, leaving behind a once and for all past.

(Davies, 1990: 18)

The most common understanding of time is that of a linear continuum that begins, perhaps at birth and ends at death or begins when one gets up in the morning and finishes the moment one goes to sleep. Certainly it is common to design research so that data is collected, or indeed data collection is avoided, according to particular time periods. These would include, for example, key points in the school year, holidays, family events, religious festivals, and so forth. In some forms of qualitative research there appears to be a positive correlation between the length of time spent in the field and assumptions of validity. Thus, the longer one has spent researching a topic, the more valid the findings are presumed to be. In research into paid employment divisions of time lead to analyses that take account of full-time and part-time working. Perhaps the most common example of time is that of age. Age is a key face sheet variable that is regularly, and often unquestionably, included as a research question (Finch, 1986).

These conceptualizations view time as measured by the clock, the days of the week, the months of the year or year dates. Davies (1990) illustrates how the emergence of the mechanical clock served religious, state, economic and capitalist interests in the Western world. This is first seen through the horarium, that is the table of hours that sets out when Matins, Lauds, Prime, Terce, Sext, None, Vespers and Compline were to be held and was the most important determinant of life in Christian Benedictine monasteries. This meant that each activity could be held at the same fixed point in time every day. This can be compared with Judaism and Islam where prayers are associated with the changing times of sunrise, noon and sunset.

Although medieval monasteries were the first to use the clock in this way, their influence soon spread to other spheres of life. The emergence of towns and cities during the British industrial revolution meant that clock time could be used to ensure that shop opening and meeting times could be regulated. The time obedience that was a feature of Benedictine monasteries became time discipline as the development of watches individualized and internalized control (Davies, 1990). Thompson (1967) illustrates the linkage between clock time, the organization of labour in capitalism, the Puritan work ethic and discipline.

Schooling is a key site where time discipline is instilled. Timetables, bells, calendars and deadlines extend the Benedictine horarium and the Puritan work ethic into the everyday lives of children. The organization of schooling is fixed according to age and calendar. The days are divided into periods and lesson activities are also planned to linear time. The length of examinations is set to specific hours and minutes. Teaching time of lessons is set aside from play time and home time. Children learn that if they have not finished their work they are taking too long or if they finish early they have not done enough. Accurately gauging the appropriate level of input in relation to the time available is a key skill. Children also learn, as Adam (1995) points out, that some people's time is thought to be more important than others.

Clock time is not only the main way through which we order and understand time in Western societies, it also provides the framework through which tasks are valued. For example, Marxist analyses of the commodification of time indicate its economic value. These analyses focus on the exchange relations of labour power and profit maximization. Monthly, weekly and hourly wages indicate how time is drawn on as a measure of labour value. Alongside labour, capital and machinery, time becomes an economic variable and allows us to speak of a time economy. '[W]e spend it, waste it, invest it, budget it and save it. We equate it, in other words, with money' (Adam, 1995: 89).

The values given to time can also be seen in rational choice models of time allocation. Becker's analysis of household economics that was introduced in Chapter 4 comprised both monetary and time aspects. Thus 'With a Becker model, a household's demand for a particular good is dependent on the market price of itself and other goods, the value of time of household members, and the household's full income' (Senauer, 1990: 152). The value that is put on women's and men's time within such an economic model of household divisions of labour relies on its estimated monetary value in the paid labour market. This has specific implications for women, given that they are mainly employed in low waged labour. Such economic analyses highlight how 'The economic status of women in society and their role and position in the household are formally linked by the value of time' (Sirianni and Negrey 2000: 64). For Sirianni and Negrey the key response to changing assumptions that it should be women who are mainly responsible for housework and family care must be to improve women's economic opportunities and investment in human capital as this would increase the value of their time.

Davies (1990) refers to linear and clock time as 'male time'. She does this because she wishes to draw attention to the 'patriarchal character of the groups and classes that have been able to influence this concept and measurement of time' (ibid.: 17). Davies argues for a greater appreciation of how 'male time' contributes to the subordination and oppression of women and how particular ways of studying time obscures women's lives. Similarly, Sirianni and Negrey (2000: 59) note that 'One of the ways time is structured is through social relations of gender, and gender inequalities are reflected in the social organization of time.' Certainly, there have been many feminist critiques of this linear model and its associated values. I highlight four of these here.

First, the linear model appears to be an 'objective' measure. Time is understood to exist as fixed units both independent of, and external to, the individual. This appearance of objectivity and measurability aligns such analyses with positivistic methodologies. Positivist methodologies argue that social science should mirror, as near as possible, the procedures of the natural sciences. The researcher should be objective and detached from the objects of research. Thus, Adam (1995) notes how a decontextualized, commodified time is the central model in social science analyses of time. She comments that:

> This socially created, artefactual resource has become so all-embracing that it is now related to as if it were time *per se*, as if there were no other times. This has the effect that even the embedded, lived times of work and non-work are understood through the mediating filter of our own creation of non-temporal time. (ibid.: 91, emphasis in original)

Second, and relatedly, as a predominant model, linear time distracts our attention from the multitude of times that exist. Thus, an event in our lives may bring back memories from the past or in the contemporary moment we might make plans for the future. At these times the past and/or future are co-existent with the present. The writing of our will extends our lives beyond death. There are also good and bad times and good and bad timing.

Third, this linear model is a gendered model that fits with men's lives. The organization of paid work into strict linear time accords with an assumption that there are no other forms of time that impact on an individual's life. In consequence, some feminists have argued that cyclical time is more reflective of women's lives. Within models of cyclical time consciousness:

> It is assumed that people pace the events of their lives according to local and natural rhythms and that the future is a perpetual recapitulation of the present. A precise time measurement is superfluous. On a day-to-day

level, people are not subject then to clock time but rather to a time that is task or process oriented. (Davies, 1990: 19)

In particular, it is women's responsibilities and role as primary carers that are drawn upon to argue that women's experiences of time are qualitatively different from those of men. Thus, Davies allocates domestic and care tasks to the sphere of cyclical time and refers to this as process time. She argues that women's care responsibilities produce a needs-oriented response whereby they have to be more flexible in relation to time. Waiting with one's child at the doctors or feeding a baby would be examples of such necessary time flexibility. Thus care:

is based on a different relation to time (although . . . it can be forced into the dominant temporal consciousness, especially when organised as wage labour). In reproductive work the clock is less important; rather it is the task at hand that is definitive . . . Care work (whether it is carried out in the home or not) is characterised by short cycles that are frequently repeated and by the fact that it is *with difficulty* subsumed under strict clock time. (Davies, 1990: 36–7, emphasis in original)

In the same way, Knights and Odih (1995) describe feminine time as relational, continuous, processual and cyclical. Feminine time exists in relation to the time demands of others and because of this women's lives are characterized by the overlapping temporalities of simultaneous actions. As this time is mediated through the needs of others, Knights and Odih argue that it is quite unlike the decontextualized, commodified and controlled linear time. And because feminine time is relational, Knights and Odih (1995: 211) also argue that 'we cannot focus solely on individual time'.

Fourth, the gendered model of linear time gives rise to gendered theories of time. Marxist analysis of the commodification of time assume that time away from work is 'free' time (Sirianni and Negrey, 2000). Feminists took up this issue in what is termed the Wages for Housework debate. Feminists arguing for Wages for Housework illustrated how domestic work was necessary reproductive work for capital and produces value/surplus value. Although within feminism there were serious divisions on this issue (see Freedman, 2001, for an accessible summary), the Wages for Housework debate made visible the unpaid work that women do. Notwithstanding, Davies (1990: 41) notes that the issue of time was never directly discussed in these debates and 'from a perspective that problematizes time, it was a debate that from the very beginning could not be solved since housework is quite simply not answerable to male time'.

Case Study 12: Time and the Weaving of the Strands of Everyday Life

Davies's (1990) study provides a phenomenological account of how 'gender relations of time were instrumental in shaping the lives and actions' (ibid.: 10) of a group of forty Swedish women who constantly moved in and out of the labour market. In this, Davies explores women's everyday lives in terms of employment, unemployment, home and community. These women were studied for a period of two and a half to three years and in-depth interviews were carried out during this period.

Davies's analysis illustrates how women's everyday lives are bound up with, and directed by, both clock and process time consciousness. For example, women's experiences of time when working in the home are bound up with the times of family members and others through which 'clock and process time weave complicated patterns' (ibid.: 131). Women of course juggled the demands of employment and family care. Wives and husbands worked different shifts to ensure that one is always available for childcare. And when women were not in paid employment, their time was given up to the time demands of others.

Davies also explores women's active and passive resistance to 'male' clock time. Here she illustrates how women's rejection of wage labour can be seen as a rejection of the 'temporal strait-jacket; as an attempt to allow more space for other forms of temporal consciousness and action' (ibid.: 204). Thus women would give priority to time rather than money by taking part-time work or becoming self-employed. Women's choice of occupation also portrayed a rejection of linear time. For example, some women chose artistic occupations because 'a central feature of artistic work is that it is structured by process time' (ibid.: 211).

Time and the Self

Psychoanalytic theories of the development of the self suggest that key events in the development of sexuality or personality occur at a fixed point in time. Freud, for example, argued that the first five years of a child's life determined sexual orientation and personality. In particular, Freud considered that at about the age of five the young child had to resolve her/his sexual identity. Lacan used the metaphor of mirror to

describe the stages of identity formation. A sense of self does not happen
immediately but 'it is during the mirror phase that the child begins to
acquire language. And it is through the entry into language that the
child is constituted as a subject' (Sarup, 1996: 36). This fixity of timing
is also evident in more recent work in the development of the plural self.
Rowan (1999) explores the development of sub-personalities in terms of
a specific time frame. Stage One occurs pre-birth when the child is in the
mother's womb. 'At this stage there is nothing wrong. Whatever is
needed is given, without the need to ask. The self is OK, and the world
is OK, and there is no need to differentiate between the two' (Rowan,
1999: 14). Stage Two occurs 'maybe pre-birth, maybe during birth,
maybe some while after birth – an event happens which indicates that I
am not in control of my world' (ibid.: 15).

Lifespan developmental psychology expands the interest in the
psychological development of individuals in childhood to that of adulthood. This work is often described in terms of stages through the life
cycle or life course. The life cycle is conceptualized through the emphasis that is placed on ages and stages in life (Allatt and Keil, 1987). Life
course theorists focus on individuals' transitions through these stages
(Allatt and Keil, 1987). Allatt and Keil indicate that life cycle theories
have generally been critiqued for their over-deterministic overtones as
they portray the individual as inhabiting a world of biological and social
inevitability. In contrast, approaches that utilize the life course are
considered to allow for much greater recognition of issues of agency.
The earliest feminist critiques of life cycle and life course analyses
highlighted how research in this field was based on men's experiences
and, as Fisher comments, ignored the particular experiences of women:

> The literature alternately refers to transitions as rites of passage, move-
> ment through life stages, bridges connecting the old and new, crisis events
> and, more generically major life change. While the study of adult tran-
> sitions has been carried out by various scholars and writers representing
> wide-ranging views, most research on the subject seems to have incor-
> porated the developmental perspective on adult maturation. This
> perspective outlines a linear, mostly chronological sequence of tasks and
> changes, and assumes a series of life cycle events, which implicitly ignore
> the possibility of distinctiveness in women's transitional experiences.
> (1989: 141)

The male model offered a picture that suggested that the experience of
transition from one stage of life to another was sporadic and short term.
It was, moreover, bounded by extensive periods of stability. Yet Fisher's
experiences of teaching these models of adult development to women

'returners' indicated that these women 'would conclude that they have been psychologically "in transit" almost all of their adult lives' (ibid.: 141).

There are therefore two points that can be made in relation to the perspectives of time that underpin these developmental models of the self. First, time is conceptualized as linear. Child and adult development is charted predominantly in terms of chronological age. For example, Erikson (1980) set out eight stages of psychosocial development. These begin in early infancy and end in late adulthood (see Arnold, 1997, for a useful summary of psychological models of adult development). Second:

> Irreversible time dominates in studies of the life cycle. This applies irrespective of whether the life cycle is conceptualised as a cumulative development of growth and decay or in terms of unidirectional successive stages; whether time is understood as internal or external to the system; whether a 'time in' or an 'in time' approach is used; whether we theorise life as being lived along time-tracks or whether we analyse social age . . . Despite the emphasis on moments of return, irreversibility and change are central to the cycles of life since no repetition is the same in its recurrence. (Adam, 1990: 99–100)

Recent work on selfhood has begun to incorporate more complex conceptualizations of time. In addition, these have also sought to go beyond the dualism of female and male time that has been a particular feature of earlier feminist work. The view of subjectivity in these conceptualizations is much closer to one 'that anticipates subjectivity as already embedded in and through time 'events' (Knights and Odih, 1995: 221). In particular, the fluidity and simultaneous nature of past, present and future time have been seen as important aspects of how selfhood is constituted. For example, Battersby (1998) offers a critique of the linearity of Gilligan's (1982) model of selfhood to illuminate the changing and diverse nature of femininities and masculinities. She does this through noting that some of the events of childhood time may inhabit the present but these are neither as unitary nor as determining as Gilligan would suggest:

> The self that I am interested in does not emerge as a 'unity' or a 'thing' in a particular slice of linear time that constitutes 'childhood development'. Instead, the self is continually established as self through responses, repetitions and habitual movements over time. It does not know itself through conscious thought, although it does, in Henry James's words, learn about itself through 'The terrible fluidity of self-revelation' (James, 1909, p. 11). Of course, during childhood some of the key dispositional responses are established; but the child's relation to the mother is not

determining of later responses in the way that Gilligan's model would seem to suggest. A 'feminine' response to a situation is not to be understood via Gilligan's monocausal account, which uses the childhood relation to the mother to explain the 'under' – or 'other'-development of the adult moral subject. Selves ('masculine' and 'feminine') are more diverse and rich than Gilligan's model would suggest. (Battersby, 1998: 207–8)

Griffiths' (1995) discussion of the authentic self similarly draws on the past as a feature of the present. To this Griffiths adds the significance of the future. Griffiths notes that although feelings of being authentic occur spontaneously, there is more to being authentic than a momentary feeling. Indeed, spontaneous feelings might rather be aspects of sentimentality or shallowness. As feelings of the moment they may be just momentary feelings. Authenticity requires something more than a momentary concern. As Griffiths (1995: 175) notes, 'the feelings of "really me", "true to myself" and "being myself" . . . seem to be indications of something more lasting than a snapshot'. The authentic self occurs because of what has happened in the past and what might happen in the future:

> the self may be experienced as feeling, acting and being, authentically, in the here and now. But there is no such 'here and now' for a self that is not a result of what has happened in the past – and what is expected in the future. It may be that we may act authentically in the present, but, if so, that authentic, spontaneous, immediacy is in fact firmly rooted in time, especially in past social interactions. (Griffiths, 1995: 176)

Moreover, Griffiths emphasizes the authentic self is not static. For Griffiths, selfhood is understood as constructed through time and as such is always in the process of construction. Thus, those aspects that are 'really me' are reconfirmed through time and also change over time:

> So, finally, what is 'authenticity'? It is to be understood in relation to agency and becoming. To be authentic requires acting at one's own behest both at a feeling level and also at an intellectual, reflective one. The feelings are the spontaneous enactment of the agency. The context of that agency in terms of the wider context needs to be taken into account. This is the intellectual reflection on the action, which may well change what future feelings arise spontaneously. So the present time remains important, but authenticity has to be achieved and re-achieved. Each action changes the context and requires understanding if authenticity is to be retained. Simply acting on what you feel will not answer. Nor will acting on what you think. Both are required, and it is difficult to know which to emphasise at any stage. (ibid.: 179)

The issue of the relationship between time and agency that Griffiths raises here is also a concern of McNay (2000). McNay views the addition of a temporal dimension as essential to overcoming some of the more deterministic elements of structuralist and poststructuralist theorizing. Time is a central aspect of McNay's analysis of a conceptualization of autonomous agency that she argues allows for a greater recognition of the creative dimensions of individuals' responses to changing social relations. Specifically, McNay argues that time has been a neglected aspect of poststructuralist work on the subject. In particular if, as poststructuralist theory would suggest, subjectivity is a process then how do we explain the coherence that we feel in our experiences of selfhood? She comments:

> A gap in constructionist accounts of subjectification is that, while suggesting that identity is composed of a multiplicity of subject positions, the coherence of the self is not really explained beyond vague and top-heavy ideas of ideological fixation. This lacuna arises partly because poststructural work on the subject is not adequately situated temporally, so that the coherence of the subject is viewed, in one-dimensional terms, as the externally imposed effect of power. (ibid.: 27)

Within poststructuralist accounts a sense of a unified identity is perceived to be an illusion of power. Yet McNay argues that the incorporation of temporality helps to explain why we might say to a friend 'I'm just the same person as I was 20 years ago'. The incorporation of time as an explanatory framework enables McNay to develop a generative account of agency and identification that is designed to overcome the dualisms of domination and resistance and identification and disidentification that contemporary ideas of agency are caught between. The impact of the past, for example, not only continues in the present. It also enables us to experience our identity as coherent:

> Although subject formations receive their shape from prevailing social conditions, certain predispositions and tendencies may still continue to effect embodied practices long after their original conditions of emergence have been surpassed. This durability partly suggests that a coherent sense of self is not just an illusion but fundamental to the way in which the subject interprets itself in time. (ibid.: 18)

In accord with both Battersby and Griffiths, and in contrast to psychoanalytic accounts outlined above that suggest that selfhood is formed at certain key points, McNay is also arguing for an understanding of identity that is dynamically constituted through time. Yet she stresses that a sense of unity and coherence are key aspects of the dynamic configuration of self. Unity is achieved by locating aspects of change about oneself as moments of disjuncture or temporal flux:

> A generative paradigm of subjectification and agency helps to [conceptualize] the coherence of the self as a simultaneity of identity and non-identity. Through a temporalization of the process of subjectification, the generative model suggests that the self has unity but it is the dynamic unity of progress in time. In other words, the identity of the self is maintained only through a ceaseless incorporation of the non-identical understood as temporal flux. (ibid.: 18–19)

McNay argues that one way of understanding how this occurs is through the narrative construction of identity. Referring to the work of Ricoeur, McNay draws attention to how the different time strands in a story that one might tell about oneself are often incompatible. This has two important implications. First that 'male' and 'female' time is not experienced in terms of discrete and separate elements. Rather, different forms of time such as clock time and task time are more fluid and in flux. Second, and relatedly, the multitude of times that exist (Adam, 1995) are actively configured and reconfigured in the stories that we tell about ourselves into a coherent narrative. Thus 'Narrative is the mode through which individuals attempt to integrate the non-synchronous and often conflictual elements of their lives and experiences' (McNay, 2000: 113).

Case Study 13: Self-transformation and the Biological Clock

The term 'biological clock' is a relatively familiar term that is applied to Western women who decide to delay child-bearing until they have established their careers. Once women reach their mid-thirties, however, time is seen to be running out. Indeed, Crouch and Manderson (1993) comment that the issue of the timing of motherhood is now seen to be intensely problematic for women. McMahon's (1995) analysis of Australian women's decisions to become mothers illustrates how time, identity and motherhood are experienced in the lives of middle- and working-class women. McMahon illustrates how the middle-class women in her study frequently referred to the problem of the 'biological clock'. However, McMahon's analysis illustrates that the relationship of time and motherhood is not simply utilitarian in the sense of an appropriate biological point. Rather, the time of the 'biological clock' was intrinsically related to future identities. Thus, McMahon comments:

> References to a biological clock were common [with regard to the
> middle-class women in the sample]. However, the data showed that what
> looked like a question of *when* to have children was often a question of
> *whether* to have them. Time did more than urge procrastinating or
> ambivalent women to make up their minds. It presented them with the
> possibility of a new and irrevocable identity – that of being permanently
> childless. (ibid.: 89, emphasis in original)

The question of when to have children was not simply to do with time
as linearity or biology. Rather, it was also related to issues of identity
and particularly adult identity. Motherhood is viewed as a key marker of
adulthood. Becoming adult, however, can also be experienced in class-
related ways. For example, Phoenix (1991) indicates that for young
working-class women becoming a mother is considered to be a route to
adulthood. However, McMahon illustrates that for middle-class women,
they considered that they had to have achieved the status of adulthood
before they could have children. In this way for middle-class women the
decision of when to have children was related to a particular conception
of the 'right' time. Thus:

> The 'right time' was frequently presented in terms of maturational, social
> and economic *achievements*. These women typically presented themselves
> as psychologically and financially ready and as having achieved readiness in
> terms of their occupational careers and relationships with partners . . .
> Ironically, being a *woman* in itself did not represent adequate grounds for
> claiming motherhood. Even for those who had always wanted children,
> becoming a mother had the character of a personal accomplishment.
> Women's adult achievements were seen as preconditions for readiness
> for children. That is, middle-class women had to *become* the sort of
> persons who could properly have children. (ibid.: 89–90)

Time–Space

> What I am about to tell you, or confide in you, today, will remain
> rather primary, loose. This is both deliberate and due to lack of
> time. But what time do I mean? The time that has not, or has not
> yet, been loosed by all that is too bound, too secondarily bound,
> thereby leaving so-called free energy chained up, in the crypt. But
> perhaps that energy is merely deprived of the space-time it needs to
> cathect, unfold, inscribe, play.

(Irigaray, 1993: 25)

As Irigaray's words convey, there are many occasions when we might have the time of the clock available to us to do something, maybe a spare half an hour here or an hour there. However, our minds and lives are too busy with other things to have the necessary time–space to *cathect, unfold, inscribe, play . . .*

The relationship between time and space has been extensively theorized in the physical and natural sciences. This relationship can be seen in Euclidean geometry and Newtonian and Einsteinian physics. Euclidean geometry and Newtonian physics view space as three-dimensional. Every point can be fixed in space in three dimensions and time is a constant continuous phenomenon experienced universally this way. Einstein argued that time and space are held in relation to each other. One's perception of both depends upon one's location. Thus, the experience of time–space was not universal. As Hawking (1988: 21) comments: 'the theory of relativity put an end to the idea of absolute time! It appeared that each observer must have his [*sic*] own measure of time, as recorded by a clock carried with him [*sic*], and that identical clocks carried by different observers would not necessarily agree.'

Adam reviews these theories and illustrates that there are three kinds of approach that are relevant for social science research:

> The first includes time as both a measure and a quantity to be measured. As such, it is used in mechanics, Newton's laws, Einstein's theories of relativity, and in the empirical studies and synchronic analyses of social scientists. The second is concerned with directional processes and events as expressed in the laws of thermodynamics, the theory of dissipative structures, some historical analyses in social science, and the work of Mead and Luhmann, The third approach is that of quantum theory which conceptualises the ultimate reality as fundamentally temporal and which has so far not had an impact on the social sciences. (1990: 49)

Because she is, in part, interested in raising questions about the impact of major theorizations of the natural and physical sciences on changing understandings of subjectivity, Grosz (1995) draws on Newton's and Einstein's conceptualizations in her exploration of time–space and the body. In accord with Adam (1990), Grosz notes two important points here:

> first representations of space have always had – and continue to have – a priority over representations of time. Time is represented only insofar as it is attributed certain spatial properties. The second is that there is an historical correlation between the ways in which space (and to a lesser

extent, time) is represented and the ways in which subjectivity represents itself. (1995: 97)

Grosz's (1995) main intention is to offer a preliminary account of the significance of time–space through which she raises some questions for the development of feminist theorizations of the body. Her work is exploratory and is intended to provoke further conceptualizations. For this reason what I outline here is relatively fragmentary and abstract. Grosz notes the work of Irigaray and Kristeva as foundational to feminist explorations of time–space relationships. She comments that in 'providing a starting point for reconceiving the ways in which sexed subjects are understood, Kristeva and Irigaray have merely opened up a terrain that needs further exploration' (ibid.: 84).

In this respect Irigaray reconceived the spatiality of women's bodies in terms of internality rather than externality and as agentic points of closure and openness rather than as passive holes awaiting penetration by the phallus. One of the ways that she did this was through a rebuke of the phallocentrism of Lacan's analysis of the mirror-stage. Lacan's analysis views women in terms of what they lack, as a 'hole', rather than in terms of what they have. The emphasis in Lacan on what can be seen, i.e. the phallus, was countered by Irigaray's use of the speculum, the curved mirror that enables internal inspection of the body. As a metaphor the speculum demonstrates that what *is* is not always on view. What woman is or could be cannot simply be known through a dominant phallocentric view represented by a looking glass mirror. The speculum allows access to those sites that are hidden from (male) view and that are beyond the phallus. Battersby (1996: 262) notes how 'Speculum as a whole reverses the direction of gaze, using woman's body as the apparatus through which to regard the philosophers' accounts of being.' For example, Irigaray opposes the Lacanian image of woman as 'hole' with the symbolic image of '*contiguity*, of the two lips touching' (Whitford, 1991: 28). This image is designed to show how woman's desire does not need to be seen through male representations but can be seen for itself.

In respect of Kristeva's analysis of identity, time and space, this illustrates issues of simultaneity rather than linearity. Identity, time and space cohabit Kristeva's (1986) conception of 'Women's Time' in terms of the politics of feminism. As Moi indicates, Kristeva provides a classic statement in relation to this:

> [Kristeva] explicitly addresses the question of feminism and its relations to femininity on the one hand, and the symbolic order on the other.

According to Kristeva female subjectivity would seem to be linked both to cyclical time (repetition) and to monumental time (eternity), at least in so far as both are ways of conceptualizing time from the perspective of motherhood and reproduction. The time of history, however, can be characterized as linear time: time as project, teleology, departure, progression and arrival. This linear time is also that of language considered as the enunciation of a sequence of words. (1986: 188)

Kristeva talks of three generations of feminists but she is not using generation solely in the sense of linear time – our grandmothers, mothers, daughters. Rather, her usage emphasizes generation in terms of occupying symbolic and corporeal space in the social order. The three generations to which Kristeva refers are, therefore, both linear – from first wave to third wave – and they also co-exist. Kristeva advocates a deconstructive approach to sexual difference where feminist struggles should be seen historically and politically in terms of the following three tiers:

1 Women demand equal access to the symbolic order. Liberal feminism. Equality.
2 Women reject the male symbolic order in the name of difference. Radical feminism. Femininity extolled.
3 Women reject the dichotomy between masculine and feminine as metaphysical. (This is Kristeva's own position.) (Moi, 1997: 249)

Moi comments that the implications for feminism are that it remains politically essential that women take up their space in human society as equals and that women also need to emphasize their difference in this space. To ignore these aspects of the feminist struggle would be to 'lose touch with the political reality of feminism' (ibid.). Kristeva's third position above has to be viewed as simultaneous, rather than linear, to these other two positions.

In recognizing the foundational work of Irigaray and Kristeva, Grosz's starting point is that the relationship between time–space and corporeality is reciprocal:

If bodies are to be reconceived, not only must their *matter and form* be rethought, but so too must their environment and *spatio-temporal location* . . . bodies are always understood within a spatial and temporal context, and space and time remain conceivable only insofar as corporeality provides the basis for our perception and representation of them. (Grosz, 1995: 84, emphasis in original)

This reciprocity leads Grosz to explore two key points. One of these is concerned with the relationship of the body to time–space. Here Grosz offers some significant points:

> space is no more 'tangible' or perceptible than time, for it is only objects in space and time which can be considered tangible and amenable to perception. Space is no more concrete than time, nor is it easier to represent. The subject is no more clearly positioned in space than in time; indeed, the immediacy of the 'hereness' of corporeal existence is exactly parallel to the 'nowness' of the subject's experience. (ibid.: 85)

A second point is the relationship between changing identities and changing conceptualizations of time–space:

> Developmentally, the child perceives and is organized with reference to a series of spatial conceptions, from its earliest access to the 'space of adherence' to the virtual space of mirror-images, the curved and plural spaces of dreams and the spatiality conferred by the primacy of vision. Historically, it can be argued (although I do not have space to do so here) that as representations of subjectivity changed, so too did representations of space and time. If space is the exteriority of the subject and time its interiority, then the ways this exteriority and interiority are theorized will affect notions of space and time. (ibid.: 99)

Thus, Grosz comments that the Kantian conception of subjectivity finds its correlate in Newtonian physics. In contrast, 'the decentred Freudian subject conforms to the relativity of an Einsteinian universe' (ibid.: 100). Grosz's attention to time–space relationships and the body indicate the potential of further reconceptualizations. For example, Benhabib's (1992) 'exile', Braidotti's (1994) 'nomad', Brah's (1996) 'diaspora space' have all been predominantly theorized in terms of spatiality. These theorizations have indicated the multiplicity of spaces that exist and the politics of space. It is perhaps the moment for these spatial metaphors to be more clearly recognized as simultaneously concerned with time.

Case Study 14: Gender Transformations

Central to Walby's (1997) research is the question 'Is the condition of women in society improving or getting worse?' Through a materialist feminist theoretical framework Walby analyses statistical data sets and the findings from survey research that gathered life history data. Her research is centrally concerned with issues of time and space in the

following ways. First, she views time as multiple and socially constructed. She comments in this respect:

> Time is no longer seen as simply the same as that shown on a clock, but as
> something which is socially perceived, constructed, refracted and impli-
> cated in complex and various ways. It is no longer of interest merely as
> the medium through which social change takes place, but has become an
> active resource in the creation of this change. (ibid.: 8)

Walby's focus on issues of space is to take account of the 'Different
patterns of gender relations [that] are found in different spatial locations.' For this reason Walby considers the role of local labour markets
and the inter-relations of the global and local in terms of the impact on
women's working lives.

Overall, Walby's analysis illustrates the complex ways through which
time and space interact in shaping women's lives. This is demonstrated
in four ways. Through:

1 The major macro-structural changes in the form of patriarchal and
   gender regimes. Here Walby extends her analysis of private and
   public patriarchy (see Walby, 1990).
2 The intersection of time and space as an analysis of the differential
   effects of change in local labour markets.
3 The significance of life-cycle events such as marriage and childcare
   on women's commitments to specific occupational and industrial
   niches. Walby's findings indicate that women remain committed
   over their lifetimes to the 'first-choice' occupations of their initial
   work placements. This is particularly the case if they are given the
   option of full or part-time working. This finding suggests that the
   personal effects of deindustrialization may not be as great as might
   be expected. New service sector jobs are largely filled by new
   entrants to the labour market.
4 The intersection of different forms of time and the different ways
   that past time impacts on the present. Walby argues that once
   certain decisions have been made, say, in terms of education and
   training and the timing and spacing of children, they are very difficult
   to undo. For example, women who have built their lives around an
   expectation that they will be primarily mothers and family carers, in
   terms of what Walby refers to as private patriarchy, are particularly
   disadvantaged in contemporary conditions. Young women are now
   planning to spend extensive periods of time in paid employment,
   within the public patriarchy regime.

Summary

In the introduction I commented that time is feminism's latent concept. Feminist research has challenged the dominance of linear clock time through analyses that illustrate how this form of time shapes our material realities and our understanding of selfhood and development. In particular, feminist research has compared masculine clock time with feminine process time through which daily cyclical activities are experienced. Feminist research has also illustrated the myriad of times that exist (Adam, 1995) and how time is imbricated in authenticity. Analyses of feminist politics and the body have provided creative conceptualizations of time–space relations. Nevertheless, although resonant in a range of analyses, time theorization is relatively under-developed. Primarily feminist analyses of time have yet to go much beyond the binary of female–male.

FURTHER READING

Adam, B. (1995) *Timewatch: The Social Analysis of Time*. Cambridge: Polity Press. Written in a very accessible way, Adam explores the varied conceptualizations of time and relates this to health, education, work, globalization and environmental change.

Davies, K. (1990) *Women, Time and Weaving the Strands of Everyday Life*. Aldershot: Gower. Davies provides a classic empirical study of the meanings of time in women's lives.

Experience 7

The meaning of experience is perhaps the most crucial site of political struggle over meaning, since it involves personal, psychic and emotional investments on the part of the individual. It plays an important role in determining the individual's role as social agent. It affects both where and how the individual acts and whether her actions are based on a consensual acceptance of the meaning and effects of an action, on conscious resistance to them, or on the demands of other external necessities. The power of experience in the constitution of the individual as social agent comes from the dominant assumption in our society that experience gives access to truth. It is assumed that we come to know the world through experience.

(Weedon, 1997: 76)

Skeggs (1997) notes that experience has been seen as *the* basis of feminism in that feminism as a social movement and as a personal politics began the moment that women began to talk to each other and make sense of their experiences as women. Indeed, de Lauretis (1994: 8) comments that we can credit feminism for conceptualizing 'experience in relation to both social-material practices and to the formation and processes of subjectivity'. This is because experience is central to feminist political, critical and textual practices through, for example, consciousness raising, critiquing scientific discourses and methodologies and imagining new forms of social organization.

The quintessential sign of the importance of experience to feminism is the slogan 'the personal is the political'. This statement is not to be understood in terms of conflating one's personal life with formal political life. For example, in Britain during the 1980s an analogy was made between Margaret Thatcher's experiences of family housekeeping and her responsibilities as Prime Minister for the nation's finances. While there may be certain skills that are common to both activities, this analogy diverts our attention away from the political situatedness of each activity. Women's roles as housekeepers can be experienced as an aspect of their subjugation and low status as they put their own needs at the bottom of any budget. Subjugation and low status are not the phrases that come immediately to mind when one reflects on prime ministerial power in relation to national finances. The phrase 'the personal is the political' was designed to draw attention to the political meanings and imperatives that derive from women's everyday experiences of their personal and private lives. Published originally in 1982, MacKinnon comments in this respect that 'the personal is the political':

> means that women's distinctive experience as women occurs within that sphere that has been socially lived as the personal – private, emotional, interiorized, particular, individuated, intimate – so that what it is to *know* the *politics* of women's situation is to know women's personal lives . . . To say that the personal is political means that gender as a division of power is discoverable and verifiable through women's intimate experience of sexual objectification, which is definitive of and synonymous with women's lives as gender female. Thus, to feminism, the personal is epistemologically the political, and its epistemology is its politics. (1997: 73–4, emphasis in original)

The centrality of the political meanings of women's personal and intimate experiences can be seen in the development of consciousness-raising groups. The purpose of such groups was to enable women to reinterpret past experiences with a view to enabling them to see their worlds in new ways. In this the political imperatives of consciousness-raising were those of enabling and facilitating women to learn that the 'anomalous, discrepant, idiosyncratic, chaotic, "crazy"' (Frye, 1996: 34) experiences that they had previously understood as their own fault or unique to them were both common and fell into regular patterns. Consciousness-raising was viewed as a way of making women's experiences of living in a world constructed by men as intelligible rather than aberrant.

The major outcome of consciousness-raising was the development of new methodologies and new ways of theorizing. Redefining women's experiences as arising from patriarchal relations facilitated the development of new theoretical perspectives and possibilities for resistance (Skeggs, 1997; Weedon, 1997). In addition, consciousness-raising represented an alternative approach to masculine forms of knowledge construction and, thereby, to accessing the truth of social relations. Specifically, consciousness-raising rejected the scientific method where knowledge claims are to be evaluated rationally and objectively and are not accepted on the basis of the status, authority or subjective view of the knower (Assiter, 2000). MacKinnon (1997: 74) comments in this respect that 'Consciousness raising not only comes to know different things as politics; it necessarily comes to know them in a different way.'

Feminist standpoint is one major strand of theorizing experience that is seen to have arisen from consciousness-raising activities and has contributed to the development of feminist epistemologies. Epistemologies are theories of knowledge that address questions such as 'who can be a "knower", what can be known, what constitutes and validates knowledge, and what the relationship is or should be between knowing and being (that is, between epistemology and ontology)' (Stanley and Wise, 1990: 26). In this 'feminist theorists have moved from the "reactive" stance of the feminist critique of social science, and into the realms of exploring what "feminist knowledge" could conceivably look like' (ibid.: 37). Two versions of standpoint theory came to prominence in the 1970s and 1980s (Hekman, 1999). These were from philosophy (Hartsock, 1983) and from sociology (Smith, 1988). Using a feminist materialist approach, Hartsock argued that women's experiences of their daily lives give them privileged access to understanding the relations of ruling. The work of Hartsock is viewed as arguing for a feminist standpoint that will in consequence justify distinctive forms of feminist knowledge and methodologies. In her focus on everyday life Smith explores the social meanings that can be derived from how women talk about their experiences. Smith (1997) is concerned to stress that her position is not to argue for a feminist standpoint that in consequence will justify feminist knowledge. Rather, she is arguing for attention to be paid to women's standpoint. By this she means that the actualities of women's lives are sites through which 'concepts and theories are examined for how they are activated in organizing social relations' (ibid.: 395).

The critiques of early versions of standpoint theory draw on developments in feminism in terms of identity politics and the influence of postmodern and poststructural theorizing. One of the most important of these has been a focus on the relationship between reality and experience that in turn invokes notions of truth. All standpoint theorists stress how problematic the idea is that we can access reality directly through experience. However, this is not to say that standpoint theorists necessarily deny that there are truths – or as Harding (1997) suggests, 'less false beliefs'. Ramazanoglu and Holland (1999: 382) describe the theoretical contestation over the place of experience in feminist theory as placing academic feminism 'between the unacceptable rock of extreme positivism and the unacceptable hard place of extreme relativism'. This is a useful analogy to portray the parameters of debate within which there will be a variety of positions although we do have to recognize that the meanings of positivism and relativism are themselves highly contestable and subject to a number of subtle other meanings. Indeed, the very nature of a dualistic framework is both its strength and problem. It is a problem because our repetitious use of dualism maintains its hegemony. In this respect Davies (1997b) remarks on the seemingly inescapable nature of binaried language in terms that even as we attempt to move beyond it, we can also be viewed as re-creating it. Yet I have not tried to escape binaries here. Rather, I have opted for a dualistic framework precisely because it is so fully inscribed within our language; dualistic frameworks are useful ready-made aids to understanding. In this regard they are heuristic and facilitate the organization of disparate and insistently untidy positions.

At the more positivistic ends of the Ramazanoglu and Holland's continuum, early versions of feminist standpoint theory suggested that reality could be accessed through political struggle and, in consequence, that there is a 'real' reality (Guba and Lincoln, 1994) to be known. This knowledge of the 'real' reality would show us the truth of social relations. Deconstructionist and discursive analyses occupy the extreme relativistic point of Ramazanoglu and Holland's continuum. For example, within poststructural theorizing Goodman and Martin (2002) comment that by undermining the notion of a coherent identity, performative views of gender of necessity trouble the category of experience. Thus, as Goodman and Martin note, rather than there being a fully constituted experiencing subject to whom experiences happen, experience is the site of subject formation. Scott (1992: 37) offers a classic statement in this regard when she comments that 'experience is at once always already an interpretation and is in need of interpretation'. The attention that is given here to the role of language as constructing rather than describing reality suggests that 'Experience is not something which language reflects. In so far as it is meaningful, experience is constituted in language' (Weedon, 1997: 81). As consciousness-raising has evidenced, by drawing on different ideas to express our experiences we can change its meanings. This suggests that if experience is a phenomenon of language, then our focus should change from looking at experiences themselves as evidence of reality and toward looking at how discourse and representation are constituting experiences (Maynard, 1998). While such a view is important in highlighting 'the constructed quality of memory and experience' (Martin, 2001: 170), Ramazanoglu and Holland's concerns are that to follow this position to its ultimate conclusion we can be led to a 'point of political indifference' (1999: 382). In part, this is because if overwhelming weight is given to a subjectivist stance on social reality, meaning 'is imposed on the object by the subject' (Crotty, 1998: 9). In such a view we simply keep reinventing reality through, for example, new forms of expression. Truth thereby also becomes an invention or another story.

This slippage between conceptualizations of reality and truth is central to contemporary political debate in feminism. As a politics feminism cannot avoid making truth claims for without them there would be no point of mobilization. However, for Ramazanoglu and Holland there remain considerable concerns around propensities to relativism that arise from postmodern perspectives. One area where such concerns are evidenced is in respect of contemporary debates about standpoint theory. Here we find the reassertion of the value of 'the power of argument' (Walby, 2000a) and the Weberian ideal type (Hekman, 1997; 1999). We also find the development of new moral concepts. For example, Assiter (2000: 337) argues for feminists to pay attention to 'emancipatory value' through which recognition is given to the needs and values that arise from our 'common humanity' and thereby contribute to removing oppressive power relations.

Despite the variety of positions within feminism on theorizing and conceptualizing experience, Griffiths (1995) draws attention to the common threads that can be found. These include paying attention to issues of values and power; the situated nature of knowledge; the role of theory; and the processual nature of knowledge. Thus Griffiths summarizes feminist epistemologies in the following terms:

- Because all feminist analyses of experience are responding to women's position in society as devalued, silenced or oppressed, they all have a moral and political stance. This means that although there is disagreement as to how they might be conceptualized or what is important, 'values' and 'power' are organizing concepts in any analysis of experience. In this, therefore, facts cannot be separated from values.
- There is no view from 'nowhere'. That is there is no 'outside', 'objective' position that can be taken. All knowledge is situated in the knower. The self, or a particular subjective position, is, therefore, the first step in formulating a feminist perspective.
- Despite considerable debate within feminism about the role of theory, all analyses of experience require engagement with theorizing. This may be no more than systematic reflection or it may lead to Grand Theory.
- Knowledge is not fixed, static or stable but should be seen much more as a spiral from which new knowledge, principles and structures emerge in a never-ending process.

To explore the terrain that Griffiths summarizes the structure of this chapter mirrors something of Ramazanoglu and Holland's (1999) concerns. I begin by outlining the key ideas of Hartsock's (1983; 1997) feminist standpoint theory. This enables me to illustrate something of the positivistic end of the rock-and-hard-place continuum noted by Ramazanoglu and Holland. The section that follows is designed to stress the standpoint view that the simple fact of having an experience is an insufficient basis on which to make claims to warrantable knowledge. This is an important point to note in respect of procedures that are used for the analysis of experience in social research. Here I discuss the central notion that standpoint has to be achieved through critical reflection, theorization and political struggle.

The second part of the chapter is primarily concerned with the challenge of postmodernist relativism. Here I outline Haraway's (1985; 1997a) conceptualization of feminist standpoint through her metaphor of the cyborg. Haraway's cyborg metaphor is viewed as bringing together postmodern and standpoint theorizing (Hekman, 1999; Walby, 2001a; Weedon, 1999). It is therefore extremely useful in illustrating how issues of multilocationality and the narrativization of experience are central to postmodern theorizing. In the fourth and final section of this chapter I turn to more contemporary debates about standpoint and the role of the personal. The feminist theorists discussed here are concerned with issues of truth and relativity and with ways of avoiding relativist and subjectivist positions. For example, Hekman (1999) has argued that it is wrong to assume that postmodernist and poststructuralist developments have left standpoint theory outmoded and irrelevant. This is because the justification that feminist knowledge provides the truth of social reality remains central to feminist politics. My discussion here focuses primarily on the arguments presented by Walby (2000a, b; 2001a, b) and Moi (1999).

The Materialism of Standpoint

In particular, I will suggest that, like the lives of proletarians according to Marxian theory, women's lives make available a particular and privileged vantage point on male supremacy, a vantage point that can ground a powerful critique of the phallocratic institutions and ideology that constitute the capitalist form of patriarchy . . . I will suggest that the sexual division of labor forms the basis for such a standpoint and will argue that, on the basis of the structures that define women's activity as contributors to subsistence and as mothers, one could begin, though not complete, the construction of such an epistemological tool. I hope to show how just as Marx's understanding of the world from the standpoint of the proletariat enabled him to go beneath bourgeois ideology, so a feminist standpoint can allow us to understand patriarchal institutions and ideologies as perverse inversions of more humane social relations.

(Hartsock, 1997: 463)

Originally published in 1983, Hartsock's essay offers a classic exposition of the role and value of experience for feminist politics. Hartsock's analysis is an adaptation of Marxist historical materialism that focuses on the centrality of class relations to capitalism. Hennessy and Ingraham (1997) indicate that materialist feminism grew out of Western Marxism and is a term that came to prominence in the late 1970s (see also Jackson, 2001; Landry and MacLean, 1993). Materialist feminism arose through 'the conjuncture of several discourses – historical materialism, marxist and radical feminism, as well as postmodern and psychoanalytic theories of meaning and subjectivity (Hennessy and Ingraham, 1997: 7). Hartsock's essay draws on analyses of the gendered division of labour and object-relations psychoanalytic theories of socialization to argue that women's experiences of being outside the dominant order can give them a privileged knowledge of social reality.

Meyers (1997) notes that what was significant about feminist standpoint theory was its grounding in women's experiences of the sexual division of labour and how it could be read as an attempt to universalize these experiences to all women. In this, Hartsock's essay draws on a number of themes that were resonant more generally at the time within second-wave materialist feminist debates. For example, Hartsock makes the case for understanding how women's household labour produces use-values for capitalism. Yet she goes further than this to suggest that women's experiences of this form of production are distinctive from the experiences of workers who produce goods for sale in the market place. The experience of motherhood as an institution, rather than simply just through individual and personal experience, creates the relational self. Thus:

Women as mothers, even more than as workers, are institutionally involved in processes of change and growth and, more than workers, must understand the importance of avoiding excessive control in order to help others grow . . . Motherhood in the large sense, i.e. motherhood as an institution rather than experience, including pregnancy and the preparation for motherhood almost all female children receive as socialization, results in the construction of female existence as centred on a complex relational nexus. (1997: 470)

Hartsock highlights how the concept of standpoint 'posits a duality of levels of reality, of which the deeper level or essence both includes and explains the "surface" or appearance, and indicates the logic by means of which the appearance inverts and distorts the deeper reality' (ibid.: 464). There are two key points here (Meyers, 1997). First, that the experience of oppression is both denied by the dominant ideology and invisible to the more advantaged people in a society. Second, that this knowledge or understanding of the reality of social relations within capitalism must be worked for at an intellectual level and through political practice. Hartsock suggests that there are five aspects to standpoint theory that are central to epistemological and political claims. These are:

1 Material life both structures and sets limits on our understanding of social relations.
2 Given the above statement, and because material life is structured in opposing ways for women and men, our view of social reality is similarly differentiated. This 'differential male and female life activity in class society leads on the one hand toward a feminist standpoint and on the other toward an abstract masculinity' (ibid.: 472). This means that those in a dominant position (i.e. men) will have a partial and perverse view of social reality.
3 It is inadequate just to dismiss as false the view of the ruling class (i.e. men) because it structures the material relations within which we live and have to work from.
4 Because of the dominance of masculine views, the truth of social relations and change must be struggled for through the use of social analysis and education. Thus, 'The ability to go beneath the surface of appearances to reveal the real but concealed social relations requires both theoretical and political activity' (ibid.: 478). Necessary theoretical developments would include a systematic critique of Marxism. Political activity would be focused on ending gendered divisions of labour.
5 The adoption of a standpoint exposes 'reality' as inhuman and is therefore potentially liberatory.

The political implications of women's experiences of connected knowledge and relationality are, according to Hartsock, central to the development of a new kind of social order:

Generalizing the activity of women to the social system as a whole would raise, for the first time in human history, the possibility of a fully human community, a community structured by connection rather than separation and opposition. One can conclude then that women's life activity does form the basis of a specifically feminist materialism, a materialism that can provide a point from which both to critique and to work against phallocratic ideology and institutions. (ibid.: 478)

The Achievement of Standpoint

Whilst personal experience undoubtedly influences one's perspective and understanding, many current references to it are determinist and essentialist. Experience/identity is substituted for, or deemed to be equivalent to, politics, as if critical awareness and understanding are inscribed on a person through forms of oppression, with an implicit or explicit presumption that such awareness is inaccessible to those who have not 'lived' such experiences. Whilst not seeking to deny differences in experience, critical consciousness involves developing a perspective on, a politics of, experience . . . One does not have to have experienced an event or a form of oppression in order to attempt to develop 'committed understanding'.

(Kelly et al., 1994: 30)

Because of the privileging of experience in feminism it is often thought that one must give precedence to the accounts of those individuals who have had direct experience of specific forms of oppressive relations. Arising from their experiences such individuals are perceived to offer a more accurate reflection of social reality. As a corollary to this it is also suggested that those who have not had such experiences cannot speak for, and cannot know, the 'real truth' of such social relations. One of the problems of such an argument is that it gives epistemic privilege to those who have direct insights and knowledge of the practices of their own contexts and those of their oppressors (Narayan, 1998; see also de Lauretis, 1997). Another problem is that it can lead us to think that direct access to an experience is sufficient for political consciousness.

Sprague (2001) comments that a significant misreading of standpoint theory is the idea that simply having an experience, say, of racism or sexism, is sufficient to claim warrantable knowledge. Sprague suggests that this has arisen because of a conflation between subjectivity and social location. For example, Narayan (1998) notes that although non-Western women may be located between two or more incompatible frameworks or perspectives on social reality this does not automatically lead to a critical stance on social relations. Similarly Sudbury (1998: 29–30) comments that there is no guarantee that sharing the same location as the researched will facilitate the production of 'truth'. She remarks: 'the fact of being a black woman researcher does not guarantee a more accurate understanding or representation of racism and oppression' (ibid.).

The achievement of a new feminist social order and knowledge of the reality of gendered relationships within capitalism that Hartsock (1997) credited standpoint theory with cannot be achieved solely through a focus on documenting women's experiences. Sprague comments in this respect: 'A standpoint is *not* how folks in a particular social location think. This point has been reaffirmed by many, if not all, of the major standpoint theorists since Hartsock took pains to specifically distinguish a standpoint from the spontaneous consciousness of social actors' (2001: 529, emphasis in original). A standpoint can only be achieved through forms of critical consciousness, reflexivity and struggle. As Sprague indicates, many of those who are defined as standpoint theorists have pointed out in various ways that standpoint is an *achievement*.

The classic commentary in this regard is that of Harding (1987) who distinguishes between feminist empiricism and feminist standpoint. Harding argues that feminist empiricism has been the main challenge to the hegemonic nature of social science as disinterested, apolitical and objective and has highlighted the masculine bias in research. However, paradoxically, it has also upheld the belief that social science *should* be objective. This has arisen from feminist empiricists' claims that the inclusion of women as both researchers and research subjects ameliorates or repairs the previous biases of male-only social science. The logical conclusion from this is that social research will be less biased and more objective through the inclusion of women's experiences and perspectives.

In contrast, Harding claims that it is not simply a question of adding women in that will create the necessary knowledge structures for a radical epistemology. This is because such an approach does not represent a challenge to existing theories of how we understand social reality given that these are based on masculine hegemony. Here standpoint theorists justify their claims of producing less distorted, and preferable, accounts of social reality though recourse to Hegelian, and subsequently Marxian, theorization that material life sets limits on human understanding. Because of this, one cannot simply claim to know the truth of experience. Knowledge only emerges through the struggles that the oppressed wage against their oppressors (Harding, 1987). A feminist standpoint is, therefore, not a perspective but an achievement . . . To achieve a feminist standpoint one must engage in the intellectual and political struggle necessary to see nature and social life from the point of view of that disdained activity which produces women's social experiences instead of from the partial and perverse perspective available from the 'ruling gender' experience of men. (ibid.: 185)

In this Harding (1991) argued for 'strong objectivity' as a hallmark of feminist research. To take up the position of 'strong objectivity', one does value the other's perspective but one does not 'go native' or merge oneself with the researched. Rather, one seeks to consider the particularity of cultural location from a critical distance. Or as Haraway also comments:

A standpoint is not an empiricist appeal to or by 'the oppressed' but a cognitive, psychological, and political tool for more adequate knowledge judged by the nonessentialist, historically contingent, situated standards of strong objectivity. Such a standpoint is the always fraught but necessary fruit of the *practice* of oppositional and differential consciousness. (1997b: 198–9, emphasis in original)

In developing her analysis of Black feminist thought, Collins (1989; 1990; 1997) gives a significant role to Black feminist scholars to look for points of synthesis and common themes between what appear to be competing epistemologies or ways of knowing. This is because, Collins argues, solely producing alternative knowledge claims or counter-discourses is insufficient. In this respect she argues that counter-knowledge claims are 'rarely threatening to conventional knowledge. Such claims are routinely ignored, discredited, or simply absorbed and marginalized in existing paradigms' (Collins, 1997: 773). Similarly, Smith comments on the importance of theorization and analysis and the role of the sociologist by distinguishing 'experience' from 'perspective':

Let me make it clear that when I speak of 'experience' I do not use the term as a synonym for 'perspective.' Nor in proposing a sociology grounded in the sociologist's actual experience, am I recommending the self-indulgence of inner exploration or any other enterprise with self as sole focus and object . . . the sociologist's investigation of our directly experienced world as a problem is a mode of discovering or rediscovering the society from within. She begins from her own original but tacit knowledge and from within the acts by which she brings it into her grasp in making it observable and in understanding how it works. She aims not at a reiteration of what she already (tacitly) knows, but at an exploration through that of what passes beyond it and is deeply implicated in how it is. (1987: 92–3)

Case Study 15: Respectable Knowledge: Experience and Interpretation*

Skeggs (1997) uses an ethnographic approach to her exploration of class and gender. She spent three years undertaking intensive participant observation and a further eight years keeping in touch with a group of working-class women who had taken a 'care' course in an English further education college. Her theoretical framework draws on post-structural theorizing and Bourdieu's concept of economic, cultural, symbolic and social capitals. Skeggs illustrates how key social divisions frame our possibilities and our access to these capitals. Her research is therefore a very useful illustration of how social mobility is restricted because of the effects of spatial framing such as those of class and gender.

Skeggs gives a very detailed account of the methodological processes and dilemmas that she faced in undertaking this work. One of those dilemmas was in respect of how she should analyse the stated experiences and perspectives of her research respondents. In particular, Skeggs notes that 'the women did not want their actions interpreted as class responses for this reproduced the position they wanted to disassociate from' (ibid.: 30). However, Skeggs also notes that 'their rejection of class did not lead me to abandon it. In fact, it did the opposite. It heightened my sensitivity to its ubiquity and made me construct theories to explain their responses' (ibid.).

Although Skeggs accepts that her respondents' understandings of class are real for them, Skeggs is taking a 'standpoint' on how to understand the experiences of class in respect of the women in her research. In support of her position Skeggs draws in part on Scott (1992: 25) who offers a poststructural theorization of experience through which she argues that 'we need to attend to the historical processes that, through discourse, position subjects and produce their experiences'. Skeggs notes, therefore, how the researcher and the researched have access to different discursive resources and configurations that in turn may produce different knowledge. She also notes that the accounts of her respondents 'are just as partial as my selections' (ibid.: 28) and that 'the process of continual selection and monitoring further contributes to the challenges to the belief that experience is an origin or foundation of knowledge that is more immediate and trustworthy than secondary knowledges' (ibid.: 29).

In part, Skeggs also draws support from the idea of researcher responsibility and accountability (see, for example, Code, 1995). She comments in this respect: 'Standpoint theory has . . . made it clear that there is no such thing as a disinterested knower and that the positions from which we speak (and how we speak) are a product of our positioning vis-à-vis forms of capital and that this informs what we decide is worthy of study' (ibid.: 26–7). Sprague (2001: 534) also comments in this respect that 'Standpoint theory, as I interpret it, identifies the authority of our experience as scholars and calls us to take responsibility for how we exercise the social power that we have. Rejecting our own authority is, from this perspective, intellectually irresponsible, as well as politically naïve.' Thus Skeggs notes:

> We cannot know ourselves so how can we expect to be the absolute knower of others, although we can be vigilant, responsible and critical? As the writer, I had the ultimate power of production but my interpretations were not produced without consultation and discussion. Rather than change my analysis to fit the analysis of the women of the research . . . I want to make a claim for using the interpretations produced through dialogue, but over which I have ultimate responsibility and which are generated in relation to the research questions I investigated. (1997: 30)

Note:
* This is the title of the methodology chapter in Skeggs (1997).

Cyborg Standpoints

> what people are experiencing [in this global world order] is not transparently clear, and we lack sufficiently subtle connections for collectively building effective theories of experience. Present efforts – Marxist, psychoanalytic, feminist, anthropological – to clarify even 'our' experience are rudimentary.
>
> (Haraway, 1997a: 519)

Alongside Benhabib's (1992) exile and Braidotti's (1994) nomad, Haraway's (1985; 1991; 1997a) cyborg is a construction of the postmodern subject. This subject is unlike the humanist subject of standpoint theory who is unified, fixed and, with the requisite degree of critical consciousness, can access and theorize her 'experience'. The cyborg is the multiply located subject of the global order. Haraway's construction of this subject starts from the premise that our experiences are constructed through the concepts that we have available to us and contemporary theories are insufficient to the task of adequately offering explanatory frameworks for understanding these. In saying this Haraway recognizes the political importance of validating women's experiences of their daily lives. However, she is critical of the totalizing tendencies of standpoint theory that suggest a shared experience of womanhood. Indeed, one of Haraway's major purposes is to illustrate how the production of universalistic theories misses the diversity of experiences and realities in a postmodern, global age of informatics.

Haraway locates the development of standpoint theory within a narrative framework that takes account of the historical discursive political necessities of its time. She therefore argues that the conceptualization of feminist standpoint should be perceived as fiction, albeit necessary, to the political context within which it was generated. Haraway comments on how it was politically necessary for feminists to construct 'women's experience' as a totalizing concept because of the invisibility of women in main/malestream science. This construction facilitated the visibility of, and recognition of the salience of, women's experiences. However, what is necessary in a postmodern global order is another kind of story that will engage the imagination and construct the possibilities for liberation. The cyborg is, therefore, both a politically motivated imaginative device and an alternative story about women's experiences. In particular, Haraway urges us 'to consider how humanity might have a figure outside the narratives of humanism. What language . . . would such a "posthumanist" figure speak?' (Brah, 1999: 5).

The aim of the metaphor of cyborg is to illustrate how postmodern feminist epistemology can be synthesized with standpoint epistemology. This is achieved through an exploration of multiple viewpoints and locations. In this way Haraway is not suggesting that the cyborg should be viewed as a totalizing theory in terms that all women experience the world in this way. Rather, she is stressing the situated and perspectival nature of knowledge (Hekman, 1999). Haraway therefore uses the cyborg as a narrative or story that points us towards a post-gender world. In this regard the cyborg is an alternative story to that offered by standpoint theorists through which Haraway does not discard our prior understandings but builds on them in order to enable women to construct their own experiences. Haraway draws on the fractured identities and plurality of feminisms. She says that she wishes to 'sketch a picture of possible unity' (1997a: 511) that draws on socialist and feminist principles of design. Thus Haraway:

> assumes that our picture of reality is a picture that includes some experiences but excludes others. She also assumes that in order to alter

this picture, another picture must be constructed, and that this picture, like the picture it replaces, is political . . . Haraway assumes that the picture that feminism constructs must be intelligible in terms of the old picture, even as it transforms it. (Hekman, 1999: 141)

In addition, Haraway suggests that the transgressive nature of cyborg imagery offers a way of moving beyond dualisms. Haraway illustrates this through the positive and negative features of the cyborg metaphor. By using a technological metaphor Haraway argues that we should not simply reject and demonize technology. From one perspective a cyborg world may imply being caught up in a grid of control over the planet and as a sign of masculinist and capitalist appropriation of women's bodies. However, from another perspective, Haraway argues that the cyborg signifies how people are not afraid to acknowledge their joint kinship with animals and machines. They are also not afraid of partial identities and contradictory standpoints. However, as Haraway argues, 'The political struggle is to see from both perspectives at once because each reveals domination and possibilities unimaginable from the other vantage points' (1997a: 506–7). The cyborg metaphor therefore encourages us to engage in the task of reconstructing 'the boundaries of daily life, in partial connection with others, in communication with all of our parts' (ibid.: 525). In consequence, the cyborg is multiplicity and contradiction, requires connection but rejects universalism and has no fear of merging the boundaries of the social, technological and natural. In this way the cyborg:

is a dream not of a common language, but of a powerful infidel heteroglossia. It is an imagination of a feminist speaking in tongues to strike fear into the circuits of the supersavers of the new Right. It means both building and destroying machines, identities, categories, relationships, spaces, stories. Though both are bound in the spiral dance, I would rather be a cyborg than a goddess. (ibid.)

Case Study 16: Theorizing Young Asian Women's Experiences

Shain (2000: 159) argues that an analysis of young Asian women's experiences means that 'race, gender, class and age divisions cannot be mechanically added or reduced to one or other of the divisions'. For this reason, Shain's research focuses on 'the complex reality of the lived experiences of young Asian women with reference to the intersections of that experience with educational institutions and frameworks'. Shain's research is based on semi-structured interviews that were conducted with 44 British-born Asian girls of Pakistani, Bangladeshi and Indian descent. Her theoretical framework would be described as broadly postcolonial and specifically it draws on Gramscian concepts of historical specificity, articulation and hegemony.

Shain notes:

> Since the experiences of young women are shaped by a multiplicity of factors . . . their responses to the situations in which they find themselves will also vary. These depend upon particular relationships between the various structural factors that shape their experiences, and also upon the subjective experience of these situations. Young women of similar religious backgrounds located in the same region within Britain, whose parents originate from the same region in Pakistan, may define their experiences of school in very different ways. This may relate to the class position of their respective families in Britain, or to the gender patterns within their households. (ibid.: 161)

For example, Shain illustrates how young women's responses to racism at school varied in terms of whether these would be perceived as mediated by a desire for survival or resistance. Nevertheless, Shain also notes that primarily their responses remained at the level of the individual rather than collective struggle. However, Shain argues:

> Although their responses were not revolutionary, the strategies of the young women cannot be viewed simply as reproductions of the apparently static cultures that are handed down to them (as in cultural pathology frameworks). Instead they reveal that young Asian women are involved in creating and shaping new identities for themselves which draw on both the various residual cultures of their parents' traditions and on the local and regional cultures that they currently inhabit. (ibid.: 171)

The Relativity of Experience

> There is then a difference between claiming that experience does not give us the truth, and concluding that experience cannot tell us anything except stories.
>
> (Ramazanoglu and Holland, 1999: 387)

Maynard (1994) comments that Harding's (1987) conceptualization of 'strong objectivity' includes a critical scrutiny of the researcher's own beliefs and cultural agendas. Indeed, one of the strong messages that come from assertions that standpoint perspectives are achieved rather than pre-given is that researchers have to develop a high level of skill in being critically reflexive. Reflexivity here does not mean merely thinking about something or turning events over in your mind. Reflexivity in this view means 'the ways in which our portrayals of social realities simultaneously describe and constitute [those] realities' (Miller, 1997: 25; see also May, 1998). Putting the researcher into the research, through, say, autobiographical notes or the use of 'I', signals how the knowledge produced is located in the perspectives of the researcher. It therefore signals how 'writing the personal [is] a political act' (Thomas and Webb, 1999: 29). It also gives a warning about the objectivity of the account by indicating the role of subjectively located knowledges. However, there are concerns that the turn to the relativism of the subjective and the personal has gone too far. There are two issues that arise here that I wish to discuss. First, there is a problem with a relativist view that all perspectives are equally viable in that it removes 'any vantage point from which to argue the superiority of its own case' (Walby, 2001a: 495). Second, there is the question of which aspects of locationality are significant and indeed if locationality always matters (Moi, 1999).

Walby (2001a, b) notes that no-one today is either an absolutist or a relativist about claims to truth. In this she is recognizing that social theorists do not occupy the extreme poles that constitute the rock of positivism and the hard place of relativism. For example, Ramazanoglu and Holland (1999: 388) stress that 'It is perfectly possible to insist that knowledge is in practice informed by accounts of experience without insisting either that experience simply tells the truth, or that theory/language constitutes all that experience is.' For all its lack of modern certainty, feminism does, therefore, claim to tell more than a few 'truths' about social relations. Feminism is not a relativistic creed in terms of its metanarratives about the power relations that arise from major social divisions. Nevertheless, giving proper and equal respect to experiences of diversity can lead to a subjectivist position that Sprague (2001) remarks is how standpoint epistemology has been popularly transformed.

One way that Walby (2000a; 2001a) links her concern about relativism is through Haraway's (1997a) storying of feminist standpoint. In this respect Walby (2001a: 489) asks 'Is "story telling" really the best that feminist social science can offer?' In response, Walby argues that the 'retreat from modernism, rationality, and science is mistaken' (ibid.). Walby's (2000a; 2001a) position draws on the following points. First, she argues that the critique of science that arises from standpoint theorization is over-simplified and sets up a stereotype. Science is neither as certain and positivistic nor as monolithic in its practices as feminist critiques of science have suggested. Rather, 'Modern scholarship within the sociology of science has shown that science-in-the making is based on constant questioning and internal critique, with knowledge claims contested – always considered provisional – and "facts" constantly being created' (2001a: 493).

Second, postmodern accounts of experience argue that our certainties should rest on the uncertainty that all knowledge is partial and located. This sets up the idea of incommensurability through which we have so little in common that we are unable to speak to each other. Walby is concerned to illustrate that individuals belong to overlapping communities through which they hold certain canons in common. In part, Walby illustrates this by arguing that, although some feminists may deny the modernism of their accounts, they 'smuggle in modernist assumptions' (ibid.: 494). Thus 'Even as they condemn "science," they actually use core aspects of its methods' (ibid.). These aspects include retaining the possibility that it is possible to evaluate knowledge claims and the superiority of a feminist method.

Third, Walby (2000b; 2001a, b) is concerned at the propensity within feminist theory to study up from the everyday experiences of women, to use qualitative approaches and the domination of feminist theory by philosophical and literary disciplines. She seeks to make a case for scientific method that she defines as 'the testing of knowledge claims against evidence and other theories' (2000b: 238). This is because Walby considers that debates within feminist theory are often under-supported by evidence and that 'Debates on questions of "what works" to change things would be improved if we had more evidence, in particular if we had more reliably comparative evidence' (ibid.). This may 'mean statistical analysis of a large and complex data set. It may mean high theory. [However] Scientific arguments are too complex for the stricture of starting from everyday lives to be appropriate' (2001b: 540).

Walby's (2001a: 503) goal is therefore for the development of a 'realist methodology, developing theories and methods that involve observations predicated on the assumption that there is a world out there that ultimately acts as a check, as a form of resistance, to the development of theory'. One of her aims here is to facilitate ways through which feminist knowledge claims can be more widely accepted. In this respect Walby argues that there is now no need to accept a marginal status for feminism, to be defensive or to reject any claims to scientific status. This is because it is widely accepted within broader scientific communities that all knowledge is provisional and open to doubt. Thus if we are to constantly stress that all feminist knowledge claims have to be seen as partial or located then we are admitting to unnecessary caveats and these will be used in the wider world to downgrade any research findings.

Walby argues that we have to put rationality and reason at the centre of our methodologies. One way in which we might do this is to reject the idea that all knowledge claims should be reduced to interests. In saying this, Walby is not suggesting that science is free from interests. Rather, she is saying that '"Reality" is not so readily subjugated to interests' (2001b: 538). Walby's position here rests on two conceptual pairs: argument–theory and persuasion–politics. Walby uses a Habermasian notion of 'argumentation' that she associates with theory. Theory here is defined as 'an attempt to explain the nature and complexities of gender inequality' (2000b: 238). Her conceptualization of argument includes the idea that there exists a consensual or widely accepted set of core principles about how to proceed. Walby seeks to demonstrate how everyday rationality is present in scientific argument through which evidence and theory are debated, evaluated and ultimately build knowledge. In terms of her linkage of persuasion–politics, Walby suggests that this relies on a different set of principles and these draw on moral and ethical exhortation. Walby accepts that in terms of political change moral and ethical stories have an important place. However, for Walby this is an insufficient basis for a broader acceptance of feminist theory.

There are several responses to Walby's position (see Felski, 2000; Harding, 2001; Knapp, 2000; Phoenix, 2000; Sprague, 2001). These generally indicate a concern that her account is overly rationalistic and overly homogenizing of the variety of positions and debates that surround the concepts of experience and standpoint. However, Walby is not alone in her concern to explore issues of argumentation. Moi (1999) is also concerned about the implications that arise from a feminist stress on the interests and perspectives that arise from locationality. Like Walby, she is critical of some forms of poststructural theorizing and the density of some theoretical languages. Moi is not, however, situating her critique within standpoint theories *per se*. Also she is not arguing the case for the scientific method. Along with other feminists, one of her concerns is the 'uncritical embrace of the personal and the subjective and an equally uncritical dismissal of the impersonal and the objective' (1999: 161). I shall illustrate Moi's responses to this concern with two examples from her text. These are the case of *ad feminam* arguments where Moi considers if and when locationality is significant and her analysis of the usefulness of some meanings of objectivity.

There are two statements in Moi's discussion on these issues that appear to me highly relevant to understanding Moi's position. These statements are that 'The personal is not the enemy of serious thought' (ibid.: 136) and there is a 'difference between claiming, as psycho-analysis does, that there is subjectivity in every belief, and claiming that every belief is purely subjective' (ibid.: 149). Moi's discussion of *ad feminam* and *ad hominem* statements is designed to illustrate how we must undertake a serious appraisal of the relevancy and purposes of why we might be concerned with an individual's location, context or speaking position. This will enable us to distinguish between an attack on the person and an attack on the argument.

Moi states: 'To argue *ad feminam* or *ad hominem* is to attack the person who makes the argument one detests, rather than the argument itself, usually in order to move the audience, to stir their passions against this abhorrent person' (ibid.: 138). The common sexist form of this is to state 'you say that because you are a woman' (ibid.). Moi notes that this is hardly an honourable intellectual approach and quite often backfires. However, Moi also comments how the recent emphasis in feminist debate about the importance of the personal has led to con-fusion. As she remarks: 'Nothing is less contentious among US literary critics today than the claim that someone's race, class, sex, sexuality, nationality, and individual experiences (of sexual abuse, rape, and racism, but also other, more innocuous experiences) affect his or her understanding of the world' (ibid.: 142). Moi is concerned with how we can avoid turning these locational shorthands into reductive and irrelevant statements that lead us to dismiss someone and their work out of hand. For example, we might be led to say 'He would say that because he is a White middle-class male' or be viewed as rejecting/ accepting a position because 'She is a heterosexual English woman'. To do this, Moi begins with the question of whether location or speaking position is always as relevant as we now appear to think it is. Principally Moi is arguing that it is not. For example, Moi asks whether we should find Judith Butler's and Luce Irigaray's respective use of Plato in *Bodies that Matter* and *Speculum of the Other Woman* problematic. This is because 'both return to Plato in order to discuss sex and gender without even mentioning the effect of his speech acts in Greek fifth-century BC society, and without saying anything about their own "location"' (ibid.: 144). Thus, if location is always relevant:

> Ought these women to have spent lots of time uncovering the effects of Plato's . . . interventions in [his] own time and society? Should they not, at the very least, have discussed the potential effects of rereading Plato in

their own time and society. If one thinks that location is *always relevant*, the answer has to be yes. (ibid.: 144, emphasis in original)

However, as Moi notes, this would be absurd and limiting. It also places too much power in the speaker to subjugate another's meaning. Moreover, we have not found it problematic that Butler and Irigaray have paid no heed to the locational aspects of Plato's texts on this occasion. This leaves us, however, with the question of when it is relevant to recognize the situated nature of knowledge. Here Moi accepts the case that power relations are relevant in this regard but she also comments that:

> All speech acts do not take place in situations of unambiguous domination. The fact that some do is no reason to claim that we must always analyse the location and position of an utterance. Even when a speech act does take place in a situation of domination, this is not always the most important thing to say about it. One still needs to give some reasons for such claims, not simply postulate them as obviously true. (ibid.: 145)

For Moi it is incumbent on us to illustrate why location is significant to any analysis. It is absolutely insufficient to invoke locationality simply because it has acquired a must-do prescriptive status. This requires us to undertake a 'fair-minded reading of the text in question' (ibid.: 147). This includes carefully establishing patterns of, say, racism or classism and then to make appropriate judgements about how issues of locationality contribute to our argument or understanding. Certainly where 'a problem of interpretation or evaluation has arisen . . . we do need to look at who is speaking, what was said, to whom it was said, under what circumstances it was said, and so on' (ibid.: 146).

In her continuing exploration of issues of locationality Moi next turns to the rise of the personal in academic debate. She notes how the personal has been placed on the positive side of a binary opposition with objectivity occupying the negative. Moi notes of course how there are varied ways in which individuals signal the personal, from brief statements about their ethnicity to expressing a liking for cappuccino and from full-blown quasi-autobiographical accounts to the use of the first person pronoun. However, overall she is concerned that 'nobody seemed to think that subjectivity can become a prison-house from which a few moments of impersonality could offer a delightful respite' (ibid.: 155). Her discussion is therefore focused on rejecting the claim that either objectivity does not exist or that it can be given no useful meaning (see also Hawkesworth, 1989).

Moi draws on the work of Cora Diamond who sets out to distinguish between strong and weak versions of the claim that all knowledge is gendered and that women's experiences give rise to a different view of reality. Diamond offers a contextualized analysis of experience that looks at different forms of objectivity in varied domains. One example that Moi uses from Diamond's work is the standard scientific conceptualization of objectivity exemplified in the 'tornado model'. The model of knowledge that meteorologists use for understanding tornadoes uses technical instruments to obtain accurate measurements of wind speed and directional changes. To develop scientific laws about tornadoes meteorologists do not want to know 'what is it like to be in a tornado' (Diamond in Moi, 1999: 156) as this will not serve their purposes of having accurate measurements from which to build models. They therefore do not want to know about people's experiences of being in a tornado particularly as these will be influenced by that very experience. The experience that is required to develop the 'tornado model' is that related to the use of sophisticated instruments. Diamond describes the tornado model as impersonal. Other impersonal forms of knowledge are rail timetables and directions given when one is lost. Such knowledge is also portable. This is because the data can be used, compared, tested and evaluated by anyone. It can also be put to the service of anyone. Thus:

> It follows that it is actually immensely useful for revolutionaries to have impersonal knowledge lying around. This is precisely the kind of knowledge that can be picked up and put into the service of projects quite different from those which originally motivated the development of that knowledge in the first place . . . Some knowledge is actually gender-free, impersonal and neutral (Diamond's example is 7 + 5 = 12). Once we recognise this, we can go on to ask whose projects this knowledge serves. This is a question which will have different answers in different cases. One of the valuable insights emerging from a reading of Cora Diamond's unjustly neglected essay is that impersonal knowledge – the tornado model – may be put to feminist as well as to non-feminist use . . . To reject 'impersonal' or 'objective' knowledge is to reject a mode of knowledge that potentially can be made more democratically available to all than 'personal' knowledge, which per definition remains tied to the person who developed it. (ibid.: 158–9)

For Moi therefore we should not reject the 'impersonal' because we assume that it must be masculine or universalizing. Rather, we would be better off asking whether or not particular modes of knowledge are suitable for our specific purposes. And Moi makes the same, it appears to me Wittgensteinean, case for the personal when she states that:

only when the personal is in the service of original thought . . . do we experience it as illuminating rather than embarrassing. In my view, the claim that every speech act has something personal in it is true, but precisely for that reason it does not justify explicitly autobiographical writing any more or less than it justifies haughtily impersonal performances. In short, the effects of the personal will depend – on the context, on what the personal is taken to mean in any given case, and on the interests the personal performance is supposed to serve. (ibid.: 164)

Summary

Riley (1988: 100) comments that 'feminism can never wholeheartedly dismantle "women's experience"'. This is because the concept of experience has been central to the development of feminist theory and feminist politics. Although the debates about experience draw on the binary of subjectivity versus objectivity, I have suggested that what we find is a conceptual trinity of experience, reality and truth. In particular I have discussed the concept of experience through its theorization as standpoint. In developments of standpoint theory I have also sought to illustrate how, on the one hand, the impact of postmodern thought has contributed to a recognition of the multilocational nature of experience and, on the other, it has created concerns about incipient and creeping relativism. The discussion in this chapter has indicated how significant debate continues around the place of the personal in feminist theory and research with some arguing that the counter-discursive movement for the personal and against objectivity has gone too far.

FURTHER READING

Hekman, S. (1999) *The Future of Differences: Truth and Method in Feminist Theory.* Cambridge: Polity Press. Specifically Chapter 2 for a detailed review of standpoint theory.

Developing Conceptual Literacy 8

> The standard idea of a philosophical quibble concerns how thinkers
> answer or respond to a problem whose answer is seen as there to be
> found, as though the question or the problem were subordinate to
> some good reason that philosophy would simply recognise (rather
> than create) . . . But feminist questions have rarely taken this form.
> On the contrary, feminist questions and concepts ask what a
> philosophy might do, how it might activate life and thought, and
> how certain problems create (rather than describe) effects . . . When
> confronted with a theory or body of thought feminism has tended to
> ask an intensely active question, not 'What does it mean?' but 'How
> does it work?' What can this concept or theory do? How can such a
> theory exist or be lived? What are its forces?
>
> (Colebrook, 2000: 7)

Social scientific training encourages us to look for systematization,
linkage, unification, and synthesis. It encourages us to ask if there is
a founding principle that will provide an explanatory framework for
understanding. This is the case even perhaps where none exists. This has
certainly been an issue for me in charting the different meanings in this
text as I have asked what kind of inter-relationships, similarities and
distinctive features might be found. My concerns began in Chapter 1
where I outlined some of the ways in which we could explain debate
over meaning and its implications for feminist research and theory.
These explanatory frameworks included the Derridean notion of non-
fixity and deferral of meaning, the dualistic framings of language and
the role of deconstruction, Wittgenstein's focus on ordinary language
use and the importance of context and Connolly's (1993) and Tanesini's
(1994) analyses of essentially contested concepts.

Something more, however, remains to be said. I need to add one
further point to these analyses that I believe is particularly relevant to
understanding the often times passionate, and many times divisive,
nature of debate over meaning within feminism. This is that concerns
over meaning within feminism have never simply been about adding to

or adopting a previous body of knowledge. Feminist concerns over meaning have arisen because of the implications for what might become or what might be created if particular meanings are taken up. Colebrook (2000: 5) comments in this respect: 'Never a stable body of thought with a grounding axiom or system, feminism has addressed theory not merely in terms of what a philosopher might offer but also in terms of what feminism might become.' Understanding feminism as a politics of becoming illustrates how much is at stake when debates over meaning arise. This is the future. When we ask, as we did in Chapter 1, 'What is "woman"?', we are of course posing both an historical and a contemporary question. Our answer, though, must also be evaluated in terms of what woman might become and who she will be.

And so it is that in this final chapter I have one primary aim. This is to apply and extend these explanatory frameworks to the development of conceptual literacy. In this my first task is to offer a synthesis of the six concepts that have been explored in this text. This draws on the key points raised in Chapter 1 and to which I am now adding Colebrook (2000). Colebrook's primary concerns are to illustrate the value of Deleuze's thought for feminism. Here Colebrook argues that Deleuze offers an active and affirmative conceptualization of thought that recognizes the creative nature of conceptual formation. Central to this is that 'In its confrontation with chaos thought creates concepts – so that concepts are the effect of active thought, and not laws by which thought ought to proceed . . . thought must *reactivate* its concepts: see concepts in terms of effects' (2000: 8). What are the effects of the concepts in this text? Figure 8.1 lists the varied conceptualizations discussed in this text. I have provided a final column entitled Implications for a Becoming Feminism. My own response, below, should not be thought of as definitive and for this reason I have inserted question marks for you to consider as you think appropriate.

I conclude my response to what I consider are the effects of the concepts in this text by turning to a set of tasks for the development of conceptual literacy. I use this form of words carefully because I find myself in a somewhat countervalent position. It is here that I have to remind myself that in the Introduction to this text I argued for a view of learning that is linked to naiveté and openness. On the one hand, therefore, I am conscious that to offer a set of tasks can be read as supplying a closed technological system that may discourage further thought. Once we believe we have 'learnt' something, we may see no reason to continue to explore or challenge that learning. Among its other meanings, the term technology, and its associated phrase tool-kit, can convey a form of knowing that Kendall and Wickham (1999: 118)

Conceptualizations Discussed	Implications for a Becoming Feminism
Equality Equal and the same Equal but different Material (in)equality Group (in)equality Politics of recognition	?
Difference No difference Equal but different Identity/group differences Poststructural différance Sexual difference Postcolonial difference	?
Choice Structuring of choice by age, class, 'race', disability, sexuality The poststructural 'choosing' subject	?

Care
Woman as carer
Care as work – paid and unpaid
Care work as divided by 'race' and
  class
Care and disability rights
Ethics of care and deconstruction of
  rights discourses
	?

Time Linear male time Cyclical feminine time Time and subjectivity Time, space and body	?
Experience Unity of gendered experiences Experiences of 'race', class, sexuality, disability, age Politicized, reflexive experiences Cyborg experiences (Im)personal experiences	?

Figure 8.1   Conceptual summary

describe as similar to 'those do-it-yourself wall-filler products that promise certain results if you just "aim and squirt", at whatever surface you care to pick'. Kendall and Wickham are rightly concerned that such short-cuts will lead to disappointing and even disastrous results. Their message, which I would echo, is that, just as in home decorating, proper prior preparation is vitally important.

On the other hand, I am mindful of, and very sympathetic to, Alvesson and Skoldberg's comments:

> Postmodernist discussion of – or attempts at – empirical research are rather limited in character. There are a number of general arguments about how *not* to conduct, for instance, ethnographic research, but more concrete guidelines or example of how it *should* be pursued are as yet few and far between. Most authors calling themselves postmodernists maintain a negative approach in this context: like the critical theorists, they are much more articulate and specific about what they are *against* than about what they are *for*. (2000: 171, emphasis in original)

It appears to me that an ethically informed pedagogy will be as explicit as possible about the technologies and skills that can be applied to analysis and *may* be useful to others. Here I therefore outline some key tasks for developing conceptual literacy. These are related to the broader field of critical literacy where the primary objective is to remain open, rather than closed, to the political implications of multiple meaning.

Towards a Synthentic Account of the Development of Conceptual Meanings

> [A]rguing about what words (ought to) mean is not a trivial business – it is not 'mere words', 'hair-splitting', or 'just semantics' – when these arguments are over what I have called socially contested terms. Such arguments are what lead to the adoption of social beliefs and the theories behind them, and these theories and beliefs lead to social action and the maintenance and creation of social worlds.
>
> (Gee, 1996: 15–16)

I began this text by noting how much concern there is in social science discourse that we are not talking about the same thing at all in our use of key concepts. Multiple meaning and divergent conceptualization are seen as particular problems for ensuring the comparability and validity of research findings. They can also be highly debilitating for learners who lose their way in a morass of contestation and interpretation. In addition, such is the postmodern emphasis on truths, rather than Truth, that it would be all too easy to say that debate over meaning is mere semantics and 'hair-splitting' (ibid.). It would be all too easy indeed. This text takes a contrary view. This is that arguments over meaning should be appraised as political acts that are designed to shape how we *should* know our social worlds. They are enacted from implicit or explicit theoretical positions based upon implicit or explicit beliefs. The outcome of these debates affects how we might proceed from here. These procedures will be both theoretical and political and they will impact on policies and practices. There are five points that have been central to understanding this view of conceptual contestation. These are:

1 Indicators ascribed to concepts are not purely descriptive but are also *appraisive*. Accordingly, indicators are value-laden.
2 Meaning needs to be considered in relation to the *contextual and theoretical* field in which it is placed. Contestation over meaning will therefore vary because the same term can have different meanings due to underlying theorization or context of use.
3 Contestation over meaning affects the *validity and truth claims* that can be made for underlying theorization.
4 Contestation arises because of the *internal complexity* of some concepts. Some concepts form webs of connection, chains of meaning or clusters with other concepts.
5 The outcome of debate directs how a field of enquiry will develop in the *future*.

These five points provide the framework for the synthesis that I offer here. In this I shall begin with what I would identify as the mistress concept of feminism. This is difference. Felski (1997) has described difference as a doxa. Difference has become so pervasive within feminist thought that it has become an orthodoxy that must always be taken into account. Certainly I can place difference centre stage and state that if we examine the varied conceptualizations of each of the six concepts we will see that different theories of difference offer a linearity of development. In this respect I noted in Chapter 3 that a major narrative in feminism is that of a movement through different forms of difference. This begins with the first difference, that between women and men, and moves to the second difference, that of identity groups divided by 'race', class, disability and so forth and finally moves towards a third difference, that of postmodernism and poststructuralism. To a large extent each of the concepts in Figure 8.1 *could* be plotted along an axis of this kind.

Why should difference be so significant? What are the features of this concept that make it so powerful. Certainly difference is a cluster concept. It is placed in a web of meaning so that when we read or hear the term difference we are making conscious and unconscious connections with other significant terms. Scott (1988) has taken a deconstructive approach to difference to illustrate how its meanings rely on meanings of equality. Evans (1995) has indicated how we need to understand difference as part of a conceptual triangle with equality and sameness. Felski (1997) has urged us to remember that the antithesis of difference is not equality but sameness. Yet the difference–equality meaning relationship appears intransigent to such reminders. In the becoming of feminism conceptualizations of difference appear intrinsically related to political outcomes for feminist egalitarianism or, as Felski puts it equality and difference 'exist in a condition of necessary philosophical and political interdependence, such that the very pursuit of difference returns one, inexorably, to the seemingly obsolete issue of equality' (ibid.: 2–3).

In addition, in the analyses that I have offered, difference would appear to have been one of the most contentious terms within feminism if not *the* most contentious. Indeed, to follow this line of thought further we might also be tempted to say that some terms are more highly developed than others. The centring of difference to all the other concepts, and the varied meanings of difference itself, could be read as a narrative of progress as we move ever forwards towards even more sophisticated understandings. However, I do not believe that this is a story of straightforward linear progression as we move from one stage to another. Rather, the debates about difference are evidence of the co-existence, rather than replacement, of disparate ideas. For example, although postcolonial conceptualizations of difference recognize the instability of identity, they do not do so unreservedly (Felski, 1997; Beasley, 1999). Rather, issues of hierarchy and difference are constantly reaffirmed in respect of 'race' and ethnicity.

In turning to care I am drawn to Thomas's (1993) comments that it may be more useful to consider care as an empirical category that requires analysis in terms of other theoretical categories. Such a point is of course pertinent to all concepts in that they have an empirical basis that will then draw on a variety of theoretical positions (Karen Phillips, personal communication). Yet the analysis I have presented about care would suggest that there is some kind of division between the empirics of doing care, as task or activity, that has primarily been the domain of sociology and care as a way of being or as an ethic that has primarily been in the domain of psychology and philosophy. The debates about the former have certainly added to the number of indicators that could/ should be included in operationalizing care. The debates about the latter have been far more voracious as they have touched upon the meanings of womanhood.

We can understand developments in sociological conceptualizations of care as illustrative of Tanesini's (1994) point that one of the purposes of meaning-claims is to prescribe changes that 'correct' previous conceptual errors. Here one of the key debates about sociological concepts of care has been to argue that these should move beyond their initial focus of 'home-based-kin-care' (Graham, 1991). In this respect issues of identity difference in particular have been significant and thus confirm Connolly's and Tanesini's points that the choice of indicators is appraisive rather than objective. Mason (1996: 17) notes that 'as feminists more generally debated questions of difference and argued more energetically about whether or not women's existence was determined in the last instance by their position in the "family", so debates about care took on these questions too'. The effect of these has expanded the notion of 'who cares' to include issues of 'race', class, sexuality and disability and the idea of women as primary carers has been challenged by empirical data that illustrates that men also undertake caring tasks. In addition, the domains of caring activity now include community and social care and workplaces more broadly. While identity difference has had the main impact on conceptualizing care, this is not to say that poststructural and decon-structive theorization have been neglected. For example, analyses of family care have been concerned to overcome the dichotomy of labour or love set out in earlier feminist theorizations (see, for example, Finch and Groves, 1983). Thus, Mason (1996: 32) argues for inclusion of the realm of the relational and feeling in order that we 'reconceptualise these aspects of care as sentient activity and active sensibility'. In addition, the collection in Silva and Smart (1999) illustrates how the linkage between discourse and identity is shaping analyses of care. Indeed, these examples are illustrative of how successful meaning-claims can shift the focus on research. Moreover they can create new fields of research. For example, 'Disability Studies' is a vibrant area of research that has explored care in respect of identity and poststructural theorization (see, for example, Morris, 1993; Thomas, 1999).

Mason's concern about relationality brings me to care as an ethics because here I believe a slightly different picture emerges in respect of the intensity of debate around conceptual meanings. The founding theorization of the sociology of care was based on connecting care to work and labour. Whilst feminists such as Mason (1996) have critiqued the binaried nature of this the foundational idea that care is also work has been broadly accepted. However, the ethics of care field has been attacked because its founding theorization was so fully focused in woman's psychology and the maternalist politics that were developed from this. Despite her claims to contrary meanings, Gilligan's (1982) classic text has normally be read as suggesting that woman's psychology is based in relationality and care for others. The work of Ruddick (1980) and Noddings (1984) developed this into a maternalist politics that argued that motherhood provided the highest example of exemplary personhood. Within such a view the primary aim of feminism is to achieve a society based on caring relationships. The problem for many feminists was that this assumed that women were innately caring. The political implications of this line of thought are that women would be held captive by their caring 'natures'. Here, more sociological definitions of care as work and care as dependency are extremely significant. Within the politics of feminism care has primarily been seen as, and indeed remains, a key part of the problem for achieving equality. For example, one of the reasons why the 'Wages for Housework' debate failed was because payment for care work would contribute to keeping women fixed in caring tasks. The perceived outcomes of an ethics of care were, therefore, in direct contradiction to what have been perceived as the more liberatory politics of gendered divisions of labour. These issues have been part of a broader concern around essentialist theorization in feminism. Essentialism is, of course, one of the 'dirty' words of feminism and we should perhaps not be surprised to note that it forms part of the dualistic meanings of difference. The outcome of this contestation has not put an end to feminist interest in an ethics of care as it did with Wages for Housework campaigns. It has for some, however, shifted the theoretical field away from maternalist politics and towards poststructural and deconstructive positions where the argument can proceed away from woman-as-caring-as-her-innate-nature to woman-as-process-of-which-caring-is-an-effect-of-discursive-relations. This literature has also sought to include men, as well as women, within caring relations (see, for example, Sevenhuijsen, 1998).

The importance attached to women's responsibilities for care is also relevant to understanding developments in the conceptualization of time. There is no doubt that time has been extensively theorized in the natural sciences yet Adam (1990; 1995) notes that theories of time are yet to impact on the development of social theory. Nowotny (1992) suggests that time is transdisciplinary and thus cannot be put under the intellectual monopoly of any discipline. However, this suggests that time may be extremely productive for feminist thought because of the concerns within feminist thought for interdisciplinary and indeed transdisciplinary perspectives. To date, however, theorization over time primarily remains within feminine and masculine dualistic framings. This is within the first difference of feminism. This is because the majority of research in this field is primarily concerned with the problems for women of fitting in with masculine conceptualizations and models of linear time. There is, of course, a very good reason for this as married women's participation rates in the paid labour force have been increasing since the Second World War (National Statistics Office, 2001) and yet their responsibilities for care have not diminished in the same way. The linear model of time is central to the organization of paid work yet caring work takes on different temporal patterns.

Seeking to more fully understand, or indeed challenge, postmodern frameworks of identity, feminists have drawn on time to understand issues of the continuity of selfhood. These have focused on the simultaneous nature of past, present and future (see for example Griffiths, 1995; McNay, 2000). More broadly in terms of feminist politics Grosz (2000) also argues for an analysis that takes account of past, present and future. Grosz comments that while there is much work being conducted on questions of time, memory and history, very little theorization is taking place in respect of time and futurity. Here Grosz argues that the common perspective in historical analysis is to learn from the lessons of the past. However, the problem of this is that the future is overwhelmingly visualized in terms of the repeatability of the past and present and, in consequence, futurity is contained by past images and issues. This means that feminism 'risks being stuck in political strategies and conceptual dilemmas that are more appropriate to the past than the future' (ibid.: 230). Finally, while issues of spatiality are an important concern and an alternative field of conceptualization time–space relationships appear to be a considerably under-developed area of feminist research.

When considering choice I think it would be fair to say that a major impetus to conceptualization is to add a necessary structural caution to accounts that give too much to agency. As a heuristic case study my focus here was on rational choice theory and feminist economists' responses to this. However, I would suggest that more broadly feminist conceptualizations of choice have also been concerned with balancing structure–agency issues. Thus research that is concerned to illustrate the complexity of choice is problematizing the predominance of rational choice models of career theory. In terms of psychological explanations, Anderson (1998) comments in this respect that models of occupational behaviour are based on economic rationality models. In this respect Evetts confirms that there is a 'continuing division of feminist researchers into opposing factions: of those who emphasize determinants and those who emphasize choice; of those who stress reproduction and continuity and those who stress change; of the perception of women as victims or women as agents' (2000: 65).

My own reading of the literature on women's careers would very much accord with that of Evetts. There is a replication of the agency–structure dualism that many feminists would both challenge and seek to go beyond. As we saw in Chapter 4, in her review of the structuring of inequalities and the complex interaction of a host of variables, Anderson (1998) suggests that we need a new language given that the term 'choice' does not convey opportunity and constraint. There is very little contestation that this is an appropriate way forward. Thus the problem is more usually posed in terms of finding a balance within the binary of agency–structure rather than an alternative framework for exploration.

One of the reasons for this is because the major conceptualizations of choice have drawn on liberal theory wherein lie the roots of feminist thought (Eisenstein, 1984). For example, liberalism and feminism both share 'some conception of individuals as free and equal beings, emancipated from the ascribed, hierarchical bonds of traditional society' (Pateman, 1987: 103). In liberal theory choice sits in a conceptual chain with individualism, rights and freedom. Thus, women's right to choice also invokes a sense of autonomy, freedom and individual rights. The important assertions of structure and the adding in of issues of class, sexuality, 'race', disability, age and gender mainly speak to the problems for women in achieving these rights and freedoms and in becoming women with choices. Indeed, although there are now extensive feminist critiques of dualistic language and growing attention to poststructural conceptions of the 'choosing subject', as Plumwood (1993: 32) comments in relation to deconstruction 'Only liberal feminism, which accepts the dominant culture, has not had much use for the concept.' This would perhaps offer some explanation for the relatively little development of conceptualizations of choice given that much work in this area has been undertaken within liberal feminist frameworks.

In placing difference as the central place for understanding how and why the other concepts have developed their meanings in the ways that they have, I am aware that experience is considered *the* basis of feminism. I do not dispute this but I believe experience has constituted a different function to that of difference. Specifically experience has been linked to new feminist methodologies and epistemologies. In Colebrook's (2000) terms experience has been about a becoming feminism in respect of the development of feminist frameworks for knowing the social world. Experience, therefore, has constituted much more of a tool for more adequate theories of knowing. As a tool for more warrantable knowledge experience has, with great similarity to the other concepts, expanded its terms of reference. It has progressed through the narratives of difference to include women's standpoint, Black feminists' standpoint and postmodern cyborg standpoints with concomitant changes to its underlying theorization.

What is perhaps surprising about the tenor of debate around experience is that so little of it has been concerned with methodological paradigms. The critique of positivism and a preference for qualitative approaches are standard across feminism. This is not to say that feminists do not do quantitative work (see, for example, Jayaratne, 1993) but Walby's (2001a) intervention to argue the case for quantitative and evidence-based approaches is relatively rare. However, when it comes to issues of relativism then widespread voices of alarm are raised. This is because as a politics, feminism cannot avoid making truth claims. Contemporary debates about the conceptualization of experience illustrate a concern for issues of truth and a critical assessment of the individualizing propensities of location and the personal. Here debates are raised about the danger of sinking within the morass of paraphernalia concerned with the anecdotal and the less than ordinary and that feminism has more to offer than mere stories. Again we could consider these interventions not as linear progression through one theoretical framework to another but as the co-existence of many frames of meaning. Thus Hekman's (1999) call for feminist science as truth invokes a rejection of relativism that is far more modern than postmodern in its tenor.

Finally, we must turn to equality. Equality has certainly been a highly contested concept. The liberal conceptualization of equality as 'the same as' has brought severe critique from feminists concerned that success is being defined for women as the achievement of certain forms of masculine lifestyle and ways of being. The cultural conceptualization of equality as 'different but equal' has evoked similarly strong reactions in respect of fears about essentialism that I have noted above. The problems of achieving equality in terms of group politics are manifest. Indeed, we might say that equality has run its course as a viable term for twenty-first-century feminism. What is interesting about equality therefore is that it is an excellent example of the politics of changing language and the limits to ever expanding meaning. For example, Griffiths

(1998) illustrates that a term such as equality can become so strongly associated with a devalued position that its use is no longer tenable. She comments in this respect: 'One reason for choosing the term "social justice" is precisely because it has been less used. As a result, it has not (yet) suffered the kind of attack as a term that the more well known terms have' (ibid.: 85). Although there is variety of meaning there are consensual limits to a word's meaning. We might be able to stretch meaning, explore multiple meanings and make new meaning but we cannot apply absolutely any meaning to a given term. The meanings of a term are rooted in negotiation between different interest groups or communities. At the heart of this negotiation are common values through which meaning is drawn. Gee (1996) comments thus:

> Meanings, and the cultural models that compose them, are ultimately rooted in negotiation between different social practices with different interests. Power plays an important role in these negotiations. The negotiations can be settled for the time, in which case meaning becomes conventional and routine. But the settlement can be reopened . . . The negotiations which constitute meaning are limited by values emanating from communities. Meanings, then, are ultimately rooted in communities. (ibid.: 81)

There are two aspects that are central to understanding the limitations of any meaning of equality. The first is that the mathematical meaning of equal as 'the same as' is predominant. Second, and the more significant issue, is that this 'same as' draws in the normative subject of masculinity into equality's frames of meaning. Within feminism the struggle for some has been to move beyond the normative male. However, the term equality always appears to pull us back to this. Within feminism equality is so strongly associated with a liberal feminist position of equality as masculine achievement and as opportunity for middle-class women that there is also strong ambivalence to the term. If we were to say that difference is a synonym for woman in this reading, equality is a synonym for White middle-class man.

What is also useful to remember, however, is that outside feminist communities these two aspects of meaning operate slightly differently. This is because the meanings are drawing in alternative discourses. Myers (2000b: 4) uses the term 'equiphobia' to denote 'an irrational hatred and fear of anything to do with equal opportunities'. She outlines media responses of 'equiphobia' to equal opportunities initiatives in schools as examples of this. However, she notes ironically that when the term equal opportunity is used in an alternative discursive domain of the perceived under-achievement of boys it does not attract the same kind of response. For example, we might say that equiphobia arises because of the linkage of equality to the term feminism. Here we do not find that 'the same as men' is heard as a foolhardy outcome for feminist politics but rather as the avowed cause. Equality is therefore taken up as a competitive slogan that will challenge male power and reduce men's spheres of influence.

What differentiates the meanings that are drawn from equality discourses between some feminist and some equiphobic communities are the implications for the future of gender relations. For some feminists the future arising from equal opportunities is, problematically, the retention of a class-based hierarchically ordered society and the further reinforcement of male-as-norm outcomes. For equiphobists the future arising from equal opportunities is a different problem. This is a diminishing male power base. Certainly these alternative communities are drawing on the same underlying meanings of equality as 'the same as men'. But this not only differentiates their responses. It also places limits on how far we can stretch equality's meanings.

Change of terminology, then, can be a highly important political act. Indeed, Griffiths commentary on equality and her choice of social justice is also significant for another reason. This is that it demonstrates so clearly that changing terminology is not merely semantic but represents an alternative theoretical or value position. Indeed, Brooks (1997: 4) notes that the shift from paying attention to equality to a much greater focus on difference is central to the politics of postfeminism and marks a conceptual change in 'feminism's conceptual and theoretical agenda'. Thus, as Griffiths further comments, social justice is not only a broader term it can actually eschew the meanings of equality in terms of the same as:

> Another reason for choosing the term is that 'social justice' is a broader term than 'equality'. There are plenty of times when strict equality would be waived for reasons of social justice. In education, the diversion of resources to children who have special needs is widely agreed to be just, whether or not it can be described in terms of formal equality. Few classroom teachers would advocate that resources or time should be distributed between children on the basis of strict equality. The converse does not hold. The claims of social justice are not waived for reasons of equality. Social justice is more fundamental than equality as a guide to how we should act in relation to society and its educational institutions. (Griffiths, 1998: 85–6)

The commentary that I have provided here on conceptual usage in feminist theory and research is clearly a product of my own developing conceptual literacy. Here I have sought to indicate how contestation over meaning can be understood in terms of attachment to particular theoretical positions and their implications for a becoming feminism. I have drawn attention to the appraisive qualities of conceptual indicators and the clearest examples of this are the addition of issues of 'race', class, sexuality, disability and age to conceptual understandings. I have also commented on how successful contestation shifts the field of enquiry and indeed can require new language to convey its distinctiveness. Finally, I have illustrated how essentially contested concepts form part of cluster concepts and webs of meaning and so widen their ambit of intentionality. However the commentary I have provided is presented *fait accompli*. Certainly I have endeavoured to make my theoretical framework explicit but much of the stimuli and feeling states that give rise to my advocacy of this framework are absent. And so I must now move to explication.

Critical Tasks in Conceptual Literacy

> As Wittgenstein teaches us, the task of freeing ourselves from the intellectual pictures that hold us captive is not only immensely hard, it is never done, for we are always going to find ourselves held by new metaphysical mirages, fall for new temptations to forsake the ordinary.
>
> (Moi, 1999: xiv)

I have described conceptual literacy as an act of sensitization to multiple meaning. I have urged that central to this sensitization is an awareness of the political implications of debate and argument over meaning. In this respect the key question that I have asked in this chapter is 'What effects does contestation have for feminist knowledge?' As I hope I have made clear in response to this question, I have drawn on particular theorists and positions. Yet there is a question that has preceded each of these. This is: 'What theoretical frameworks can enable me to understand the politics of how text and stories work on me to produce my intellectual responses of agreement, rejection, joy, passion, depression, disbelief, loss and transformation?' For me this question is central and it is here that I turn to critical literacy. Through critical literacy 'we come to know how enchanting language is, we learn to revel in the enchantment of knowing ourselves in the world through language. At the same time as we learn to be transgressive, we develop the skills of critical imagination through which we open up new possibilities, think the as yet unthinkable, beyond and outside dead language' (Davies, 1997a: 29). Davies (1994; 1996; 1997a; 2000) has illustrated how critical literacy is a set of practices that draws on poststructural theories of selfhood and language. It encourages the development of skills and habits but does not seek to separate theory from practice. Rather, as Davies remarks, critical literacy is concerned with developing a reflexive awareness of how speaking-as-usual constructs our understandings of ourselves and of others. It is, in this regard, concerned with the relationship between the construction of selves and regimes of truth. To do critical literacy we need to develop the capacities through which we can read against the grain of dominant discourses and the privileged positions that are constructed within them. In this we must learn to look beyond the content of the text and to see, and critique, how this content works upon us to shape meaning and desire. Davies (1997a) has set out five inter-related tasks that we need to undertake to develop critical literacy. I have adapted these for the development of conceptual literacy.

Know Well Dominant Forms of Thought . . .

Feminism has been extremely critical of the masculinity of Cartesian rationality and the concomitant separation of body and mind. In coming to learn this we might be encouraged to think that as feminists we therefore do not need to 'know' masculine forms of rationality as they have been ruled outside legitimate ways of feminist being and knowing. We might also believe that once we have learnt that a theory or principle is problematic then it will no longer have power over or within us. However, we need to recognize that although we might *now* critique how rationality has been constructed in this way we have been encouraged, through, for example, our schooling, to master its discourses (Davies et al., 2001). When Walby (2001a: 494) comments in her critiques of experience that feminists 'smuggle in modernist assumptions' she is alerting us to how we have both been taken up by and take up the reason of mainstream science. We cannot assume that even if we so desire we can free ourselves so easily, and certainly never totally, from such powerfully dominant discourses.

Brah (1999: 8) suggests that the Althusserian idea of interpellation is useful as it makes sense of 'being situated and "hailed" socially, culturally, symbolically, and psychically, all at once [and thus] it takes seriously the relationship between the social and the psychic'. Indeed, while we should seek to thoroughly know rational thought and how it works on us to persuade, we should also apply these principles to dominant discourses within feminism. How have we been hailed or situated by this, and other, discourses? To answer this question it is not necessary to reject these discourses, although we might, but it is necessary to know how dominant discourses work on us and on others and why we are so powerfully committed to or rejecting of such discourses. This will help us come to understand why we might take up, or we might be persuaded by, particular forms of argumentation.

. . . Move Beyond Dominant Forms of Thought to Embrace Multiple Ways of Knowing

The second task that Davies suggests is to move beyond linear and rational thought and to embrace and celebrate multiple and contradictory ways of knowing. This is because this will help us to undermine the power of dominant discourses. It will also encourage movement through openness and openings and raise questions for us about the truth of different ways of knowing. This text has many examples of the multiple discourses of feminism and relatedly the many ways of conceptualizing. This raises the question of how research and theorization changes through different conceptual usage and the effects this has for developing feminist knowledge and feminist politics. It also raises questions for research design and analysis. In this respect Alvesson and Skoldberg (2000: 194–5) offer a set of 'pragmatic postmodern principles' that may be useful for thinking about the application of multiple meaning and pluralism in terms of the conduct of research. These are:

- Pluralism in the potential of different identities or voices associated with different groups, individuals, positions or special interests which inform, and can be seen in, research work and research texts.
- Receptiveness to pluralism and variation in what individual participants in the research process convey (the possibility of multiple representations by one and the same individual participant).
- Alternative presentations of phenomena (for instance, the use of different sorts of descriptive language).
- Command of different theoretical perspectives (root metaphors), as well as a strong familiarity with the critique of and problems with these. This enables openness and different sorts of readings to surface in the research.

Alvesson and Skoldberg comment that it would not be feasible to achieve a high degree of pluralism and a minimum degree of exclusion in any one text by covering all four of the above dimensions. It is possible, however, to maximize one or two of these. Overall what they suggest is that 'What is crucial is the production of an open text, which stimulates active interpretation on the part of the reader; researchers should avoid "closing" their texts by placing themselves too firmly between the reader and the voices researched' (ibid.: 195). Coffey (2001: 115) offers a summary of research in the postmodern and notes how Haw's (1998) text on the education of Muslim girls is 'an exemplary example of a feminist collaborative approach to the writing (and researching) task'.

. . . Read, Speak and Write Oneself into the Possibilities of Different Discourses

Millard's (1997) research illustrates the great variety of reading practices that young people engage in both within and outside school. In this respect the third task that Davies urges is that we should read and speak ourselves into the possibilities of different discourses and contexts. We might, for example, ask what a cyborg conceptualization of experience means for our sense of identity. Or what conceptualizations of postcolonial difference mean for a becoming feminism. Or indeed what kinds of future feminist politics can be envisaged that are based on a conceptualization of care as an ethic or care as work. In addition, we might also write ourselves into different discourses and contexts.

A focus on authorship in postmodern enquiry has illustrated how researchers shape meanings in the presentation of their findings. Atkinson (1990) illustrates how the believability of the research report is not a given that just comes with the data. It is formed through the researcher's use of a variety of literary devices and narrative strategies that depict rhetorical figures, use descriptive vocabulary to evoke the scenes within which these characters live their lives and which rely on the selection of appropriate illustrative material. Nevertheless, authorial authority is never guaranteed. Poststructuralism has challenged the idea that there exists 'a single, literal reading of a textual object, the one intended by the author' (Barone, 1995: 65). Although some readings are certainly more privileged than others, interpretation cannot be controlled. Readers bring their own knowledges, experiences, values and meanings to the text. This means that as author I cannot guarantee the authority of my words.

The focus in postmodern scholarship on these issues has brought a greater consciousness of narrative devices and strategies of persuasion in the dissemination of research. This heightened consciousness may of course lead to attempts to reinforce researcher authority through becoming more expert in the various techniques of writing. Yet this heightened consciousness has also led researchers to take more risks and to become more 'playful' in the styles that are used for written dissemination. One of the purposes of this playfulness has been to open up and make more explicit how knowledge is constructed through research. For example, Perriton (1999) uses two, unequal, columns that separate first and third person pronouns. The authoritative voice of the third person mirrors the personal voice of the first person to convey that they are the voices of the same author. Yet the greater space given to the third person discussion replicates how ideas of the neutral researcher continue to predominate.

However, within the research methodology literature the issue of writing is either ignored or is considered primarily in technical terms of, say, style, format, writing drafts and thinking about potential audiences. Perry (2000) notes that educators have paid very little attention to the role of writing in the development of critical consciousness. A standard view of writing is that this is an act of *transcription* of one's thinking where one needs to engage in the act of thinking prior to putting those thoughts onto paper. In contrast Perry's central point is that writing *is* thinking. One not only becomes conscious of one's thinking through writing but writing shapes and transforms our thinking. As with critical literacy more generally, Perry's work is strongly influenced by Freirean pedagogies. Perry argues that it is necessary for learners 'to become aware of what it means for them to write in order to establish a new relationship with writing' (ibid.: 186). This means that learners need to engage in a variety of 'risk-free' writing tasks that include

> focused and unfocused freewriting, sustained exploratory writing to discover what they know and think about topics and issues, loop writing to discover the depth of their thinking on topics/issues/events not apparent at the outset of the writing [and discussion of] the politics and the power of language use in and out of the academy. (ibid.)

With some similarity to Perry, Lillis's (2001) research into critical literacy and student writing is focused on what she describes as the essayist literacy that is required of higher education students. Lillis notes that 'social and personal identity are bound up with ways of meaning making in fundamental ways' (ibid.: 169). She suggests that the following questions are central to understanding the effects of this.

These are: 'What kinds of identities are privileged through existing practices? How can traditionally excluded identities be foregrounded and including in teaching, learning and meaning making? What kinds of identities do we want to encourage in higher education, and why?' (ibid.). Of course, we might want to extend Lillis's questions to other spheres and domains and to both writing and reading.

. . . Engage in Moral and Philosophical Critique

Fourth, and relatedly, Davies indicates how we need to engage in moral and philosophical critique of discourse. This is not, however, to assert our moral superiority or ascendancy over others but it is to more fully understand how truth is constructed at different points in time and in different discourses. Gee (1996) points out how contestation over meaning always invokes moral argumentation. Thus with conceptually contested terms he comments that 'it is pointless to ask what they "really" mean. What is to the point is to say what you *choose* to take them to mean, after careful, thoughtful, and ethical reflection' (ibid.: 16). In this Gee offers two principles that he argues should form the basis of ethical human discourse. These are that we should ensure that any conceptualization that we choose should not harm someone else and that we have an ethical obligation to make explicit any tacit theory if we have reason to believe that this theory will give us an advantage over another. This means that we also need to make our conceptualizations known to those with whom we work. As we have learnt we cannot assume that we share the same meanings of particular concepts. Indeed, as Lankshear et al. (1997) comment, we can usually safely assume that such meanings are not shared. It is, therefore, important when people, particularly from different backgrounds or discursive traditions, come together to work collectively. Lankshear et al. note:

> This is especially important where words which have positive connotations and generate strong allegiances across discursive borders are being employed in discursive contexts where projects of willing visions into reality are being enacted. In such contexts there are real dangers of being co-opted into agendas we might subsequently wish we had resisted, but where we could/did not resist because we failed to appreciate the extent to which the meanings of others were not our own meanings; possibly we did not even realize exactly how others with the power to ensure that their meanings prevailed were, in fact, framing what appeared to be shared concepts. (ibid.: 92)

For example, many feminists have had an enormous commitment to equality and have worked with a variety of policy-makers and organizational leaders to realize their visions. However, they have commented on how the 'business' case, rather than the 'moral' case, has been far more persuasive as a reason for organizations to become involved in equal opportunities work. Thus, Shaw (1995: 224) comments: 'A feature of the 1990s has been the attempt to show that a wider sense of social responsibility makes good business sense.' The 'business' case argues that 'the workforce consists of a diverse population of people [and] harnessing these differences will create a productive environment in which everybody feels valued, where their talents are being fully utilised and in which organisational goals are met' (Kandola and Fullerton, 1994: 8). Here, therefore, feminist equality discourses come together with the needs of capitalism. As research in the equal opportunities, and diversity management, fields indicate the focus has been on 'glass ceiling' work that has been mainly beneficial to middle-class women working within professional and management fields. As Shaw remarks:

> [M]uch equal opportunities work is irrelevant to the bulk of women who are nowhere near managerial grades. The individualistic strategies advocated for potential high-fliers may be effective, but they do not touch the working conditions of the majority. Indeed, if they did, there is a good chance that they would be abandoned, for equality of opportunity, in and of itself, implies no commitment to equality. (1995: 215)

The implication of this in terms of conceptual literacy and critical language awareness is that we must ask what constructions of equality are operating within each field and what are the consequences of these. To do this we need to tease out the various sets of meanings of socially contested terms. This will enable us to raise questions and issues for debate and dialogue and will deepen our understanding of the 'values and ideological loadings that are at stake in any Discourse' (Lankshear et al., 1997: 93). This will also help us to understand the grounds that exist for making, or indeed not making, common cause in the creation of a more socially just world (ibid.).

. . . Recognize the Limits of Critique and Potential Transformation

The fifth task that Davies notes is that we have to recognize the limits of any critique or potential transformation. Central to this is developing a reflexive awareness of ourselves as sentient beings and the place of language and meaning in the production of feeling. In this respect Lankshear et al. (1997: 83) describe how fast capitalist texts promote visions of '"enchanted workplaces" where hierarchy is dead and "partners" engage in meaningful work amidst a collaborative environment of mutual commitment and trust'. Central to this are discourses of empowerment and self-direction that work on the subject to produce similarly enchanted employees. While critical literacy is concerned to develop skills and knowledges that enable us to at least recognize enchantment when it occurs, Moi's (1999) comments remind us about the difficulties of freeing ourselves from the pictures and mirages that hold us captive. Moi reflects on her earlier published work *Sexual/ Textual Politics* and comments that there are 'many traces of the metaphysics I now want to escape' (ibid.: xiv). She comments:

> I appear to believe that there is something intrinsically wrong with being part of a binary opposition (on what evidence? I ask myself today), I am quite insufficiently nuanced about when essentialism is a bad thing and when it doesn't matter, and I spend too much time using words like 'signifier' when 'word' would have been quite adequate. (ibid.: xiv–xv)

More contemporarily Moi is 'concerned with the ordinary and the everyday. I now see poststructuralism as a form of thought that is too eager to lose itself in metaphysics . . . In short, the two new essays collected in Part I show why I would now challenge the mindset that produces the need to place scare quotes around words such as "reality" or "social beings"' (ibid.: xiv). However, she notes that these new essays 'also show how hard the task of justifying this feeling intellectually actually is' (ibid.). Nevertheless, this does not stop Moi from attempting such a task. Thus, impossible though it may be to forsake new metaphysical mirages for the ordinary unless we constantly strive to 'move beyond the intellectual pictures that hold us captive' (ibid.) we will neither understand the power of linguistic forms nor develop the capacity to use them well (Davies, 1994; 1996; 1997a; 2000).

Case Study 17: Constructing and Deconstructing Masculinities through Critical Literacy

Davies's (1997a) focus on critical literacy highlights the importance of equipping learners not simply with knowledge but with the tools through which they can become their own knowledge producers. Davies is working within a poststructuralist framework and the research discussed here is based on observational data. Davies gives us the case of Mr Good, a teacher, who is not resistant to the idea of disrupting gender identities. Indeed, as Davies's pseudonym indicates, Mr Good appears to engage in the essential strategies of deconstruction that might lead to the acquisition of new identities. Nevertheless, Davies argues that Mr Good's pedagogic approach remains flawed.

Mr Good seeks to challenge stereotypes of macho masculinity by making it possible for boys to take themselves up as literate, oral beings. He does this in a number of ways. For example, Mr Good draws on his own personal interests and feelings to indicate that he is not a detached bystander to knowledge. He also challenges, in a supportive way, displays of macho masculinity when they are evidenced in the classroom. Indeed, through his various responses Mr Good suggests that there are many ways in which masculinity can be 'done'. Much of this incorporates the notion of the 'new man' within traditional forms of masculinity. Thus, boys in Mr Good's class were able to read poetry without feeling self-conscious. They were able to play football and to know about wars and planes. They were able to engage with philosophical and moral issues and speak about their feelings.

However, Davies argues that Mr Good does not go far enough. This is because Mr Good does not offer the children in his class 'the kind of reflexive knowledge that would allow them to see what is happening and to critique the various discourses that are made available to them' (ibid.: 25). Essentially, Mr Good does not hold in play the variety of meanings ascribed to masculinity. He does not explore the ways in which these meanings rely on each other. Nor does he explore the potential to create new meanings. In this, then, Mr Good does not give the children in his classroom the tools through which to become fully critically literate and thereby able to understand how their positioning could change through resisting dominant meanings or changing them. Here there are three pedagogic tasks that could be undertaken. First, there is a need to generate a level of critical literacy that enables learners to recognize multiple discourses. Second, there is a need to facilitate a critical awareness of the ways in which the self is contradictorily positioned as colonized and colonizer and as oppressed and oppressive within these discourses. Third, there is a need to embrace, as one's own, the multiplicity of positions with which one wishes to identify.

Summary

I have indicated that central to conceptual contestation is a concern about the effects of meaning. Feminism's relationship with becoming gives a particular weight to the political implications of the language and terms that we use to frame our theory and our research. Through the language of conceptual literacy this text has explored only one part of this. The effects of conceptual contestation are real as they produce what become acceptable ways of knowing, theorizing and doing. We are each caught up in, and actively take up, these webs of meaning. They are productive of our passions and commitments. As Moi (1999) wrestles to free herself from the intellectually learnt search for deep meaning, she demonstrates what is for me a central feminist ethic. This is the development of skills in:

> catching language in the act of formation and in recognising and assessing the effects of that formation [through which] language is no longer a dead tool for the maintenance of old certainties, but a life-giving set of possibilities for shaping and reshaping a complex, rich, fluid social world. A critically and socially [and conceptually] literate [personhood] would not be caught up, as some might fear, in a mindless, relativist spiral. Rather, in the very visibility and analysability of language, and its effects, lies the possibility of being open to a philosophical and moral critique of the many and multiple meanings and modes of being embedded in and created through different uses of language. (Davies, 1997a: 29)

I offer this text in that spirit.

FURTHER READING

Clearly, the work of Bronwyn Davies has been central to this chapter and I can only urge you to follow up the references here. More broadly, however, I would further suggest you consult first-hand *all* the texts cited in this book that are relevant to your own research. This way you will not be reliant on my own (mis)readings and (mis)interpretations!

References

Adam, B. (1989) 'Feminist social theory needs time: reflections on the relation between feminist thought, social theory and time as an important parameter in social analysis', *The Sociological Review*, 37: 458–73

Adam, B. (1990) *Time and Social Theory*. Cambridge: Polity Press.

Adam, B. (1995) *Timewatch: The Social Analysis of Time*. Cambridge: Polity Press.

Allatt, P. and Keil, T. (1987) 'Introduction', in P. Allatt, T. Keil, A. Bryman and B. Bytheway (eds), *Women and the Life Cycle: Transitions and Turning-Points*. Basingstoke: Macmillan, pp. 1–12

Alvesson, M. and Skoldberg, K. (2000) *Reflexive Methodology: New Vistas for Qualitative Research*. London: Sage.

Anderson, P. (1998) 'Choice: can we choose it?', in J. Radford (ed.), *Gender and Choice in Education and Occupation*. London: Routledge, pp. 141–61.

Ang, I. (1997) 'Comment on Felski's "The Doxa of Difference": the uses of incommensurability', *SIGNS: Journal of Women in Culture and Society*, 23(1): 57–69.

Arber, S. and Gilbert, N. (1989) 'Men: the forgotten carers', *Sociology*, 23(1): 111–18.

Arber, S. and Ginn, S. (1990) 'The meaning of informal care: gender and the contribution of elderly people', *Ageing and Society*, 10: 429–54.

Arnold, J. (1997) *Managing Careers into the 21st Century*. London: Paul Chapman.

Ashiagbor, D. (1999) 'The intersection between gender and "race" in the labour market: lessons for anti-discrimination law', in A. Morris and T. O'Donnell (eds), *Feminist Perspectives on Employment Law*. London: Cavendish Publishing, pp. 139–60.

Assiter, A. (2000) 'Feminist epistemology and value', *Feminist Theory*, 1(3): 329–45.

Atkinson, J. (1985) *Flexibility, Uncertainty and Manpower Management*. Report 89, Brighton: Institute of Manpower Studies.

Atkinson, P. (1990) *The Ethnographic Imagination: Textual Constructions of Reality*. London: Routledge.

Bacchi, C. (1990) *Same Difference: Feminism and Sexual Difference*. St Leonards, NSW: Allen and Unwin.

Bacchi, C. (1996) *The Politics of Affirmative Action: 'Women', Equality and Category Politics*. London: Sage.

Bailey, L. (2000) 'Bridging home and work in the transition to motherhood: a discursive study', *The European Journal of Women's Studies*, 7(1): 53–70.

Bainbridge, C. (2001) 'Luce Irigaray', in A. Elliott and B. Turner (eds), *Profiles in Contemporary Social Theory*. London: Sage, pp. 184–93.

Ball, S. and Gewirtz, S. (1997) 'Girls in the education market: choice, competition and complexity', *Gender and Education*, 9(2): 207–22.

Barkan, E. and Shelton, M. (eds) (1998) *Borders, Exiles and Diasporas*. Stanford, CA: Stanford University Press.

Barone, T. (1995) 'Persuasive writings, vigilant readings and reconstructed characters: the paradox of trust in educational story sharing', in J. Hatch and R. Wisniewski (eds), *Life History and Narrative*. London: Falmer, pp. 63–74.

Barrett, M. (1987) 'The Concept of "Difference"', *Feminist Review*, 26: 29–41.

Battersby, C. (1996) 'Her blood and his mirror: Mary Coleridge, Luce Irigaray, and the female self', in R. Eldridge (ed.), *Beyond Representation: Philosophy and Poetic Imagination*. Cambridge: Cambridge University Press, pp. 249–72.

Battersby, C. (1998) *The Phenomenal Woman: Feminist Metaphysics and the Patterns of Identity*. Cambridge: Polity Press.

Beasley, C. (1999) *What is Feminism? An Introduction to Feminist Theory*. London: Sage.

Bechhofer, F. and Paterson, L. (2000) *Principles of Research Design in the Social Sciences*. London: Routledge.

Becker, G. (1991) *A Treatise on the Family*. Cambridge, MA: Harvard University Press.

Belcher, A. (1999) 'Equal opportunities, staff development and assertiveness', in A. Morris and T. O'Donnell (eds), *Feminist Perspectives on Employment Law*. London: Cavendish Publishing, pp. 43–60.

Benhabib, S. (1992) *Situating the Self: Gender, Community and Postmodernism in Contemporary Ethics*. Cambridge: Polity Press.

Bergmann, B. (1995) 'Becker's theory of the family: preposterous conclusions', *Feminist Economics*, 1(1): 141–50.

Berik, G. (2000) 'Mature export-led growth and gender wage inequality in Taiwan', *Feminist Economics*, 6(3): 1–26.

Bettie, J. (2000) 'Women without class: *chicas, cholas*, trash, and the presence/absence of class identity', *SIGNS: Journal of Women in Culture and Society*, 26(1): 1–35.

Blackmore, J. (1997) 'Disciplining feminism: a look at gender-equity struggles in Australian higher education', in L. Roman and L. Eyre (eds), *Dangerous Territories: Struggles for Difference and Equality in Education*. New York: Routledge, pp. 75–98.

Blackmore, J. (1999) *Troubling Women: Feminism, Leadership and Educational Change*. Buckingham: Open University Press.

Blackwell, L. (2001) 'Occupational sex segregation and part-time work in modern Britain', *Gender, Work and Organization*, 8(2): 146–63.

Blaxter, L. and Hughes, C. (2000) 'Social capital: a critique', in J. Thompson (ed.), *Stretching the Academy: The Politics and Practice of Widening Participation in Higher Education*. Leicester: NIACE, pp. 80–93.

Blaxter, L., Hughes, C. and Tight, M. (2001) *How to Research*, 2nd edn. Buckingham: Open University Press.

Blaxter, L. and Tight, M. (1994) 'Juggling with time: how adults manage their time for lifelong education', *Studies in the Education of Adults*, 26(2): 162–79.

Blaxter, L. and Tight, M. (1995) 'Life transitions and educational participation by adults', *International Journal of Lifelong Education*, 14(3): 231–46.

Blyton, P., Hassard, J., Hill, S. and Starkey, K. (1989) *Time, Work and Organization*. London: Routledge.

Bock, G. and James, S. (eds) (1992) *Beyond Equality and Difference: Citizenship, Feminist Politics and Female Subjectivity*. London: Routledge.

Bohan, J. (1997) 'Regarding gender: essentialism, constructionism and feminist psychology', in M. Gergen and S. Davis (eds), *Toward a New Psychology of Gender: A Reader*. New York: Routledge, pp. 31–47.

Boyne, R. (1990) *Foucault and Derrida: The Other Side of Reason*. London: Unwin Hyman.

Brabeck, M. (1993) 'Moral judgement: theory and research on differences between males and females', in M. Larrabee (ed.), *An Ethic of Care: Feminist and Interdisciplinary Perspectives*. New York: Routledge, pp. 33–48.

Bradley, H. (2000) 'Social inequalities: coming to terms with complexity', in G. Browning, A. Halcli and F. Webster (eds), *Understanding Contemporary Society: Theories of the Present*. London: Sage, pp. 476–88.

Brah, A. (1990) 'Difference, diversity and differentiation', in J. Donald and A. Rattansi (eds), *'Race', Culture and Difference*. London: Sage, pp. 126–48.

Brah, A. (1996) *Cartographies of Diaspora: Contesting Identities*. London: Routledge.

Brah, A. (1999) 'The scent of memory: strangers, our own, and others', *Feminist Review*, 61: 4–26.

Braidotti, R. (1994) *Nomadic Subjects: Embodiment and Sexual Difference in Contemporary Feminist Theory*. New York: Columbia University Press.

Braidotti, R. (1997) 'Comment on Felski's "The doxa of difference": working through sexual difference', *SIGNS: Journal of Women in Culture and Society*, 23(1): 23–40.

Brine, J. (1999) *Under-Educating Women: Globalizing Inequality*. Buckingham: Open University Press.

Brooks, A. (1997) *Postfeminisms: Feminism, Cultural Theory and Cultural Forms*. London: Routledge.

Brownmiller, S. (1999) *In Our Time: Memoir of a Revolution*. New York: The Dial Press.

Bryson, V. (1998) 'Citizen warriors, workers and mothers: women and democracy in Israel', in N. Charles and H. Hintjens (eds), *Gender, Ethnicity and Political Ideologies*. London: Routledge, pp. 127–45.

Bulbeck, C. (2000) 'The "space between" or why does the gap between "us" and "them" look like an unbridgeable chasm?', *Asian Journal of Women's Studies*, 6(3): 36–64.

Burgess, R. (1984) *Key Variables in Social Investigation*. London: Routledge and Kegan Paul.

Butler, J. (1990) *Gender Trouble: Feminism and the Subversion of Identity*. New York: Routledge.

Butler, J. (1995) 'Contingent foundations', in S. Benhabib, J. Butler, D. Cornell and N. Fraser (eds), *Feminist Contentions: A Philosophical Exchange*. New York: Routledge, pp. 35–57.

Butler, J. (1999) *Gender Trouble: Feminism and the Subversion of Identity*, 2nd edn. New York: Routledge.

Butler, J. and Scott, J. (eds) (1992) *Feminists Theorize the Political*. New York: Routledge.

Cantillon, S. and Nolan, B. (2001) 'Poverty within households: measuring gender differences using nonmonetary indicators', *Feminist Economics*, 7(1): 5–23.

Carby, H. (1982) 'White women listen! Black feminism and the boundaries of sisterhood', in Centre for Contemporary Cultural Studies (eds), *The Empire Strikes Back*. London: Hutchinson.

Cavarero, A. (1992) 'Equality and sexual difference: amnesia in political thought', in G. Bock and S. James (eds), *Beyond Equality and Difference: Citizenship, Feminist Politics and Female Subjectivity*. London: Routledge, pp. 32–47.

Chalude, M., de Jong, A. and Laufer, J. (1994) 'Implementing equal opportunity and affirmative action programmes in Belgium, France and The Netherlands', in M. Davidson and R. Burke (eds), *Women in Management: Current Research Issues*. Liverpool: Paul Chapman, pp. 289–303.

Charles, N. (1993) *Gender Divisions and Social Change*. Hemel Hempstead: Harvester Wheatsheaf.

Charles, N. (2000) *Feminism, the State and Social Policy*. Basingstoke: Macmillan.

Chodorow, N. (1978) *The Reproduction of Mothering: Psychoanalysis and the Sociology of Gender*. Berkeley, CA: University of California Press.

Cixous, H. (1997) 'Sorties: out and out: attacks/ways out/forays', in C. Belsey and J. Moore (eds), *The Feminist Reader*. Basingstoke: Macmillan, pp. 91–103.

Code, L. (1995) *Rhetorical Spaces: Essays on Gendered Locations*. London: Routledge.

Coffey, A. (1994) 'Timing is everything: graduate accountants, time and organizational commitment', *Sociology*, 28(4): 943–56.

Coffey, A. (2001) *Education and Social Change*. Buckingham: Open University Press.

Colebrook, C. (2000) 'Introduction', in I. Buchanan and C. Colebrook (eds), *Deleuze and Feminist Theory*. Edinburgh: Edinburgh University Press, pp. 1–17.

Coleman, J. (1987) 'Norms as social capital', in G. Radnitzky and P. Bernholz (eds), *Economic Imperialism: The Economic Method Applied Outside the Field of Economics*. New York: Pragon, pp. 133–56.

Coleman, J. (1988a) 'Social capital in the creation of human capital', *American Journal of Sociology*, 94: 945–1558.

Coleman, J. (1988b) *Foundations of Social Theory*. Cambridge, MA: Harvard University Press.

Coleman, M. (2000) 'The female secondary headteacher in England and Wales: leadership and management styles', *Educational Research*, 42(1): 13–27.

Colley, A. (1998) 'Gender and subject choice in secondary education', in J. Radford (ed.), *Gender and Choice in Education and Occupation*. London: Routledge, pp. 18–36.

Collins, P. (1989) 'The social construction of Black feminist thought', *SIGNS: Journal of Women in Culture and Society*, 14(4): 745–73.

Collins, P. (1990) *Black Feminist Thought*. London: Routledge.

Collins, P. (1997) 'Comment on Hekman's "Truth and method: feminist standpoint theory revisited": where's the power?', *SIGNS: Journal of Women in Culture and Society*, 22(2): 375–81.

Connolly, W. (1993) *The Terms of Political Discourse*, 3rd edn. Oxford: Blackwell.

Cornell, D. (1997) 'Comment on Felksi's "The doxa of difference": diverging differences', *SIGNS, Journal of Women in Culture and Society*, 23(1): 41–56.

Corti, L., Laurie, H. and Dex, S. (1994) *Caring and Employment*. Research Series 39, Sheffield: Department of Employment.

Cotterill, P. (1994) *Friendly Relations? Mothers and Their Daughters-in-Law*. London: Taylor and Francis.

Crick, M. (1976) *Explorations in Language and Meaning: Towards a Semantic Anthropology*. London: Malaby Press.

Crotty, M. (1998) *The Foundations of Social Research: Meaning and Perspective in the Research Process*. London: Sage.

Crouch, M. and Manderson, L. (1993) *New Motherhood: Cultural and Personal Transitions in the 1980s*. Sydney, NSW: Gordon and Breach Science.

David, M., Davies, J., Edwards, R., Reay, D. and Standing, K. (1997) 'Choice within constraints: mothers and schooling', *Gender and Education*, 9(4): 397–410.

Davies, B. (1989) *Frogs and Snails and Feminist Tales: Preschool Children and Gender*. Sydney, NSW: Allen and Unwin.

Davies, B. (1991) 'The concept of agency: a feminist poststructuralist analysis', *Social Analysis*, 300: 42–53.

Davies, B. (1994) *Poststructuralist Theory and Classroom Practice*. Geelong: Deakin University Press.

Davies, B. (1996) *Power/Knowledge/Desire: Changing School Organisation and Management Practices*. Canberra: Department of Employment, Education, Training and Youth Affairs.

Davies, B. (1997a) 'Constructing and deconstructing masculinities through critical literacy', *Gender and Education*, 9(1): 9–30.

Davies, B. (1997b) 'The subject of post-structuralism: a reply to Alison Jones', *Gender and Education*, 9(3): 271–84.

Davies, B. (2000) *(In)scribing Body/Landscape Relations*. Walnut Creek: AltaMira Press.

Davies, B., Dormer, S., Gannon, S., Laws, C., Taguchi, H., McCann, H. and Rocco, S. (2001) 'Becoming schoolgirls: the ambivalent project of subjectification', *Gender and Education*, 13(2): 167–82.

Davies, K. (1990) *Women, Time and Weaving the Strands of Everyday Life*. Aldershot: Gower.

Davis, K. and Lutz, H. (2000) 'Open forum: life in theory: three feminist thinkers on transition(s)', *The European Journal of Women's Studies*, 7(3): 367–78.

de Lauretis, T. (1994) 'The essence of the triangle or, taking the risk of essentialism seriously: feminist theory in Italy, the U.S. and Britain', in N. Schor and E. Weed (eds), *The Essential Difference*. Bloomington and Indianapolis: Indiana University Press, pp. 1–39.

de Lauretis, T. (1997) 'Aesthetic and feminist theory: rethinking women's cinema', in S. Kemp and J. Squires (eds), *Feminisms*. Oxford: Oxford University Press, pp. 27–36.

de Vaus, D. (2001) *Research Design in Social Research*. London: Sage.

Dunne, G. (1997) *Lesbian Lifestyles: Women's Work and the Politics of Sexuality*. Basingstoke: Macmillan.

Edwards, R. (1993) *Mature Women Students: Separating or Connecting Family and Education*. London: Taylor and Francis.

Eisenberg, A. (2000) 'Cultural pluralism today', in G. Browning, A. Halcli and F. Webster (eds), *Understanding Contemporary Society: Theories of the Present*. London: Sage, pp. 385–401.

Eisenstein, H. (1984) *Contemporary Feminist Thought*. London: Unwin.

Eisenstein, Z. (1993) *The Radical Future of Liberal Feminism*. Boston: Northeastern University Press.

England, P. (1993) 'The separative self: androcentric bias in neoclassical assumptions', in M. Ferber and J. Nelson (eds), *Beyond Economic Man: Feminist Theory and Economics*. Chicago: University of Chicago Press, pp. 37–53.

Erikson, E. (1980) *Identity and the Life Cycle: A Reissue*. New York: W.W. Norton.

Ermath, E. (1989) 'The solitude of women and social time', in F. Forman with C. Sowton (eds), *Taking our Time: Feminist Perspectives on Temporality*. Oxford: Pergamon Press, pp. 37–46.

Evans, J. (1995) *Feminist Theory Today: An Introduction to Second-Wave Feminism*. London: Sage.

Evans, M. (ed.) (1994) *The Woman Question*. London: Sage.

Evetts, J. (ed.) (1994) *Women and Career: Themes and Issues in Advanced Industrial Societies*. London: Longman.

Evetts, J. (2000) 'Analysing change in women's careers: culture, structure and action dimensions', *Gender, Work and Organization*, 7(1): 57–67.

Fagan, C. (2001) 'Time, money and the gender order: work orientations and working time preferences in Britain', *Gender, Work and Organization*, 8(3): 239–66.

Felski, R. (1997) 'The doxa of difference', *SIGNS Journal of Women in Culture and Society*, 23(1): 1–21.

Felski, R. (2000) 'Being reasonable, telling stories', *Feminist Theory*, 1(2): 225–9.

Field, D., Hockey, J. and Small, N. (eds) (1997) *Death, Gender and Ethnicity*. London: Routledge.

Figes, K. (1994) *Because of Her Sex: The Myth of Equality for Women in Britain*. London: Pan Books.

Finch, J. (1986) 'Age', in R. Burgess (ed.), *Key Variables in Social Investigation*. London: Routledge and Kegan Paul, pp. 12–30.

Finch, J. (1989) *Family Obligations and Social Change*. Cambridge: Polity Press.

Finch, J. and Groves, D. (eds) (1983) *A Labour of Love: Women, Work and Caring*. London: Routledge and Kegan Paul.

Finch, J. and Mason, J. (1993) *Negotiating Family Responsibilities*. London: Routledge.

Fine, B. (1999) 'The development state is dead – long live social capital?', *Development and Change*, 30: 1–19.

Fine, B. and Green, F. (2001) 'Economics, social capital, and the colonization of the social sciences', in S. Baron, J. Field and T. Schuller (eds), *Social Capital: Critical Perspectives*. Oxford: Oxford University Press, pp. 78–93.

Fine, M. (1998) 'Working the hyphens: reinventing self and other in qualitative research', in N. Denzin and Y. Lincoln (eds), *The Landscape of Qualitative Research*. Thousand Oaks, CA: Sage, pp. 130–55.

Fineman, S. (ed.) (1993) *Emotion in Organizations*. London: Sage.

Finlayson, A. (1999) 'Language', in F. Ashe, A. Finlayson, M. Lloyd, I. MacKenzie, J. Martin and S. O'Neill (eds), *Contemporary Social and Political Theory: An Introduction*. Buckingham: Open University Press, pp. 47–87.

Fisher, B. and Tronto, J. (1990) 'Towards a feminist theory of caring', in E. Abel and M. Nelson (eds), *Circles of Care: Work and Identity in Women's Lives*. New York: State University of New York Press, pp. 35–62.

Fisher, J. (1989) 'Teaching "time": women's responses to adult development', in F. Forman with C. Sowton (eds), *Taking our Time: Feminist Perspectives on Temporality*. Oxford: Pergamon Press, pp. 136–49.

Flax, J. (1997) 'Forgotten forms of close combat: mothers and daughters revisited', in M. Gergen and S. Davis (eds), *Towards a New Psychology of Gender: A Reader*. New York: Routledge, pp. 311–24.

Folbre, N. (1994) *Who Pays for the Kids? Gender and the Structures of Constraint*. London: Routledge.

Forman, F. (1989) 'Feminizing time: an introduction', in F. Forman with C. Sowton (eds), *Taking our Time: Feminist Perspectives on Temporality*. Oxford: Pergamon Press, pp. 1–9.

Forseth, U. and Dahl-Jorgensen, C. (2001) 'Understanding changes among interactive service workers', paper presented at Rethinking Gender, Work and Organization Conference, University of Keele, 27–29 June.

Foucault, M. (1972) *The Archaeology of Knowledge*. London: Tavistock Publications.

Francis, B. (1998) *Power Plays: Primary School Children's Constructions of Gender, Power and Adult Work*. Stoke-on-Trent: Trentham Books.

Francis, B. (1999) 'Modernist reductionism or post-structuralist relativism: can we move on? An evaluation of the arguments in relation to feminist educational research', *Gender and Education*, 11(4): 381–94.

Franzway, S. (2000) 'Women working in a greedy institution: commitment and emotional labour in the union movement', *Gender, Work and Organization*, 7(4): 258–68.

Fraser, N. (1995) 'From redistribution to recognition: dilemmas in justice in a post-socialist age', *New Left Review*, 212: 68–93.

Fraser, N. and Gordon, L. (1994) 'A geneaology of dependency: tracing a keyword in the U.S. welfare state', *SIGNS*, 19(2): 309–36.

Freedman, J. (2001) *Feminism*. Buckingham: Open University Press.

Friedman, M. (1993) 'Beyond caring', in M. Larrabee (ed.), *An Ethic of Care: Feminist and Interdisciplinary Perspectives*. New York: Routledge, pp. 258–73.

Frye, M. (1996) 'The possibility of feminist theory', in A. Garry and M. Pearsall (eds), *Women, Knowledge and Reality: Explorations in Feminist Philosophy*. New York: Routledge, pp. 34–47.

Gardiner, J. (1997) *Gender, Care and Economics*. Basingstoke: Macmillan.

Gedalof, I. (2000) 'Identity in transit: nomads, cyborgs and women', *The European Journal of Women's Studies*, 7(3): 337–54.

Gee, J. (1996) *Social Linguistics and Literacies: Ideology in Discourses*, 2nd edn. London: Taylor and Francis.

Gewirtz, S., Ball, S. and Bowe, R. (1995) *Markets, Choice and Equity in Education*. Buckingham: Open University Press.

Giddens, A. (1991) *Modernity and Self-identity: Self and Society in the Late Modern Age*. Cambridge: Polity Press.

Gilligan, C. (1982) *In a Different Voice*. Cambridge, MA: Harvard University Press.

Gilligan, C. (1993) 'Reply to critics', in M. Larrabee (ed.), *An Ethic of Care: Feminist and Interdisciplinary Perspectives*. New York: Routledge, pp. 207–14.

Gilligan, C. (1998) 'Hearing the difference: theorizing connection', in M. Rogers (ed.), *Contemporary Feminist Theory: A Text/Reader*. Boston: McGraw-Hill, pp. 341–6.

Goodman, J. and Martin, J. (2002) 'Introduction', in J. Goodman and J. Martin (eds), *Gender, Colonialism and Education*. London: Woburn Press.

Graham, H. (1990) *Time, Energy and the Psychology of Healing*. London: Jessica Kingsley.

Graham, H. (1991) 'The concept of caring in feminist research: the case of domestic service', *Sociology*, 25(1): 61–78.

Graham, H. (1993) *Hardship and Health in Women's Lives*. London: Harvester Wheatsheaf.

Griffiths, M. (1995) *Feminisms and the Self: The Web of Identity*. London: Routledge.

Griffiths, M. (1998) *Educational Research for Social Justice: Getting Off the Fence*. Buckingham: Open University Press.

Grosz, E. (1990a) 'Contemporary theories of power and subjectivity', in S. Gunew (ed.), *Feminist Knowledge: Critique and Construct*. London: Routledge, pp. 59–120.

Grosz, E. (1990b) 'Conclusion: a note on essentialism and difference', in S. Gunew (ed.), *Feminist Knowledge: Critique and Construct*. London: Routledge, pp. 332–44.

Grosz, E. (1995) *Space, Time and Perversion*. New York: Routledge.

Grosz, E. (2000) 'Deleuze's Bergson: duration, the virtual and a politics of the future', in I. Buchanan and C. Colebrook (eds), *Deleuze and Feminist Theory*. Edinburgh: Edinburgh University Press, pp. 214–34.

Guba, E. and Lincoln, Y. (1994) 'Competing paradigms in qualitative research', in N. Denzin and Y. Lincoln (eds), *Handbook of Qualitative Research*. Thousand Oaks, CA: Sage, pp. 105–17.

Haraway, D. (1985) 'A manifesto for cyborgs: science, technology and socialist feminism in the 1980s', *Socialist Review*, 80: 65–108.

Haraway, D. (1991) *Simians, Cyborgs and Women: The Reinvention of Nature*. London: Free Association Books.

Haraway, D. (1997a) 'A manifesto for cyborgs: science, technology, and socialist feminism in the 1980s', in D. Meyers (ed.), *Feminist Social Thought: A Reader*. New York: Routledge, pp. 502–31.

Haraway, D. (1997b) *Modest_Witness@Second_Millennium FemaleMan©_-Meets_OncoMouse^{TM}*. New York: Routledge.

Harding, S (ed.) (1987) *Feminism and Methodology: Social Science Issues*. Bloomington and Milton Keynes: Indiana University Press/Open University Press.

Harding, S. (1991) *Whose Science? Whose Knowledge? Thinking from Women's Lives*. Milton Keynes: Open University Press.

Harding, S. (1997) 'Comment on Hekman's "Truth and method: feminist standpoint theory revisited"; whose standpoint needs the regimes of truth and reality?', *SIGNS: Journal of Women in Culture and Society*, 22(2): 382–91.

Harding, S. (2001) 'Comment on Walby's "Against epistemological chasms: the science question in feminism revisited": can democratic values and interests ever play a rationally justifiable role in the evaluation of scientific work?', *SIGNS: Journal of Women in Culture and Society*, 26(2): 511–27.

Hartmann, H. (1981) 'The unhappy marriage of Marxism and feminism: towards a more progressive union', in L. Sargent (ed.), *Women and Revolution: The Unhappy Marriage of Marxism and Feminism*. London: Pluto Press, pp. 1–42.

Hartsock, N. (1983) 'The feminist standpoint: developing the ground for a specifically feminist historical materialism', in S. Harding and M. Hintikka (eds), *Discovering Reality*. Dordrecht: Kluwer Academic Publishers, pp. 283–310.

Hartsock, N. (1997) 'The feminist standpoint: developing the ground for a specifically feminist historical materialism', in D. Meyers (ed.), *Feminist Social Thought: A Reader*. New York: Routledge, pp. 462–83.

Hasibuan-Sedyono, C. (1998) 'She who manages: the Indonesian woman in management', in P. Drake and P. Owen (eds), *Gender and Management Issues in Education: An International Perspective*. Stoke-on-Trent: Trentham Books.

Hatt, S. (1997) *Gender, Work and Labour Markets*. Basingstoke: Macmillan.

Haw, K. with contributions from Shah, S. and Hanifa, M. (1998) *Educating Muslim Girls: Shifting Discourses*. Buckingham: Open University Press.

Hawkesworth, M. (1989) 'Knowers, knowing, known: feminist theory and claims to truth', *SIGNS: Journal of Women in Culture and Society*, 14(3): 533–57.

Hawking, S. (1988) *A Brief History of Time: From the Big Bang to Black Holes*. London: Bantam Press.

Heidegger, M. (1977) *On Time and Being*. New York: Harper Colophon.

Heidegger, M. (1980) *Being and Time*. Oxford: Blackwell.

Hekman, S. (1994) 'The feminist critique of rationality', *The Polity Reader in Gender Studies*. Cambridge: Polity Press, pp. 50–61.

Hekman, S. (1997) 'Truth and method: feminist standpoint theory revisited', *SIGNS: Journal of Women in Culture and Society*, 22(2): 341–65.

Hekman, S. (1999) *The Future of Differences: Truth and Method in Feminist Theory*. Cambridge: Polity Press.

Hennessy, R. and Ingraham, C. (eds) (1997) *Materialist Feminism: A Reader in Class, Difference, and Women's Lives*. New York: Routledge.

Henwood, F. (1996) 'WISE choices? Understanding occupational decision-making in a climate of equal opportunities for women in science and technology', *Gender and Education*, 8(2): 199–214.

Hewitt, P. (1993) *About Time: The Revolution in Work and Family Life*. London: Institute for Public Policy Research.

Hochschild, A. (1983) *The Managed Heart: Commericalization of Human Feeling*. Berkeley, CA: University of California Press.

Hochschild, A. (1997) *The Time Bind: When Work Becomes Home and Home Becomes Work*. New York: Metropolitan Books.

Homans, G. (1990) 'Rational-choice theory and behavioural psychology', in C. Calhoun, M. Meyer and W. Scott (eds), *Structures of Power and Constraint: Papers in Honor of Peter M Blau*. Cambridge: Cambridge University Press, pp. 77–90.

hooks, b. (1997) 'Feminism: a movement to end sexist oppression', in S. Kemp and J. Squires (eds), *Feminisms*. Oxford: Oxford University Press, pp. 22–6.

Hughes, B. (1990) 'Quality of life', in S. Peace (ed.), *Researching Social Gerontology: Concepts, Methods and Issues*. London: Sage, pp. 46–58.

Hughes, C. (2001) 'Developing conceptual literacy in lifelong learning research: a case of responsibility', *British Educational Research Journal*, 27(5): 601–14.

Hughes, C. (2002) *Women's Contemporary Lives: Within and Beyond the Mirror*. London: Routledge.

Iganski, P., Mason, D., Humphreys, A. and Watkins, M. (2001) 'Equal opportunities and positive action in the British National Health Service: some lessons from the recruitment of minority ethnic groups to nursing and midwifery', *Ethnic and Racial Studies*, 24(2): 294–317.

Irigaray, L. (1985) *Speculum of the Other Woman*, transl. G. Gill. Ithaca, NY: Cornell University Press.

Irigaray, L. (1993) *Sexes and Genealogies*. New York: Columbia University Press.

Jackson, S. (2001) 'Why a materialist feminism is (still) possible – and necessary', *Women's Studies International Forum*, 24(3–4): 283–93.

Jayaratne, T. (1993) 'The value of quantitative methodology for feminist research', in M. Hammersley (ed.), *Social Research: Philosophy, Politics and Practice*. London: Sage, pp. 109–23.

Johnson, C. (2000) *Derrida*. London: Phoenix.

Jones, A. (1997) 'Teaching post-structuralist feminist theory in education: student resistances', *Gender and Education*, 9(3): 261–70.

Josselson, R. (1996) *The Space Between Us: Exploring the Dimensions of Human Relationships*. Thousand Oaks, CA: Sage.

Kandola, R. and Fullerton, J. (1994) *Managing the Mosaic: Diversity in Action*. London: IPD.

Kaplan, M. (1992) *Mothers' Images of Motherhood*. London: Routledge.

Kelly, A. (ed.) (1987) *Science for Girls?* Milton Keynes: Open University Press.

Kelly, L., Burton, S. and Regan, L. (1994) 'Researching women's lives or studying women's oppression? Reflections on what constitutes feminist research', in M. Maynard and J. Purvis (eds), *Researching Women's Lives from a Feminist Perspective*. London: Taylor and Francis, pp. 27–48.

Kendall, G. and Wickham, G. (1999) *Using Foucault's Methods*. London: Sage.

Klein, W. (1994) *Time in Language*. London: Routledge.

Knapp, A. (2000) 'More power to argument', *Feminist Theory*, 1(2): 207–24.

Knights, D. and Odih, P. (1995) '"It's about time!" The significance of gendered time for financial services consumption', *Time and Society*, 4(2): 205–31.

Kristeva, J. (1986) 'Women's time', in T. Moi (ed.), *The Kristeva Reader*. Oxford: Basil Blackwell, pp. 187–213.

Landry, D. and MacLean, G. (1993) *Materialist Feminisms*. Oxford: Blackwell.

Lane, N. (2000) 'The low status of female part-time NHS nurses: a bed-pan ceiling?', *Gender, Work and Organization*, 7(4): 269–81.

Lankshear, C. with Gee, J., Knobel, M. and Searle, C. (1987) *Changing Literacies*. Buckingham: Open University Press.

Lather, P. (1991) *Getting Smart: Feminist Research and Pedagogy with/in the Postmodern*. New York: Routledge.

Laws, C. and Davies, B. (2000) 'Poststructuralist theory in practice: working with "behaviourally disturbed" children', *Qualitative Studies in Education*, 13(3): 205–21.

Legge, K. (1995) 'HRM: rhetoric, reality and hidden agendas', in J. Storey (ed.), *Human Resource Management: A Critical Text*. London: Routledge, pp. 33–62.

Letherby, G. (2001) 'Researching non-motherhood in higher education: an attempt at a reflexive auto/duo/biographical approach', paper presented at the Politics of Gender and Education Third International Conference, Institute of Education, University of London, 4–6 April.

Lewis, S., Izraeli, D. and Hootsmans, H. (1992) *Dual-Earner Families: International Perspectives*. London: Sage.

Lillis, T. (2001) *Student Writing: Access, Regulation, Desire*. London: Routledge.

Lloyd, G. (1996) 'The man of reason', in A. Garry and M. Pearsall (eds), *Women, Knowledge and Reality: Explorations in Feminist Philosophy*. New York: Routledge, pp. 151–65.

Luke, C. (ed.) (1996) *Feminisms and Pedagogies of Everyday Life*. New York: SUNY.

MacKinnon, C. (1997) 'Feminism, Marxism, method, and the state: an agenda for theory', in D. Meyers (ed.), *Feminist Social Thought: A Reader*. New York: Routledge, pp. 64–91.

Martin, J. (2001) 'Reflections on writing a biographical account of a woman educator activist', *History of Education*, 30(2): 163–76.

Mason, J. (1996) 'Gender, care and sensibility in family and kin relationships', in J. Holland and L. Adkins (eds), *Sex, Sensibility and the Gendered Body*. Basingstoke: Macmillan, pp. 15–36.

May, T. (1998) 'Reflexivity in the age of reconstructive social science', *International Journal of Social Research Methodology*, 1(1): 7–24.

Maynard, M. (1994) 'Methods, practice and epistemology: the debate about feminism and research', in M. Maynard and J. Purvis (eds), *Researching Women's Lives from a Feminist Perspective*. London: Taylor and Francis, pp. 10–26.

Maynard, M. (1995) 'Beyond the "big three": the development of feminist theory into the 1990s', *Women's History Review*, 4(3): 259–81.

Maynard, M. (1998) 'Feminists' knowledge and the knowledge of feminisms: epistemology, theory, methodology and method', in T. May and M. Williams (eds), *Knowing the Social World*. Buckingham: Open University Press, pp. 120–37.

McGinn, M. (1997) *Wittgenstein and the Philosophical Investigations*. London: Routledge.

McMahon, M. (1995) *Engendering Motherhood: Identity and Self-Transformation in Women's Lives*. New York: Guilford Press.

McNay, L. (2000) *Gender and Agency: Reconfiguring the Subject in Feminist and Social Theory*. Cambridge: Polity Press.

Meehan, D. (1999) 'The under-representation of women managers in higher education: are there issues other than style?', in S. Whitehead and R. Moodley (eds), *Transforming Managers: Gendering Change in the Public Sector*. London: UCL Press, pp. 33–49.

Meyers D. (ed.) (1997) *Feminist Social Thought: A Reader*. New York: Routledge.

Meyers, D. (2001) 'The rush to motherhood – pronatalist discourse and women's autonomy', *SIGNS: Journal of Women in Culture and Society*, 26(3): 735–74.

Miles, M. and Huberman, A. (1994) *Qualitative Data Analysis: An Expanded Sourcebook*, 2nd edn. Thousand Oaks, CA: Sage.

Millard, E. (1997) 'Differently literate: gender identity and the construction of the developing reader', *Gender and Education*, 9(1): 31–48.

Miller, G. (1997) 'Building bridges: the possibility of analytic dialogue between ethnography, conversation analysis and Foucault', in D. Silverman (ed.), *Qualitative Research: Theory, Method and Practice*. London: Sage, pp. 24–44.

Min, X. (1999) 'Who prepares dinner tonight?', *Asian Journal of Women's Studies*, 5(1): 140–54.

Mitchell, J. (1974) *Psychoanalysis and Feminism*. Harmondsworth: Penguin.

Mohanty, C. (1991) 'Cartographies of struggle: Third World women and the politics of feminism', in C. Mohanty, A. Russon and L. Torres (eds), *Third World Women and the Politics of Feminism*. Bloomington, IN: Indiana University Press, pp. 1–47.

Mohanty, C. (1997) 'Preface: dangerous territories, territorial power, and education', in L. Roman and L. Eyre (eds), *Dangerous Territories: Struggles for Difference and Equality in Education*. New York: Routledge, pp. ix–xvii.

Moi, T. (ed.) (1986) *The Kristeva Reader*. Oxford: Basil Blackwell.

Moi, T. (1997) 'Feminist, female, feminine', in S. Kemp and J. Squires (eds), *Feminisms*. Oxford: Oxford University Press, pp. 246–50.

Moi, T. (1999) *What is a Woman?* Oxford: Oxford University Press.

Mongia, P. (ed.) (19??) *Contemporary Postcolonial Theory: A Reader*. London: Arnold.

Moore, H. (1994) *A Passion for Difference: Essays in Anthropology and Gender*. Cambridge: Polity Press.

Morris, J. (1993) *Independent Lives: Community Care and Disabled People*. Basingstoke: Macmillan.

Munro, P. (1998) *Subject to Fiction: Women Teachers' Life History Narratives and the Cultural Politics of Resistance*. Buckingham: Open University Press.

Myers, K. (2000a) 'Lessons learned?', in K. Myers (ed.), *Whatever Happened to Equal Opportunities in Schools? Gender Equality Initiatives in Education* Buckingham: Open University Press, pp. 217–30.

Myers, K. (2000b) 'How did we get here?', in K. Myers (ed.), *Whatever Happened to Equal Opportunities in Schools? Gender Equality Initiatives in Education*. Buckingham: Open University Press, pp. 1–10.

Nagl, L. and Mouffe, C. (eds) (2001) *The Legacy of Wittgenstein: Pragmatism or Deconstruction*. Frankfurt: Peter Lang.

Narayan, U. (1998) 'The project of feminist epistemology: perspectives from a non-western feminist', in M. Rogers (ed.), *Contemporary Feminist Theory: A Text/Reader*. Boston: McGraw-Hill, pp. 82–9.

National Statistics (2001) *Labour Market Dataset*. http://www.statistics.gov.uk/ukin_figs/Data_labour.asp (accessed 15 January 2001).

Negrey, C. (1993) *Gender, Time, and Reduced Work*. New York: State University of New York Press.

Nelson, J. (1993) 'The study of choice or the study of provisioning? Gender and the definition of economics', in M. Ferber and J. Nelson (eds), *Beyond Economic Man: Feminist Theory and Economics*. Chicago: University of Chicago Press, pp. 23–36.

Nicolson, P. (1996) *Gender, Power and Organisation*. London: Routledge.

Noddings, N. (1984) *Caring: A Feminine Approach to Ethics and Moral Education*. Berkeley, CA: University of California.

Norris, C. (2000) 'Post-modernism: a guide for the perplexed', in G. Browning, A. Halcli and F. Webster (eds), *Understanding Contemporary Society: Theories of the Present*. London: Sage, pp. 25–45.

Nowotny, H. (1992) 'Time and social theory: towards a social theory of time', *Time and Society*, 1(3): 421–54.

O'Connell, H. (1996) *Equality Postponed: Gender, Rights and Development*. Oxford and London: WorldView Publishing/One World Action.

Oliver, K. (2001) 'Julia Kristeva', in A. Elliott and B. Turner (eds), *Profiles in Contemporary Social Theory*. London: Sage, pp. 174–83.

Orr, P. (2000) 'Prudence and progress: national policy for equal opportunities (gender) in schools since 1975', in K. Myers (ed.), *Whatever Happened to Equal Opportunities in Schools? Gender Equality Initiatives in Education*. Buckingham: Open University Press, pp. 13–26.

Ozga, J. and Deem, R. (2000) 'Carrying the burden of transformation: the experiences of women managers in UK higher and further education', *Discourse: Studies in the Cultural Politics of Education*, 21(2): 141–54.

Ozga, J. and Walker, L. (1995) 'Women in education management: theory and practice', in D. Limerick and B. Lingard (eds), *Gender and Changing Educational Management*. Rydalmere, NSW: Hodder Education.

Paechter, C. (2000) *Changing School Subjects: Power, Gender and Curriculum*. Buckingham: Open University Press.

Parker, G. (1993) *With This Body: Caring and Disability in Marriage*. Buckingham: Open University Press.

Pateman, C. (1987) 'Feminist critiques of the public/private dichotomy', in A. Phillips (ed.), *Feminism and Equality*. Oxford: Basil Blackwell, pp. 103–26.

Peace, S. (ed.) (1990) *Researching Social Gerontology: Concepts, Methods and Issues*. London: Sage.

Pears, D. (1971) *Wittgenstein*. London: Collins.

Perriton, L. (1999) 'The provocative and evocative gaze upon women in management development', *Gender and Education*, 11(3): 295–308.

Perry, P. (2000) *A Composition of Consciousness: Roads of Reflection from Freire to Elbow*. New York: Peter Lang Publishers.

Phillips, A. (1987) *Feminism and Equality*. Oxford: Blackwell.

Phillips, A. (1993) *Democracy and Difference*. Cambridge: Polity Press.

Phoenix, A. (1991) *Young Mothers?* Cambridge: Polity Press.

Phoenix, A. (2000) 'Aspiring to a politics of alliance: response to Sylvia Walby's "Beyond the politics of location: the power of argument in a global era"', *Feminist Theory*, 1(2): 230–5.

Pilcher, J. (1999) *Women in Contemporary Britain: An Introduction*. London: Routledge.

Piper, C. (1993) *The Responsible Parent: A Study of Divorce Mediation*. London: Harvester Wheatsheaf.

Plummer, K. (2000) 'Intimate choices', in G. Browning, A. Halcli and F. Webster (eds), *Understanding Contemporary Society: Theories of the Present*. London: Sage, pp. 432–44.

Plumwood, V. (1993) *Feminism and the Mastery of Nature*. London: Routledge.

Pollert, A. (ed.) (1991) *Farewell to Flexibility?* Oxford: Basil Blackwell.

Poovey, M. (1988) 'Feminism and deconstruction', *Feminist Studies*, 14(1): 51–64.

Porter, P. (1995) 'The need for a spring clean: gendered educational organisations and their glass ceilings, glass walls, sticky floors, sticky cobwebs and slippery poles', in B. Limerick and B. Lingard (eds), *Gender and Changing Educational Management*. Rydalmere, NSW: Hodder Education, pp. 234–43.

Pratt, G. (1993) 'Reflections on poststructuralism and feminist empirics, theory and practice', *Antipode*, 25(1): 51–63.

Press, J. and Townsley, E. (1998) 'Wives' and husbands' housework reporting: gender, class and social desirability', *Gender and Society*, 12(2): 188–218.

Ramazanoglu, C. and Holland, J. (1999) 'Tripping over experience: some problems in feminist epistemology', *Discourse: Studies in the Cultural Politics of Education*, 20(3): 381–92.

Raphael Reed, L. (1999) 'Troubling boys and disturbing discourses on masculinity and schooling: a feminist exploration of current debates and interventions concerning boys in school', *Gender and Education*, 11(1): 93–110.

Reskin, B. and Padavic, I. (1994) *Women and Men at Work*. Thousand Oaks, CA: Pine Forge Press.

Ribbens, J. (1994) *Mothers and their Children: A Feminist Sociology of Childrearing*. London: Sage.

Riddell, S., Baron, S. and Wilson, A. (1999) 'Social capital and people with learning difficulties', *Studies in the Education of Adults*, 31(1): 49–65.

Riley, D. (1988) *'Am I That Name?' Feminism and the Category of 'Women' in History*. Basingstoke: Macmillan.

Robson, A. and Robson, J. (eds) (1994) *Sexual Equality: Writings by John Stuart Mill, Harriet Taylor Mill and Helen Taylor*. Toronto: University of Toronto Press.

Rowan, J. (1999) 'The normal development of subpersonalities', in J. Rowan and M. Cooper (eds), *The Plural Self: Multiplicity in Everyday Life*. London: Sage, pp. 11–27.

Ruddick, S. (1980) 'Maternal thinking', *Feminist Studies*, 6(2).

Ruddick, S. (1997) 'Maternal thinking', in D. Meyers (ed.), *Feminist Social Thought: A Reader*. New York: Routledge, pp. 583–603.

Sarup, M. (1996) *Identity, Culture and the Postmodern World*. Edinburgh: Edinburgh University Press.

Scheurich, J. (1997) *Research Method in the Post-Modern*. London: Falmer.

Schor, N. and Weed, E. (eds) (1994) *The Essential Difference*. Bloomington and Indianapolis: Indiana University Press, pp. 151–84.

Schreuder, P. (1999) 'Gender in Dutch general education: the case of "taking care"', *Gender and Education*, 11(2): 195–206.

Scott, J. (1988) 'Deconstructing equality-versus-difference: or, the uses of poststructuralist theory for feminism', *Feminist Studies*, 14(1): 33–50.

Scott, J. (1992) '"Experience"', in J. Butler and J. Scott (eds), *Feminists Theorize the Political*. New York: Routledge, pp. 22–40.

Scott, J. (2000) 'Rational choice theory', in G. Browning, A. Halcli and F. Webster (eds), *Understanding Contemporary Society: Theories of the Present*. London: Sage, pp. 126–38.

Searle, C. (1998) *None but Our Words: Critical Literacy in Classroom and Community*. Buckingham: Open University Press.

Senauer, B. (1990) 'The impact of the value of women's time on food and nutrition', in I. Tinker (ed.), *Persistent Inequalities: Women and World Development*. Oxford: Oxford University Press, pp. 150–61.

Sevenhuijsen, S. (1998) *Citizenship and the Ethics of Care: Feminist Considerations on Justice, Morality and Politics*. London: Routledge.

Shain, F. (2000) 'Culture, survival and resistance: theorizing young Asian women's experiences and strategies in contemporary British schooling and society', *Discourse: Studies in the Cultural Politics of Education*, 21(2): 156–74.

Shaw, J. (1995) 'Conclusion – feminization and new forms of exploitations: the changing language of equal opportunities', in J. Shaw and D. Perrons (eds), *Making Gender Work: Managing Equal Opportunities*. Buckingham: Open University Press.

Silva, E. and Smart, C. (eds) (1999) *The New Family?* London: Sage.

Sirianni, C. (1987) 'Economies of time in social theory: three approaches compared', *Current Perspectives in Social Theory*, 8: 161–95.

Sirianni, C. and Negrey, C. (2000) 'Working time as gendered time', *Feminist Economics*, 6(1): 59–76.

Skeggs, B. (1997) *Formations of Class and Gender*. London: Sage.

Skeggs, B. (2001) 'The toilet paper: femininity, class and mis-recognition', *Women's Studies International Forum*, 24(3–4): 295–307.

Smart, C. (1989) *Feminism and the Power of Law*. London: Routledge.

Smith, D. (1987) 'Women's perspective as a radical critique of sociology', in S. Harding (ed.), *Feminism and Methodology: Social Science Issues*. Bloomington and Milton Keynes: Indiana University Press/Open University Press, pp. 84–96.

Smith, D. (1988) *The Everyday World as Problematic: A Feminist Sociology*. Milton Keynes: Open University Press.

Smith, D. (1997) 'Comment on Hekman's "Truth and method: feminist standpoint theory revisited"', *SIGNS: Journal of Women in Culture and Society*, 22(2): 392–8.

Smith, L. (1999) *Decolonizing Methodologies: Research and Indigenous Peoples*. London: Zed Books.

Spelman, E. (1988) *Inessential Woman: Problems of Exclusion in Feminist Thought*. London: Women's Press.

Spivak, G. (1988) 'Can the subaltern speak?', in C. Nelson and L. Grossberg (eds), *Marxism and the Interpretation of Culture*. London: Macmillan, pp. 271–313.

Spivak, G. (2001) *Political Discourse: Theories of Colonialism and Postcolonialism*. http://landow.stg.brown.edu/post/poldiscourse/spivak/spivak1.html (accessed 3 March 2001).

Spivak, G. with Rooney, E. (1994) 'In a word, *Interview*', in N. Schor and E. Weed (eds), *The Essential Difference*. Bloomington and Indianapolis: Indiana University Press, pp. 151–84.

Sprague, J. (2001) 'Comment on Walby's "Against epistemological chasms: the science question in feminism revisited": structured knowledge and strategic methodology', *SIGNS: Journal of Women in Culture and Society*, 26(2): 527–36.

Stambaugh, J. (1977) 'Introduction', in M. Heidegger, *On Time and Being*. New York: Harper Colophon, pp. vii–xi.

Stanley, L. and Wise, S. (1990) 'Method, methodology and epistemology in feminist research processes', in L. Stanley (ed.), *Feminist Praxis: Research, Theory and Epistemology in Feminist Sociology*. London: Routledge, pp. 20–62.

Stern, D. (1995) *Wittgenstein on Mind and Language*. New York: Oxford University Press.

Strachan, J. (1999) 'Feminist educational leadership: locating the concepts in practice', *Gender and Education*, 11(3): 309–22.

Strassman, D. (1993) 'Not a free market: the rhetoric of disciplinary authority in economics', in M. Ferber and J. Nelson (eds), *Beyond Economic Man: Feminist Theory and Economics*. Chicago: University of Chicago Press, pp. 54–68.

Sudbury, J. (1998) *Other Kinds of Dreams: Black Women's Organisations and the Politics of Transformation*. London: Routledge.

Sullivan, C. and Lewis, S. (2001) 'Home-based telework, gender and the synchronization of work and family', *Gender, Work and Organization*, 8(2): 123–45.

Swanton, C. (1985) 'On the "Essential contestedness" of political concepts', *Ethics*, 95(4): 811–27.

Sylvester, C. (1999) '"Progress" in Zimbabwe: is "It" a "Woman"?', *International Feminist Journal of Politics*, 1(1): 89–118.

Tanesini, A. (1994) 'Whose language?', in K. Lennon and M. Whitford (eds), *Knowing the Difference: Feminist Perspectives in Epistemology*. London: Routledge, pp. 203–16.

Tanton, M. and Hughes, C. (1999) 'Editorial: gender and (management) education', *Gender and Education*, 11(3): 245–50.

Thomas, C. (1993) 'De-constructing the concept of care', *Sociology*, 27(4): 649–69.

Thomas, C. (1999) *Female Forms: Experiencing and Understanding Disability*. Buckingham: Open University Press.

Thomas, L. and Webb, E. (1999) 'Writing from experience: the place of the personal in French feminist writing', *Feminist Review*, 61: 27–48.

Thompson, E.P. (1967) 'Time, work-discipline and industrial capitalism', *Past and Present*, 36: 52–97.

Thornley, C. (1996) 'Segmentation and inequality in the nursing workforce: re-evaluating the evaluation of skills', in R. Crompton, D. Gallie and K. Purcell (eds), *Changing Forms of Employment: Organisations, Skills and Gender*. London: Routledge, pp. 160–81.

Thornton, M. (1986) 'Sex equality is not enough for feminism', in C. Pateman and E. Gross (eds), *Feminist Challenges: Social and Political Theory*. Sydney, NSW: Allen and Unwin.

Tight, M. (1996) *Key Concepts in Adult Education and Training*. London: Routledge.

Tripp, A. (2000) 'Rethinking difference: comparative perspectives from Africa', *SIGNS: Journal of Women in Culture and Society*, 25(3): 649–75.

Tronto, J. (1993) *Moral Boundaries: A Political Argument for an Ethic of Care*. London: Routledge.

Tronto, J. (1995) 'Women and caring: what can feminists learn about morality from caring?', in J. Held (ed.), *Justice and Care: Essential Readings in Feminist Ethics*. Boulder, CO: Westview Press, pp. 101–16.

Umansky, L. (1996) *Motherhood Reconceived: Feminism and the Legacies of the Sixties*. New York: New York University Press.

Walby, S. (1990) *Theorizing Patriarchy*. Oxford: Basil Blackwell.

Walby, S. (1997) *Gender Transformations*. London: Routledge.

Walby, S. (2000a) 'Beyond the politics of location: the power of argument in a global era', *Feminist Theory*, 1(2): 189–206.

Walby, S. (2000b) 'In search of feminist theory', *Feminist Theory*, 1(2): 236–8.

Walby, S. (2001a) 'Against epistemological chasms: the science question in feminism revisited', *SIGNS: Journal of Women in Culture and Society*, 26(2): 485–510.

Walby, S. (2001b) 'Reply to Harding and Sprague', *SIGNS: Journal of Women in Culture and Society*, 26(2): 537–40.

Walkerdine, V. (1990) *School Girl Fictions*. London: Verso.

Walkerdine, V. (1994) 'Femininity as performance', in L. Stone (ed.), *The Education Feminism Reader*. New York: Routledge, pp. 57–69.

Walsh, D. (1998) 'Structure/agency', in C. Jenks (ed.), *Core Sociological Dichotomies*. London: Sage.

Weedon, C. (1997) *Feminist Practice and Poststructuralist Theory*, 2nd edn. Oxford: Blackwell.

Weedon, C. (1999) *Feminism, Theory and the Politics of Difference*. Oxford: Blackwell.

Whitford, M. (ed.) (1991) *The Irigaray Reader*. Oxford: Basil Blackwell.

Williams, F. (1993) 'Anthology: care', in J. Bornat, C. Pereira, D. Pilgrim and F. Williams (eds), *Community Care: A Reader*. Basingstoke: Macmillan/ Open University, pp. 81–95.

Williams, R. (1993) 'Race, deconstruction, and the emergent agenda of feminist economic theory', in M. Ferber and J. Nelson (eds), *Beyond Economic Man: Feminist Theory and Economics*. Chicago: University of Chicago Press, pp. 144–52.

Wilson, M. (ed.) (1997) *Women in Educational Management: A European Perspective*. Liverpool: Paul Chapman.

Winch, C. and Gingell, J. (1999) *Key Concepts in the Philosophy of Education*. London: Routledge.

Wisker, G. (2000) *Post-Colonial and African American Women's Writing: A Critical Introduction*. Basingstoke: Macmillan.

Witherell, C. and Noddings, N. (1991) *Stories Lives Tell: Narrative and Dialogue in Education*. New York: Teachers College Press.

Wittgenstein, L. (1958) *Philosophical Investigations*, transl. G.E.M. Anscombe. Oxford: Blackwell.

Wohl, A. (2001) *Race and Class Overview: Parallels in Racism and Class Prejudice*. http://landow.stg.brown.edu/victorian/race/rcov.html (accessed 3 September 2001).

Woollacott, A. (2000) 'The colonial flaneuse: Australian women negotiating turn-of-the-century London', *SIGNS: Journal of Women in Culture and Society*, 25(3): 761–87.

Young, I. (1990) *Justice and the Politics of Difference*. Princeton, NJ: Princeton University Press.

Young, S. (1997) *Changing the Wor(l)d: Discourse, Politics and the Feminist Movement*. London: Routledge.

Index

Weedon, C. 13, 14, 16, 57, 65, 69, 71, 72, 76, 82, 95, 151, 152, 154, 156
Western feminism 75–81
Whiteness, normative category of 63
Whitford, M. 146
Williams, F. 107, 110, 111
Williams, R. 92
Wilson, M. 115, 116
Winch, C. and Gingell, J. 21
Wisker, G. 75, 77, 78
Witherell, C. and Noddings, N. 126
Wittgenstein, L. 6, 13, 22, 174; language games 20–22

Wollacott, A. 80–81
Wollstonecraft, M. 7, 40, 46, 57
Woman, as deconstructed 73; as mother 47, 116–117; as relational 108; as superior 46; meanings of 11–31
Woman-centred feminism 52
Women 'returners' 139–140
Women's Time 146
Writing, as thinking 191

Young, I. 129
Young, S. 63–65